MW00590630

The Three Battles of
SAND CREEK

In Blood, in Court,
and as the End of History

Gregory F. Michno

Savas Beatie

California

First Edition, first printing

Library of Congress Cataloging-in-Publication Data

Names: Michno, Gregory, 1948- author.
Title: Three battles of Sand Creek: In Blood, in Court, and as the End of History / by Gregory F. Michno.
Description: First edition. | El Dorado Hills, California : Savas Beatie LLC, 2017. | Includes bibliographical references and index.
Identifiers: LCCN 2016019329| ISBN 9781611213119 (hardcover : alk. paper) | ISBN 9781611213126 (ebk.)
Subjects: LCSH: Sand Creek Massacre, Colo., 1864. | Cheyenne Indians--Wars, 1864. | Arapaho Indians--Wars.
Classification: LCC E83.863 .M533 2017 | DDC 978.8004/97353--dc23
LC record available at https://lccn.loc.gov/2016019329

SB

Published by
Savas Beatie LLC
989 Governor Drive, Suite 102
El Dorado Hills, CA 95762

Phone: 916-941-6896
Web: www.savasbeatie.com
E-mail: sales@savasbeatie.com

Savas Beatie titles are available at special discounts for bulk purchases in the United States by corporations, institutions, and other organizations. For more details, please contact Savas Beatie, P.O. Box 4527, El Dorado Hills, CA 95762, or you may e-mail us at sales@savasbeatie.com, or visit our website at www.savasbeatie.com for additional information.

Proudly published, printed, and warehoused in the United States of America.

"History is a pack of lies we play on the dead."

— Voltaire (1694-1778)

Table of Contents

Table of Contents (continued)

III. THE END OF HISTORY

*Maps, Photos, and Illustrations are placed throughout
the book for the convenience of the reader.*

Preface

After spending nearly half a century studying the western Indian wars, I finally achieved a sense of "enlightenment," that moment when the little "Eureka" light bulb pops on and a richer and fuller understanding is achieved. Ironically, this milestone of sorts also produced a dichotomy, because it has finally become clear that there are no definitive answers to be realized. It is extremely difficult to write accurate history. Studying and writing good history on Sand Creek is nearly impossible.

Others have already written extensively on the Sand Creek incident. I use the word "incident" because the words "fight," "battle," or "massacre" more often than not spark an argument before a discussion on the merits even begins. Almost every major historical event experiences interpretive shifts over the years. Examples abound, such as the causes of Civil War, Custer's actions at the Battle of the Little Bighorn, or the depiction of the American Indian.

The manner in which Sand Creek has been portrayed, however, has remained remarkably static. Politicians, investigative committees, and the Eastern press hailed it as a massacre almost from the start, and most of the general public today who hears the words "Sand Creek" add the word "massacre" to the end. The only "good" press about Sand Creek came from a few eyewitnesses, but they are usually depicted as apologists or liars. Even some of those men changed their minds when the tide of disgust grew too high to withstand. The Sand Creek affair was a tragic event in American history, but after all the ink spilled writing about it, we still don't know what really happened beyond the most general brush strokes.

Many questions arise when discussing Sand Creek: Were the Indians peaceful? Did they capture and hold white prisoners? Were they under the protection of the soldiers? Was this a battle or a massacre? Were excessive numbers of women and children killed? Were bodies mutilated? Did the Indians fly an American flag? Did the chiefs die stoically in front of their tipis? Were white scalps found in the village? Did Sand Creek trigger the beginning of the extensive and bloody Indian Wars?

Three formal hearings were conducted to find answers to these and other questions. The body of evidence produced by these inquiries is large. Unfortunately, a close study of the evidence only muddies the water and makes it more difficult to reach firm conclusions.

In a fit of unwarranted optimism, I thought I would be able to clear the water when I wrote *Battle at Sand Creek: The Military Perspective* (Upton & Sons) in 2004. As a historian, I believed that a presentation of the facts would allow readers to objectively evaluate the complicated situation, make an educated assessment, and perhaps see the affair in a different light—or at least realize there were two sides to the story. Since the incident is almost universally portrayed as a massacre, I tried to swing the historical pendulum more to the middle by illuminating the points that would lend credence to the minority view that an actual battle had occurred, albeit one that was accompanied by horrible atrocities.

I was wrong. Critics of *Battle at Sand Creek* argued I was too "pro-white." Ari Kelman, the author of *A Misplaced Massacre: Struggling Over the Memory of Sand Creek* (Harvard University Press, 2013), for example, represented me as a modern defender of Colonel John Chivington and seems to view everyone who defends some of the actions of white settlers and/or soldiers as "culture warriors." When I wrote *Lakota Noon: The Indian Narrative of Custer's Defeat* (Mountain Press, 1997), however, criticism erupted that I was too "pro-Indian." Since both sides of the spectrum are angry with me, perhaps I am doing something right.

I am by no means a Chivington defender. In fact, I cannot countenance the historical man. I find almost all of our military actions taken against the Native Americans in the name of Manifest Destiny to be a hollow cover-up for a blatant land-grab. Our treatment of the tribes was appalling. But facts are facts, and as I noted above, I firmly believed that evidence would persuade readers to see different points of view.

What I didn't fully appreciate was that the truth becomes more elusive the deeper and more detailed we drill into the history of an event. As we move from macro history to micro history, uncovering more facts and evidence on events large and small, the more difficult it is to organize these facts into a coherent narrative—particularly when individual memories are involved. Memories are often faulty. We make poor eyewitnesses, and sometimes (often?) enhance or alter our memories without ever realizing it when additional suggestions or information is interjected after an event. Sometimes we subconsciously do what the rest of the herd does. We are slaves to our prejudices, experiences, and belief systems. Sometimes our beliefs conflict with our behaviors. For better or worse, we filter information through our individual lenses, and we sometimes don't let truth get in the way of what we already think. We often see what we believe, and often ignore concrete evidence that contradicts what we believe. The participants in the Sand Creek affair were also human, and so not immune to any of this.

*   *   *

The Three Battles of Sand Creek is divided in three sections. The first, "In Blood," unfolds the story of Sand Creek. It is shorn of much of the background information that was included in my earlier book *Battle at Sand Creek*, but maintains a reconstituted version of the events of November 29-30 1864. It is the most comprehensive account of that day published to date.

The second section, "In Court," focuses on the three investigations into the Sand Creek affair, illustrates some of the biases involved, and presents some of the contradictory testimony.

The third section, "The End of History," is an attempt to put my Eureka moment into book form by shedding light on the significant challenge of sorting fact from fiction when particular details and human memory are involved. To accomplish this, I use contemporary examples and several modern psychological- and memory-related tests, intertwined with applicable Sand Creek examples, in an effort to determine the reliability of eyewitness testimony. I believe the results will surprise some readers, and make them think about how we interpret not only historical events, but events of our own lives. As will be readily understood, the obstacles encountered utilizing eyewitness memory testimony make writing accurate and detailed history very difficult, and perhaps impossible.

My hope is that readers new to the story of Sand Creek appreciate the varied aspects of the incident and complications involved in using memory to put the pieces together in a coherent narrative, and that readers already familiar with it will reassess their beliefs about what may or may not have happened there. Where will the "facts" presented herein take them? Will initial conceptions be cemented into place by the end of the book, or changed by the telling of the tale? In particular, will confirmation bias—the tendency to interpret or recall information in a way that confirms one's beliefs—lead readers to throw out the non-confirmatory evidence and thus further reinforce original beliefs or initial reactions?

Perhaps there is some penitence about writing history, like the medieval flagellants who walked the European streets whipping themselves with flails. Ultimately, the journey through the sources, the discoveries, and the stories carry me to some higher meaning of understanding and help me continue rowing against the current.

Gregory F. Michno
Frederick, Colorado

Part I:

IN BLOOD

Chapter 1

Colonel Chivington Takes Command

No one really knew if Col. John M. Chivington hated Indians or not. Born in 1821 near Lebanon, Ohio, the Scotch-Irish Chivington family moved from town to town while John grew to manhood, becoming a Mason and a Methodist preacher in the process. In 1848, he moved with his own family to Quincy, Illinois, where he delivered his first sermon. Thereafter, he preached in Illinois, Missouri, and Nebraska.

Chivington opposed slavery and got in many hot arguments during the free-soil fighting in Kansas in the 1850s. In 1854, he organized the first Masonic lodge in the Kansas Territory, an organization in which the majority of members were Wyandot Indians. According to Chivington, they "seemed eagerly seeking some word of God, some light in the darkness of failure to understand the Almighty." Speaking with a tolerance that might sound anachronistic, he added that "Manitou is merely the Indian conception of the Supreme Being, and I find that conception is not unlike our idea of God."[1]

A large, imposing, barrel-chested man at six feet, four inches tall and 260 pounds, Chivington preached the Word as he saw it. When he talked of abolition in the churches of Platte County, Missouri, he was threatened with tar

---

1 Reginald S. Craig, *The Fighting Parson: The Biography of Colonel John M. Chivington* (Tucson, AZ, 1959), 21-30, 40, 66; Gary Roberts, "Sand Creek: Tragedy and Symbol," A Dissertation Submitted to the Graduate Faculty in Partial Fulfillment of the Requirements for the Degree of Doctor of Philosophy (Norman, OK, 1984), 114-16, 120.

Colonel John M. Chivington,
First Colorado

Although vilified today, in the 1860s
Chivington was a hero in many circles.

The Denver Public Library

and feathers, but the next Sunday Chivington marched to the pulpit, set down his Bible and two pistols next to it, and announced, "By the grace of God and these two revolvers, I am going to preach here today."

Chivington stayed in Platte County until 1860, when he moved his family to Denver, Colorado, where he would be the presiding Methodist elder in the Rocky Mountain District. On August 29, 1861, when Governor William S. Gilpin announced the formation of the First Colorado Regiment to fight for the Union in the young Civil War, Chivington offered his services. "I will be glad to appoint you as the chaplain of the regiment," said Gilpin. "I appreciate your offer," Chivington replied, but he wanted to fight against slavery, not preach against it. "Therefore, I must respectfully decline an appointment as a non-combatant officer, and at the same time urgently request a fighting commission instead." Gilpin made him a major.[2]

Chivington experienced hard fighting against the Rebels in the New Mexico Territory, became the military district commander in Colorado, and was often engaged against various Plains Indians, who had a notion they could drive the invading whites out of their territory. Keeping the roads and vital supply lines open was a constant headache, and 1864 erupted with nearly continuous

2 Gary Roberts, "Sand Creek: Tragedy and Symbol," A Dissertation Submitted to the Graduate Faculty in Partial Fulfillment of the Requirements for the Degree of Doctor of Philosophy (Norman, OK, 1984), 114-16, 120.

fighting. Chivington was badgered by civilian complaints as well as military expectations that he ought to do more to control the Indians. The West had a way of shoving problems in his face that he didn't have to deal with back East. If Chivington hadn't hated Indians before he moved to Colorado, he soon changed his mind. "Nits make lice" is a statement always attributed to him. It meant that he would just as soon kill all the Indian children before he they grew up and procreated.[3]

Sometime in October 1864, the harried colonel made up his mind to do something about controlling the Indians. The stagecoach king, Ben Holladay, was tired of Indians attacking his stagecoaches and stock and wired Secretary of War Edwin M. Stanton in the middle of the month demanding immediate relief. Believing that the officers and men currently patrolling the lines could not provide aid, he noted, "I most respectfully urge that General Connor be assigned to this duty at once." Conner, he added, "was the man for the work of punishing these marauders."

"General Connor" was Patrick Edward Connor, who had been promoted to brigadier general after his winter victory over the Indians at Bear River, Idaho. The next day the Army's general-in-chief, Maj. Gen. Henry W. Halleck, ordered Connor to give all possible protection to the road between Fort Kearny and Salt Lake City. In the last days of October, Connor's California troops began moving east while he took a Holladay stage to Denver to investigate conditions there and meet with Chivington. Before he began the trip, Connor wired Chivington to let him know he was coming. "Can we get a fight out of the Indians this winter?" he asked.[4]

Any procrastination about Indian troubles was approaching its end. Elements of the First and Third Colorado regiments assembled and headed for

---

3 The source of Chivington's "Nits" statement may have come from District Attorney Samuel E. Browne, one of Chivington's enemies, who claimed the colonel said it at a rally in Denver in September 1864. The phrase was common during the nineteenth century. Denmark Vesey, a black freedman accused of plotting a rebellion in South Carolina in 1822, was also said to have uttered, "What's the sense of killing the louse and leaving the nit?" when discussing killing all the white children.

4 Raymond G. Carey, "Colonel Chivington, Brigadier General Connor, and Sand Creek," *Westerners Brand Book 1960*, Guy M. Herstrom, ed. (Boulder, CO, 1961), 117-18, 120. Hereafter cited as "Chivington, Connor, and Sand Creek"; J. V. Frederick, *Ben Holladay the Stagecoach King* (Glendale, CA, 1940. Reprint, Lincoln, NE, 1989), 198-99; James F. Varley, *Brigham and the Brigadier: General Patrick Connor and his California Volunteers in Utah and Along the Overland Trail* (Tucson, AZ, 1989), 191.

Fort Lyon in southeast Colorado. On October 16, Chivington wrote Maj. Edward W. Wynkoop, in charge of Fort Lyon, that he was coming to take the regiment on a campaign against the Indians, but he needed more weapons. "The rascal who started with them left them at Atchison and took on some mining machinery," he complained. "This leaves us with nothing but our muskets for the Third. Send as quick as possible those Starr carbines. I have moved the Third out sixty miles, and will be after the Indians as soon as we can get those carbines."[5]

At Fort Lupton on the same day, Maj. Hal Sayr, Third Colorado, received orders to send Company B to Bijou Basin. Companies E, H, I, K, L, and M had already moved there from Denver on October 14, and constructed Camp Elbert, which became the field headquarters of the Third Colorado. Major Sayr and Capt. Harper M. Orahood moved Company B to Denver and up Cherry Creek. They marched southeast and camped on Running Creek, which was nearly deserted because the settlers had been frightened away after the Hungate killings there the previous June. The next day they crossed the divide over to Kiowa Creek and marched southeast into Bijou Basin. "There is now Seven Companies here," Sayr wrote in his diary. After shuffling a few more companies around, they settled down to wait for Chivington's final order to move out.

It began snowing on October 30, and Bijou Basin was locked in by the bad weather. Sayr recorded that the snow was two feet deep and still falling. They searched for a man named Washington Watson, Company B, who was lost and feared frozen to death. He was found the next day about ten miles from camp. Both of his feet were badly frozen, but he survived. Not so lucky was one of the Latino soldiers from Lt. Mariano Autobees's Company H, who froze to death on the night of November 2. He was buried the next day by his comrades, "without a coffin," recalled Sayr. "Nothing but a handkerchief tied over his face."[6]

The long cold wait in Bijou Basin went more quickly for William M. Breakenridge, a 17-year-old boy from Wisconsin who had come to Colorado for adventure and enlisted in the Third Regiment because he believed it was his

5 Chivington to Wynkoop, October 16, 1864, in *The War of the Rebellion: A Compilation of the Official Records of the Union and Confederate Armies*, 128 vols. (Washington, DC, 1880-1901), Series 1, vol. 41, pt. 4, 23-24. Hereafter OR. All references are to Series 1 unless otherwise noted.

6 Lynn I. Perrigo, "Major Hal Sayr's Diary of the Sand Creek Campaign," *Colorado Magazine* (March 1938), 15, no. 2, 51-53.

patriotic duty to fight Indians. Billy was detailed as courier to carry dispatches between the Basin and Denver. He complained about the old muzzle-loading musket he received, but remedied it by trading for a Sharps carbine. With a fast horse and a better weapon, he took the back trail to Denver. To avoid being spotted by Indians, Breakenridge rode all night, stopped at a ranch about half way to Denver for a short sleep, and reached the city in the evening. He would be kept busy in that manner for the next three weeks.[7]

In Camp Baxter, about five miles below Pueblo, Company G waited for its equipment. Irving Howbert complained of the great snowstorm that began the last day of October. "The snowfall at our camp was twenty inches in depth," he said, "at Colorado City it was over two feet on the level, and on the Divide still deeper." The camp was out of food in a few days. Captain Oliver Baxter told everyone who had a home nearby to go there and remain until further notice. Howbert and a half-dozen men started north along Fountain Creek toward Colorado City. They followed the tracks of a solitary wagon through the crusty snow and arrived at a ranch late at night, utterly exhausted. One more day's march brought the tired men to their homes. There, they waited almost two weeks before receiving word to rejoin the company.

In the meantime, Company A trekked from the Pike's Peak area over to Bijou Basin. Private Alston K. Shaw did not like the change of camp. "Here the men did not feel so good natured," he observed. "It was cold and stormy, bedding was scarce and rations were low. Captain [Theodore] Cree had brought straw to feed the horses, but the soldiers used some of it to lie on and cover with their blankets." Cree placed blankets on his horse, but soldiers kept stealing them. After attending to business in Denver, Col. George L. Shoup of the Third Colorado rode north to collect the remaining troops along the South Platte. He hurried Companies C, D, and F of the Third Colorado and Company H of the First Colorado, off toward Denver. Captain David H. Nichols started with his Company D on November 4, but another blizzard trapped them on the plains for four days. Huddled in Bijou Basin, Captain Sayr wrote, "Monday Nov 7th. Commenced snowing last evening and has snowed all day with a cold wind from N.E." The men of the Third Colorado faced their toughest test to date battling the elements. One man went snow blind, one lost his mind, three died,

---

7   William M. Breakenridge, *Helldorado: Bringing the Law to the Mesquite* (Lincoln, NE, 1992), 30, 33, 41.

and eleven deserted. By mid-November the regiment had only about 500 men —but those that remained were ready to fight.[8]

Colonel Chivington was also ready to fight. His companies were nearly all congregated in Bijou Basin or marching there. The ball was rolling because they all believed the citizens of Colorado Territory were in deadly danger from the Indians, who had been raiding and killing all spring and summer, albeit with provocation. As noted, Chivington and Colorado Territorial Governor John Evans were constantly bombarded by complaints to do something about the violence and theft. The Denver press was becoming as anxious as the people. Editorials appearing in the *Daily Union Vedette*, the post newspaper published at Camp Douglas, Utah, General Connor's home base, exacerbated the situation. The paper argued that Chivington needed to take matters into his own hands and solve the problem. "Prompt and energetic action is demanded," continued the paper, and only 300 well-armed men were needed to keep the roads open and prove that "the brave soldier fighting for law and right, is more than a match for two redskins." In a final barb, the *Vedette* declared that if Colorado troops couldn't do the job, there were "a considerable number of California Volunteers in the District of Utah . . . who would esteem it a great satisfaction, could they be allowed the opportunity of wiping out the scoundrels who have lately been and are now infesting the Overland road East."

Chivington might take civilian complaints with some tolerance, but it was unendurable to be the object of military sarcasm reflecting on his own competence. With an increased sense of urgency, especially knowing that General Connor might be approaching to take over, Chivington quickened his pace. He was fairly certain he knew where the Indians were located. According to Chivington, "the hostile Indians had proceeded south from the Platte and were almost within striking distance of Fort Lyon." On November 12, Chivington told Shoup to get his regiment moving.[9]

---

8 Perrigo, "Sayr's Diary," 51-53; Luella Shaw, *True History of Some of the Pioneers of Colorado* (Hotchkiss, CO, 1909), 63-64; Irving Howbert, *The Indians of the Pike's Peak Region* (New York, NY, 1914. Reprint, Glorieta, NM, 1970), 95-96; Carey, "Chivington, Connor and Sand Creek," 131. Some claim Chivington lowered the number of his men in his reports to make his victory at Sand Creek look more glorious, but he never could field the entire Third Regiment for lack of mounts and equipment, while deaths, sickness, and desertion cut deeply into his available men.

9 Carey, "Chivington, Connor and Sand Creek," 121, 123-24; Perrigo, "Sayr's Diary," 53; Chivington to Curtis, December 16, 1864, *OR* 41, pt. 1, 948-49, 954.

The soldiers were already in motion and Chivington was about to ride out to join them when General Connor pulled into town. Delayed because of the early snowstorms, Connor left his California cavalry behind at Fort Bridger and rode with Ben Holladay on a stagecoach to Denver. They arrived at the Planter's House on November 14. The next day, the First Colorado's band serenaded them and Chivington observed official etiquette by visiting. General Halleck had informed Connor that he was not to take over command of troops in Chivington's district, but they were to cooperate with each other. There is no official record of the conversation between the two men, but it was certain Chivington was not amenable to letting Connor borrow his troops (and by this time most of the regiment was as far south as Fountain Creek).

On November 19, before Chivington started on his journey to catch up with the troops, Connor told him that he was confident the Indians were in for "a most terrible threshing if you catch them, and if it was in the mountains, and you had them in a canyon and your troops at one end of it"—Connor had trapped the Shoshones at Bear River in just that manner. "But," he continued, "I am afraid on these plains you won't do it."

"Possibly I may not," Chivington admitted, "but I think I shall."

Connor asked him to wire back if he managed to catch the Indians, and Chivington promised he would do so. "Colonel," Connor asked, "where are these Indians?"

"General," Chivington answered, "that is the trick that wins in this game, if the game is won. There are but two persons who know their exact location, and they are myself and Colonel George L. Shoup."

"But I won't tell anybody," Connor protested.

"I will bet you don't," said Chivington.

Connor began to leave, but turned and said, "Well, I begin to believe that you will catch those Indians."[10]

Chivington did not know exactly where the Indians were, but more people than he and Shoup knew where many of them had been camping of late.

---

10 Carey, "Chivington, Connor and Sand Creek," 125, 127-30; Varley, *Brigham and the Brigadier*, 195.

Chapter 2

The Road to Sand Creek

The area that became the Colorado Territory began as a land white Europeans usually only passed through on their way to somewhere else—"fly-over" country might ben the term used today. That quickly changed when gold was discovered along the Front Range of Colorado, a mountainous area located in the central part of the territory. A few fur traders were replaced by miners, and merchants, businessmen, farmers, and ranchers arrived. The lure of easy riches had a way of making the idea of Manifest Destiny more palatable to those who deigned to consider its ramifications. Trails and stagecoach lines veered toward central Colorado and railroads would soon be on the way. Denver was on the road to becoming a metropolis of the mountains. Unfortunately for them, the Indian tribes refused to quietly exit the stage.

The previously sporadic fighting increased when gold-seekers entered the region. Up in Minnesota in 1862, the Sioux had fought back, killing as many as 600 white settlers and soldiers. The military retaliation spilled over into the Dakotas, turning once-neutral tribes there into enemies. The turmoil and fighting spread farther west and south. In 1863, the US Army conducted major campaigns in the Dakotas, while in Colorado, Governor John Evans and Colonel Chivington were wringing their hands worrying that the war would spread to their domain. Rumors of raiding abounded.

In November 1863, Robert North, a white man living with the Arapahos, gave the governor a shocking report: Bands of Comanche, Apache, Kiowa, Arapaho, Sioux, and Cheyenne had pledged to each other to go to war with the whites in the spring of 1864, as soon as they could get enough ammunition and guns to do so. Since Robert North had an Arapaho wife, the Indians had asked him to join the uprising, but he had demurred. "I am yet a white man," he replied, "and wish to avoid bloodshed."

Governor Evans sent the alarming news to Commissioner of Indian Affairs William P. Dole, and added that corroborating evidence was received from Indian Agent Samuel Colley. In September, Evans had instructed the military commanders to not allow Indians to loiter about the forts or purchase supplies. Now he ordered Colley to stop supplying them with guns. With the trouble in 1863 and the news of threatened warfare in the spring, the coming winter would be a time of apprehension. It was a hard season, and the Indians in Colorado Territory took shelter in the sparsely timbered bottoms, relatively snug beneath their lodge skins and buffalo robes, as were the settlers and miners in their lodges of wood or adobe.[1]

The white settlers found more to worry about in January 1864, when the Second Colorado Cavalry was ordered to the Missouri border to guard against Confederate bushwhackers. With only the First Colorado to defend the territory, Governor Evans and many citizens grew increasingly anxious about the approaching spring. Evans believed a massive attack on the scale of the Minnesota uprising would surely occur. He wanted more troops, but was told to utilize the militia if the need arose. This late in the war, though, few men were willing to join a militia unit. Evans was quickly becoming aware that Coloradans were generally not cut out to be soldiers. As the *Rocky Mountain News* lamented, that "About ninety-nine hundredths of the citizens of Denver who are able to bear arms are constitutionally opposed to doing so."[2]

Governor Evans continued to forward his concerns to Maj. Gen. Samuel H. Curtis, in charge of the Department of Kansas, of which the Colorado Territory was now a part. Curtis had his own problems, and was also being bombarded with pleas from Kansas citizens for protection along the Fort Scott and Santa Fe roads. On March 18, he wrote to his boss, Maj. Gen. John Pope, "An immense emigration is concentrating in the Platte Valley en route for the Bannock mines, and they are liable to create trouble with the tribes northwest of Laramie, whose territory they will undoubtedly invade." Most of all, there was a

1 Evans to Dole, November 10, 1863, *OR* 34, pt. 4, 100; Harry E. Kelsey, Jr., *Frontier Capitalist: The Life of John Evans* (Denver, CO, 1969), 135.

2 Roberts, "Sand Creek," 201-02.

continuing need for troops to counter the bushwhackers and Rebels on the borders of Missouri, Arkansas, and Indian Territory. Colorado was of secondary concern. Curtis wrote back to Evans, "I am glad to have transmitted to my notice all intelligence of a credible nature Your Excellency can send me, and I will take due notice and govern myself accordingly." Not only would Curtis not send more soldiers to Colorado, be he also informed Evans, "I am obliged to draw every man who can be spared from the Indian frontier to operate against rebels who have devastated this State of Kansas."[3]

Evans would have to make do on his own. By April, some of his fears were realized. In Bijou Basin, a circular valley about 65 miles southeast of Denver, government freighters Irwin and Jackman fattened up their herd for the spring hauling, but Cheyenne Indians drove off 175 cattle. Herders trailed the stolen stock, following tracks leading eastward to Sand Creek. They eventually gave up and returned to Denver with the news of the thefts. General Curtis was notified and orders went back to Colonel Chivington as well as Lt. Col. William Collins at Fort Laramie: "Handle the scoundrels without gloves if it becomes necessary." Chivington dispatched Lt. George S. Eayre after the culprits. Lieutenant Eayre, along with Capt. William McLain, who commanded an independent artillery battery, left on April 8 with 54 men of the battery, two 12-pounder mountain howitzers, and 26 men of the First Colorado. They picked up the trail, crossed the divide between the waters of the Platte and Arkansas, and moved down Sand Creek.[4]

While Eayre was searching, rancher W. D. Ripley rode into Camp Sanborn on the South Platte River to report that Cheyenne were stealing his stock along Bijou Creek. Lieutenant Clark Dunn and 40 men of Companies C and H of the First Colorado went with Ripley to recover the stock. On April 12, about three miles from Fremont's Orchard, Dunn spotted about 15 Cheyenne driving horses across the South Platte. Ripley announced that the horses were his. Dunn and 15 troopers confronted the warriors while Ripley and four men went after the stock. The Cheyenne approached Dunn in an effort to shake hands to prove they were friendly. Dunn was wary, however, and made the mistake of trying to disarm them. Shooting began, the Indians bolted, and Dunn tried to catch them. Each side claimed the other fired first. The chase continued for

3   Curtis to Pope, March 18, 1864, Curtis to Evans, March 26, 1864, *OR* 34, pt. 2, 652, 742-43.

4   Eayre to Chivington, April 23, 1864, *OR* 34, pt. 1, 881; Mitchell to Commanding officer, Fort Laramie, April 7, 1864, *OR* 34, pt. 3, 85.

nearly 15 miles before Dunn gave up. Four of his men were wounded—two of them fatally—and the Cheyenne took four casualties.[5]

Meanwhile, Lieutenant Eayre was trailing cattle into eastern Colorado. On April 15 at the headwaters of the South Fork Republican they found a five-lodge Cheyenne camp. The inhabitants were already fleeing, and a few warriors were riding their way. Soldiers tried to capture them, but the warriors shot and wounded one. When McLain unlimbered the battery, all the Indians fled. Eayre rode into the abandoned camp and burned it. The next day they found and burned another deserted camp and recovered 19 cattle said to belong to Irwin and Jackman. With the army mules breaking down from the strain of pulling their heavy wagons, Eayre returned to Denver. The Plains War of 1864 had begun.[6]

The Coloradans' preemptive strikes may have only made things worse. Major Jacob Downing, of the First Colorado, rode out with Lieutenant Dunn and 60 men looking for more Indians. Downing's column rode a circuitous route of 140 miles before returning to Camp Sanborn empty-handed. "Everything indicates the commencement of an Indian war," he wrote in a letter to Chivington. "Active measures should at once be adopted to meet them on all sides, or the emigration will be interrupted. The people along the Platte are generally very much terrified."[7]

Downing tried again. On May 1 near American Ranch on the South Platte, he captured a half-Lakota man named Spotted Horse. Under threat of death, they forced him to lead the soldiers to the nearest Indian camp. With 40 men of Companies C and H, Downing rode north to Cedar Canyon and, on May 3, found a 14-lodge camp. Downing moved to cut off the pony herd from the camp and his troops killed two young herders in the process. Ten men were detailed to guard the ponies while Downing divided his small command to move against the Indians. Most of them hurried for cover. While several warriors fired from behind some rocks, the women and children headed up the canyon. Downing had a tough time advancing against the warriors' fire. He

---

5 Gregory F. Michno, *Encyclopedia of Indian Wars Western Battles and Skirmishes, 1850-1890* (Missoula, MT, 2003), 134-35.

6 General Curtis at Fort Leavenworth was also getting edgy. On April 19, he wired Brig. Gen. Benjamin Alvord, commanding the District of Oregon, in an effort to coordinate their efforts. Curtis wrote that a "vast army of immigrants" was converging on the Platte Valley and he was not sure he could protect them. Ibid.

7 Downing to Chivington, April 20, 1864, *OR* 34, pt. 3, 233, 242, 250-52.

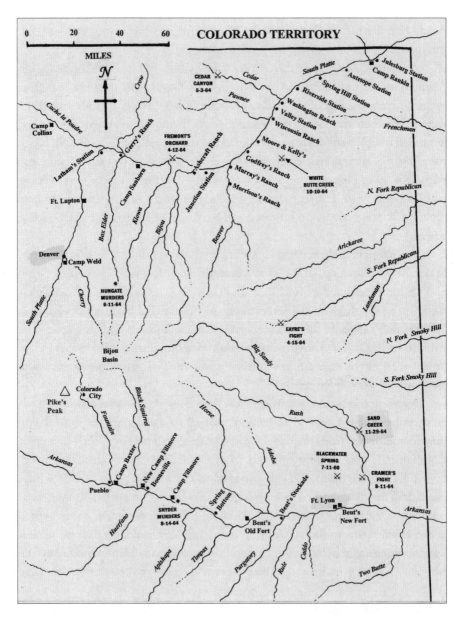

tried to draw them out, but they would not be baited. After a three-hour fight, one of his soldiers was killed and one was wounded. Downing had enough, and with "the carbine ammunition getting rather scarce, and the Indians so concealed that after fifty shots I could scarcely get a man, I concluded to return" to American Ranch. Downing took 100 captured horses with him. He claimed to have killed 25 Indians and wounded 35 more—which was probably more people than were in the entire village at that time. The Cheyenne acknowledged only two women and two boys killed. An excited Downing sent a note to Chivington immediately upon his return: "Send me more troops; I need them. The war has commenced in earnest."[8]

Any war that had begun was mostly due to the efforts of the Colorado soldiers. General Curtis began to realized that matters were spiraling out of control and cautioned Governor Evans to tone it down. "I hope, therefore," Curtis wrote, "Your Excellency will dispense with all the Federal troops you can spare, and use your utmost efforts, by kindness and militia force, to keep down Indian troubles and side issues that draw away men" Curtis would rather use with better effect in Kansas and Missouri. For the time being, Evans and Chivington were to cool their heels with the Plains tribes.[9]

Unfortunately, Lt. George Eayre was out once more hunting Indians. The lieutenant had returned to Denver for reinforcements. This time with lighter wagons, 84 men, and McLain's battery, his column headed east to the Smoky Hill River in Kansas. Eayre effectively disappeared for almost two weeks, and his superiors wondered where in the world he had gone. It was May 16 when the command stumbled into about 250 Cheyenne lodges at Big Bushes, some 40 miles northwest of Fort Larned at the junction of Big Timber Creek and the Smoky Hill.

When a line of warriors appeared on a hill ahead, Eayre hurriedly tried to form his cavalry into line. Lean Bear, who had met with President Abraham Lincoln the previous year and was given a silver peace medal, was apprehensive, but nevertheless rode out to see what the soldiers wanted. He probably did not recall Uncle Abe's words, "You know it is not always possible for any father to have his children do precisely as he wishes them to do." Lean Bear and his companion, Star, rode downhill as other warriors began moving around the flanks. Private Asbury Bird watched the men approach. "When the two Indians came to meet us they appeared friendly, but when they saw the command coming on a lope they ran off. No effort was made by Lieutenant Ayres to hold a talk with the Indians." In a flash, related Bird, "we were attacked by about seven hundred Indians."

---

8 Downing to Chivington, May 3, 1864, *OR* 34, pt. 1, 907-08; Doris Monahan, *Destination: Denver City The South Platte Trail* (Athens, OH, 1985), 142-43. American Ranch was also known as "Moore & Kelley's."

9 Curtis to Evans, May 9, 1864, *OR* 34, pt. 3, 531.

The Cheyenne Wolf Chief told a different story. According to him, Lean Bear told them to stay where they were so they would not frighten the soldiers and rode forward to shake their hands. "When the chief was only within twenty or thirty yards of the line," he continued, "the officer called out in a very loud voice and the soldiers all opened fire on Lean Bear and the rest of us." Lean Bear and Star were shot off their horses and the troops pumped round after round into them. They were so engrossed with the Indians in their front that they did not realize that hundreds of other warriors had gotten around their flanks. "They were so close that we shot several of them with arrows," continued, Wolf Chief. "Two of them fell backwards off their horses. . . . More Cheyennes kept coming up in small parties, and the soldiers were bunching up and seemed badly frightened."

As troops and warriors merged—Eayre estimated the Indians numbered from 400 to 500—the scene became a vortex of shouts, shots, and confusion. The howitzers, loaded with small pieces of lead, rumbled up and were unlimbered on level prairie, but the artillerymen could not elevate their pieces high enough to hit the warriors on the hillsides. "The grapeshot struck the ground around us," said Wolf Chief, "but the aim was bad."

Soon, Black Kettle arrived and frantically rode among the warriors calling, "Stop the fighting! Do not make war!" "But," said Wolf Chief, "it was a long time before the warriors would listen to him. We were very mad." Black Kettle may have prevented serious losses on both sides. He reined in many warriors and a lull ensued. Eayre saw the opportunity to strengthen his position. When the wagons came up, he organized his men and the howitzers inside a makeshift square of dismounted cavalry. The most persistent attacks were over, but a moving fight continued for seven hours and about seven miles before the last of the warriors gave up the chase. The Cheyenne lost three killed and several wounded, while Eayre claimed he had killed three chiefs and 25 warriors. Eayre lost four killed and three wounded, and 15 saddled cavalry horses were captured. Eayre headed south toward Fort Larned, where he arrived on May 19. The war was about to be kicked into high gear.[10]

---

10 Wynkoop to Maynard, May 27, 1864, OR 34, pt. 1, 934-35; Wynkoop to Maynard, June 3, 1864, Alfred Gay to G. O'Brien, June 10, 1864, OR 34, pt. 4, 208, 403, 460-62; U.S. Congress, Senate. "The Chivington Massacre," *Report of the Joint Special Committee on the Condition of the Indian Tribes*, Senate Report 156, 39th Congress, 2nd Session (Washington, DC, 1867), 72, 75; Savoie Lottinville, ed., *Life of George Bent Written From His Letters* (Norman, OK, 1968), 131-32; Peter John Powell, *People of the Sacred Mountain*, Vol. I (San Francisco, CA, 1981), 263-64.

Lieutenant Eayre had his fill of Indian hunting, but the Cheyenne, who had engaged in some sporadic raiding up to this point, were now infuriated. Heavy raiding immediately began along the Santa Fe Trail, as was usual almost every year when the grass grew green for the ponies and the weather warmed. The routine spring raiding began concurrently with Eayre's encounter.

Charles Rath owned the Walnut Creek Ranch 20 miles northeast of Fort Larned and 40 miles east of the Big Bushes fight. The day of the that fight, Cheyenne rode to Rath's ranch and stole his Cheyenne wife, telling him they were going "to kill all the whites they could find." Rath gathered all the goods he could pile into his wagons and sent them east with a few of his men. He and two employees, meanwhile, built a defensive position on the roof of the ranch house. The next morning the Cheyenne returned, stole horses and mules, and carried off whatever remaining goods they could find. The three white men decided to let well enough alone and escaped with their lives after the raiders left.

Other Indians hit Curtis' and Cole's Ranch at the Great Bend of the Arkansas, and the Cow Creek Ranch about 15 miles northeast of Rath's. Indians also hit settlers and merchants along the roads east to Salina. By May 18, citizens had sworn out affidavits that depredations were being committed between Fort Larned and Fort Riley. Settlers fled their homes in the Smoky Hill country and congregated as far east as Abilene. One civilian deposition concluded, "The terror among the frontier settlements is general, and unless aid is afforded the probability is that all the settlements will be abandoned, if the settlers are not murdered."[11]

Many Indians were involved in the May raids, but only a minority could blame their marauding on retaliation for Eayre's killing of Lean Bear. Eayre, however, added fuel to the fire that was already smoldering. As such, he became a convenient patsy as the man who started an Indian war—until a bigger culprit in the person of John Chivington stepped in six months down the road.

At this time, Curtis wanted all available troops moved east to deal with the larger Confederate threat, while Chivington and Governor Evans shuffled their meager forces to deal with what they believed was a full-scale Indian uprising. Chivington was certain bloodshed was the only answer. "The Cheyenne will

---

11 Donald J. Berthrong, *The Southern Cheyennes* (Norman, OK, 1963), 188; Louise Barry, "The Ranch at Walnut Creek Crossing," *Kansas Historical Quarterly* (Summer 1971), 37, no. 2, 143-44; Louise Barry, "The Ranch at Great Bend," *Kansas Historical Quarterly* (Spring 1973), 39, no. 1, 96-98; *OR* 34, pt. 3, 661.

Major Edward W. Wynkoop,
First Colorado

He tried to bring peace, but his actions
led to the Sand Creek incident.

The Denver Public Library

have to be soundly whipped before they will be quiet," he cautioned Maj. Edward W. Wynkoop, who was in command at Fort Lyon, on the last day of May. "If any of them are caught in your vicinity kill them, as that is the only way." On May 28 Evans wrote to General Curtis explaining his predicament. Colorado troops had been sent out of the territory, and "Now we have but half the troops we then had, and are at war with a powerful combination of Indian tribes, who are pledged to sustain each other and drive the white people from this country." Evans believed his prediction had come true. "The depredations have commenced precisely as foretold in my communications to the Departments last fall."[12]

It was something of a self-fulfilling prophesy. The Coloradans were so certain the Indians would go to war that when the inevitable (and not uncommon) stock thefts occurred, it was seen as something different: The beginning of a great uprising. White retaliation resulted in Indian reprisals, and a snowball became an avalanche. In early June, when Indian raiders drove off 150 cattle and horses along the South Platte, the telegraph operator at Junction Station tapped off the sarcastic question, "Where is Chivington and his bloodthirsty tigers?"[13]

---

12 Evans to Curtis, May 28, 1864, *OR* 34, pt. 4, 98, 151.

13 Monahan, *Denver City*, 151.

The Denverites were already on edge when the latest news arrived from Running Creek. On June 11, a band of perhaps a dozen Arapaho were in the area stealing horses from ranches and freighters and paid a visit to Isaac Van Wormer's place 35 miles southeast of Denver, a ranch being operated by Van Wormer's hired man Nathan Hungate. Perhaps the Indians believed the ranch would be easy pickings, but Nathan had other ideas. The raiders were running off some stock when a hail of gunfire rang out from the ranch house. One or more Indians may have been hit, and the Arapaho decided to teach the defiant hired hand a lesson. Bullets blasted the ranch house while Hungate's two little daughters cowered in a corner and his wife Ellen bravely loaded several available weapons. Ellen may also have been firing, for the pair put up quite a defense. Frustrated, the Arapaho set the house on fire, and the Hungates had no choice but to flee the burning structure. Ellen and the children were cut down within a few hundred yards. The angry warriors vented their rage upon them, raping Mrs. Hungate before stabbing and scalping her. The two young girls, one an infant of three or four months and the other two years old, had their heads nearly severed, and the infant was disemboweled. Nathan made it another mile, working his Henry rifle before succumbing to wounds. The Indians desecrated his corpse and disappeared east onto the plains.[14]

On June 15, the Hungates' bodies were carried into Denver and displayed in a wagon box. *The Commonwealth,* a Denver newspaper, printed a clarion call cal arms:

A HORRIBLE SIGHT! The bodies of those four people who were massacred by the Cheyennes on Van Wormer's ranch, thirty miles down the Cut-off, were brought to town this morning, and a coroner's inquest held over them. It was a most solemn sight indeed, to see the mutilated corpses stretched in the stiffness of death, upon that wagon bed, first the father, Nathan Hungate, about 30 years of age, with his head scalped and his cheeks and eyes chopped in as with an axe or tomahawk. Next lay his wife, Ellen, with her head also scalped through from ear to ear. Alongside of her lie two small children, one at her right arm and one at her left, with their throats severed completely, so that their handsome little heads and pale innocent countenances had to be stuck on, as it were, to preserve the humanity of form. Those that perpetuate such unnatural, brutal butchery as this ought to be hunted to the farthest bounds of these

14 Jeff Broome, "Indian Massacres in Elbert County, Colorado New Information on the 1864 Hungate and 1868 Dietemann Murders," *The Denver Westerners Roundup* (January-February 2004), 11-15.

broad plains and burned to the stake alive, was the general remark of the hundreds of spectators this afternoon.[15]

The slaughter put Denver into an uproar. Mobs broke into the ordnance stores demanding guns and ammunition. On the night of the 19th, a panic swept through town when horsemen came tearing down the streets, Paul Revere-like, shouting that the Indians were coming. At Camp Weld, Mollie Sanford rushed for her door at the furious pounding and opened it to see a soldier with "his eyes almost starting from their sockets."

"Run, wimmen!" he cried. "Run for your lives, the Injuns are coming three thousand strong! Run for the brick building at Denver! Governor's orders! But don't get skeered."

"I was already about paralyzed," Mollie admitted, but another woman who shared the quarters with her "immediately went into hysterics."

Mollie spread the word around the barracks and soon all the women were shrieking. She wanted to flee but decided to wait for her husband, Lt. Byron H. Sanford. When he arrived, they gathered their two children and some essentials and walked to town. By daylight the streets were filled with families, but there were no traces of Indians and the scare petered out. Mollie later learned that it had all begun when some folks living outside town saw some Mexican cattle drivers and thought they were Indians. The Denver *Commonwealth* elaborated:

> The great panic of last night will never be forgotten by anyone who witnessed or shared it. It was terrible as causeless, and as unreasonable. . . . There are dangers, but none which preparation will not avert. It may require some sacrifice of time and comfort, but in mercy to poor women, don't let us make them suffer another such a fright.[16]

---

15 Scott C. Williams, ed., *Colorado History Through the News (a context of the times.) The Indian Wars of 1864 Through the Sand Creek Massacre* (Aurora, CO, 1997), 44. The effect of the Hungate killings on Denver was powerful and long-lasting. Stephen Decatur, who later fought at Sand Creek, testified that he had counted with real satisfaction the number of dead Indians after that event. "I was at the house of Mrs. Hungate only a few days before she was murdered, and I became attached to her and her babes, and I wished her friends to know how many of the bloody villains we had killed," explained Decatur. U.S. Congress, Senate. "Sand Creek Massacre," *Report of the Secretary of War*, Senate Exec. Doc. 26. 39th Congress, 2nd Session (Washington, DC, 1867), 198.

16 Mollie D. Sanford, *Mollie: The Journal of Mollie Dorsey Sanford in Nebraska and Colorado Territories 1857-1866* (Lincoln, NE, 1976), 187-88; Williams, *Through the News*, 59.

Exaggerated as it may have been, the Indian menace was real enough to the Coloradans, and rumor believed is reality. Governor Evans began organizing the militia and wrote the War Department for permission to raise another regiment of volunteers. On June 27, Evans decided to wait no more and issued an ultimatum addressed "To the Friendly Indians of the Plains":

> Agents, interpreters, and traders will inform the friendly Indians of the plains that some members of their tribes have gone to war with the white people. They steal stock and run it off, hoping to escape detection and punishment. In some instances they have attacked and killed soldiers and murdered peaceable citizens. For this the Great Father is angry, and will certainly hunt them out and punish them, but he does not want to injure those who remain friendly to the whites. He desires to protect and take care of them. For this purpose I direct that all friendly Indians keep away from those who are at war, and go to places of safety. . . . The object of this is to prevent friendly Indians from being killed through mistake. None but those who intend to be friendly with the whites must come to these places. The families of those who have gone to war with the whites must be kept away from among the friendly Indians. The war on hostile Indians will be continued until they are all effectually subdued.

Evans and almost every citizen of Colorado Territory were sure there was a war on. There was no doubt the soldiers were on a war footing. The Cheyenne and Arapaho were certainly aware of the war, and even the Lakota, when in council with the US Army at Fort Cottonwood in June, remarked that they would try to keep their people out of the way "until this war is over between the whites and Cheyennes."[17]

The Army command, however, appeared to be in denial about the matter. General Curtis ordered Chivington to move his troops to central Kansas. He believed "a good company or two, with two howitzers well attended, is no doubt sufficient to pursue and destroy any band of Indians likely to congregate anywhere on the plains, and it is bad economy to divert needless numbers in pursuit of Indians."

On July 5, having grown tired of Evans's constant cry for help, Curtis finally snapped:

> I may not have all you have seen and heard, but I am sure I have great deal on the subject which you have not seen nor heard, and I am obliged to Your Excellency for all

17 Kelsey, *Frontier Capitalist*, 143; Washington Henman, June 8, 1864, *OR* 34, pt. 4, 459.

the intelligence which you have sent me. . . . While prepared for the worst as far as possible we may not exhaust our efforts in pursuit of rumors, and I, therefore, request you to send me telegraphic information of outrages which were fully ascertained.[18]

After Evans issued his ultimatum, he told Agent Sam Colley to employ John Smith, his son Jack, and William Bent to spread the word to get the peaceful Indians together because the non-complying Indians would be treated as hostile and bent on mischief. While some heeded the warning, others were out raiding. In mid-July, Satanta and his Kiowa attacked Fort Larned and stole about 170 horses. Kiowa, Comanche, and Arapaho raiders attacked wagon trains in the Great Bend area, killing 10 teamsters and plundering the wagons. The friendly Arapaho Left Hand rode to Fort Larned to talk, but the nervous soldiers shot at him, which only further served to anger many young warriors. Cheyenne and Arapaho raided ranches along the South Platte in Colorado.

In August, Indians attacked a wagon train at Lower Cimarron Springs in Kansas, killing five men. There was fighting across the Central Plains and down into Texas. With so many Indians in non-compliance with Evans's ultimatum, Agent Colley weighed his possibilities. With a war on, he could probably hold back the annuity goods—food and other supplies the US government provided to the Indians in exchange for land—he had been stockpiling, even though Maj. Scott Anthony at Fort Lyon had already forced him to distribute much of it. When he learned of the increasing depredations, the Indians's "good friend" Sam wrote to Governor Evans, "I now think a little powder and lead is the best food for them."[19]

There was plenty of fighting prior to August 1864, but early that month the conflict increased another notch. Along a 60-mile stretch of the Little Blue River in Nebraska between August 7-9, hundreds of Cheyenne and Lakota warriors devastated the ranches and roads. When the assault was over, 38 settlers were dead, nine were wounded, and five were captured. On August 8 farther west along Plum Creek near the Platte River, Cheyenne attacked wagon trains and stagecoach stations, leaving 13 people dead and capturing two more.[20]

18 Curtis to Chivington, June 29, 1864, *OR* 34, pt. 4, 595; Curtis to Evans July 5, 1864, *OR* 41, pt. 2, 53.

19 Kelsey, *Frontier Capitalist*, 144.

20 Michno, *Encyclopedia of Indian Wars*, 147-49.

Like Governor Evans, Governor Alvin Saunders of Nebraska and Governor Thomas Carney of Kansas cast about for help. General Robert B. Mitchell reacted, writing to General Curtis, "I find the Indians at war with us through the entire District of Nebraska from South Pass to the Blue, a distance of 800 miles and more, and have laid waste the country, driven off stock, and murdered men, women, and children in large numbers. In my humble opinion," he continued, "the only way to put a stop to this state of things will be to organize a sufficient force to pursue them to the villages and exterminate the leading tribes engaged in this terrible slaughter."[21]

A frustrated Governor Evans nullified his June proclamation to the friendly Indians, and on August 11 issued a new one in the *Rocky Mountain News*:

> All citizens of Colorado, either individually or in such parties as they may organize, to go in pursuit of all hostile Indians on the plains, scrupulously avoiding those who have responded to my said call to rendezvous at the points indicated, also to kill and destroy as enemies of the country wherever they may be found, all such hostile Indians. And further, as the only reward I am authorized to offer for such services, I hereby empower such citizens, or parties of citizens, to take captive, and hold to their own private use and benefits, all property of said hostile Indians that they may capture.[22]

Evans had just given *carte blanche* to raid and kill Indians, and unfortunately, few Indians subscribed to the newspaper. "All good citizens," concluded the proclamation, "are called upon to do their duty for the defense of their homes and families." Coincidentally, that same day the War Department in Washington authorized Evans to raise a 100-days regiment of cavalry or infantry at his discretion. The papers trumpeted the news. To many, it finally appeared as though Colorado had been given the means for its salvation.[23]

---

21 Mitchell to Curtis, August 15, 1864, *OR* 41, pt. 2, 722. Many orders were issued to exterminate Indians. General James H. Carleton gave orders to Kit Carson to kill all male Indians. Colonel Patrick Connor gave orders to his troops to kill all the males. General George Crook issued orders to hunt down and kill all Apaches. Generals Pope, Mitchell, Blunt, Curtis, Sherman, and Sheridan used phrases that contained the words "kill" or "extermination," but genocide was never formal policy. William Dole, in *Report of the Commissioner of Indian Affairs 1862*, 188, expressed the official viewpoint: "The idea of exterminating all these Indians is at once so revolting and barbarous that it cannot for a moment be entertained." Yet, perhaps we are walking the line between *de jure* and *de facto* policy.

22 Williams, *Through the News*, 118-19, 124-27.

23 Williams, *Through the News*, 118-19, 124-27.

With Evans issuing a proclamation that sanctioned open season on the Indians, there was no telling what would happen. On August 11 near Sand Creek, Lt. Joseph Cramer of the First Colorado led 15 troopers in a chase against Neva and a small band of Arapaho on their way to Fort Lyon to talk peace. Neva carried a copy of Evans's initial armistice proposal, but Cramer's aggression drove him off in a running skirmish.

From that time on, it would not be easy for Indians to demonstrate their goodwill. At Fort Lyon, Major Wynkoop wrote to Chivington that two of his men had been recently murdered. He also complained that his carbines were "absolutely worthless," but he intended to present a bold front. "At all events," he added, "it is my intention to kill all Indians I may come across until I receive orders to the contrary from headquarters."

Sam Colley also painted a pessimistic picture in a letter to Governor Evans. "The Indians are very troublesome," he complained, writing of the Cramer affair. He believed large war parties were nearby. Contractors were working on a new agency at Point of Rocks, but Colley feared it "will have to be abandoned if troops cannot be obtained to protect it. I have made application to Major Wynkoop for troops. He will do all he can, but the fact is we have no troops to spare from here. . . . I fear that all the tribes are engaged." The Arapaho he had been feeding, added Colley, "have not been in for some time. It looks at present as though we shall have to fight them all."[24]

On August 14, Arapaho under Little Raven's son had just stolen stock from Point of Rocks Agency when they came across a wagon making its way to Fort Lyon from Denver. The Indians attacked and killed three men, including John Snyder, a soldier stationed at the fort who had been allowed to ride in the wagon to Denver to pick up his wife. Anna Snyder was captured in the attack and taken to a camp on the upper Solomon in Kansas. Only a short time after she arrived there she tried to escape, but was recaptured. The distraught woman had watched her husband slaughtered and despaired of ever being released. One night she tore up her calico dress into strips, twisted them into a rope and hanged herself from the crossed tipi poles in a lodge. Some thought the Arapaho had killed her.[25]

---

24 Wynkoop to Maynard, August 13, 1864, *OR* 41, pt. 1, 237-40; Colley to Evans, August 12, 1864, *OR* 41, pt. 2, 673.

25 Gregory F. Michno, *Battle at Sand Creek The Military Perspective* (El Segundo, CA, 2004), 138-39.

War parties were still out. In north-central Kansas in early August, four homesteaders—John and Thomas Moffitt, John Houston, and James Tyler—picked a bad time to go on a buffalo hunt and died for their efforts. On August 21, Cheyenne under Little Robe attacked a large number of freight wagons camped at Cimarron Crossing of the Arkansas River, killing 11 men and driving off about 130 mules.[26]

The various tribal camps spread across the Central Plains were becoming loaded with contraband goods, stolen horses, mules, and captive white women and children, but the raiding season would come to an end. Winter was a time to take shelter in isolated creek bottoms and wait out the weather in comparative safety and comfort. Peace negotiations were essential. In Black Kettle's Cheyenne camp, George Bent, the mixed-blood son of the white trader William Bent, and Edmund Guerrier, another mixed-blood married to George's sister Julia, wrote two (nearly) identical letters—one to Agent Colley and the other to the commanding officer at Fort Lyon. Here was what the wrote:

Cheyenne Village, August 29, 1864

Sir:

We received a letter from Bent, wishing us to make peace. We held a council in regard to it; all came to the conclusion to make peace with you, providing you make peace with the Kiowas, Comanches, Arapahoes, Apaches and Sioux. We are going to send a message to the Kiowas and to the other nations about our going to make peace with you. We heard that you have some prisoners at Denver; we have seven prisoners of yours which we are willing to give up, providing you give up yours. There are three war parties out yet, and two of the Arapahoes; they have been out some time and expected in soon. When we held this council there were few Arapahoes and Sioux present. We want true news from you in return, that is a letter.

Black Kettle and other Chiefs[27]

26 Gregory F. Michno and Susan J. Michno, *Forgotten Fights Little-Known Raids and Skirmishes on the Frontier, 1823 to 1890* (Missoula, MT, 2008), 205-07.

27 Report of the Secretary of War, 1867, Exec. Doc. 26, 39th Congress, 2nd Session, xi, 169, hereafter referred to as "Sand Creek Massacre." This letter has been reprinted with various spellings.

Some of the tribes were suing for peace, but the Coloradans still had nightmares of being tomahawked in their sleep. They may have gotten some relief knowing that a new regiment was being organized, but it seemed as if they had been calling for help forever and most of their warnings had been ignored as trivial complaints. Some historians have disregarded their pleas as no more than crying "wolf," or as a plot by Evans and William N. Byers, editor of the *Rocky Mountain News*, to stir up a war for their own political ends.[28] Although the terror may have been unfounded, a century and more later it is easy to overlook the very real fears felt by the isolated white population.

Initially, volunteers responded well to Governor Evans's call for troops. Sixty men from the mining camp of Central City signed up in one afternoon after a recruiting promotion made by mining engineer Hal Sayr and future senator Henry M. Teller. In a few days, 44 more men had joined and marched to Denver to be mustered in as Company B, Third Colorado. In similar fashion, four companies were raised in Denver and one in Boulder. In the *Rocky Mountain News* of August 24, a line read, "Over seven hundred men are enlisted for the new regiment. Pretty good recruiting for a single week." The initial recruiting may have gone well, but most Coloradans were not convinced that their survival depended on flocking to the colors. On August 18, Colonel Chivington proclaimed martial law, closed down businesses, and made additional efforts to get more men. Enough joined in the counties of Pueblo and El Paso to form Company G. There was little gear for them and many waited for almost two months before they received adequate arms, equipment, and horses.

Despite the relatively successful recruitment effort, most Coloradans were not enthusiastic Indian fighters. They had moved there to begin a new life, get rich, or escape the Civil War. The territories were havens for draft dodgers. General Curtis had expressed his concern. Every time there was a gold discovery, it impacted the dwindling population's available to fight. "It is hard to tell whether love of gold or fear of the draft has the longest end of the singletree," Curtis wrote. It took another month to raise the remaining companies.

---

28 Margaret Coel, *Chief Left Hand: Southern Arapaho* (Norman, OK, 1981), 181, 186-92, 197; Berthrong, *Southern Cheyennes*, 169, 171; Dee Brown, *Bury My Heart at Wounded Knee* (New York, NY, 1970), 74-75; David H. Bain, *Empire Express Building the First Transcontinental Railroad* (New York, NY, 1999), 185-88.

Ultimately, a total of 1,149 men enrolled. Of the approximately 800 men whose occupations were known, more than 500 were farmers and miners, and about 200 were laborers, clerks, teamsters, carpenters, engineers, printers, and merchants. The men were not the dregs of society as some have claimed, but a typical cross-section of citizens. And most of them, some enthusiastically and others reluctantly, were ready to fight Indians if they could get weapons and find a target before peace or winter prevented it.[29]

The Third Colorado began assembling in late August at Camp Evans, a post on the South Platte a few miles north of Denver. Because of logistics and supply problems, however, the entire regiment never did gather in one place. There were simply not enough supplies and mounts for them. From the start, only about 375 horses were available to mount the new regiment. Captain Cyrus L. Gorton, assistant quartermaster, scrambled to purchase 120 more horses on the open market, which, he said, "was entirely irregular" for he had no authority to buy them. Eventually they got about 725 horses, which still left some 300 soldiers without mounts. They only got enough horses to mount the entire regiment in December—when the enlistments expired. The regiment was issued two howitzers, 1,103 used rifles and muskets (mostly old .54 calibers), and 103 used pistols. Colonel George L. Shoup assumed command on September 21.[30]

The Third Colorado was as ready for action as it would ever be.

29 Michno, *Battle at Sand Creek*, 144-46.

30 "Sand Creek Massacre," 160-62, 175.

Chapter 3

Camp Weld Conference

As the Third Colorado formed up, the Cheyenne hurried their peace letters to Fort Lyon. The courier was Lone Bear, whom the whites called One Eye.

It was natural that One Eye would carry the peace letters to Major Wynkoop or Agent Colley because the Cheyenne had been in the spy for the US Army for some time, and moved easily between the adversaries. It was also a lucrative job, for he received $125 per month plus rations for his efforts. Chivington was aware of his good services. When One Eye voiced concern that he might be taken for an enemy, Agent Colley assured him otherwise because Chivington had written out a certificate of his good character stating that "he was a friendly Indian. Colley also told him that if he came across any soldiers to simply "show that to them." One Eye, continued the agent, "was an Indian we relied upon for a great deal for information." Virtually everyone at Fort Lyon knew of One Eye's duties "as a government employee."[1]

One Eye had been to the fort scores of times, and this was just another routine trip. His friend Minimic (Eagle Head) and Minimic's wife rode along for the company. Their arrival at Fort Lyon on September 4 set off a series of events that inexorably led to the fighting at Sand Creek. Wynkoop ordered the

---

1 U.S. Congress, Senate, "Massacre of Cheyenne Indians," *Report of the Joint Committee on the Conduct of the War*, 38th Congress, 2nd Session (Washington, DC, 1865), 21, 30, 32, hereafter "Massacre of Cheyenne Indians"; "Sand Creek Massacre," 141.

Indians off their horses and reprimanded a sergeant for not shooting them. Only then did he take a look at the peace letter. According to Wynkoop, the letter indicated that the Indians "had never desired to be at war, but had been driven to it by the whites, that they had made various efforts to communicate with the Fort but had always been fired upon and driven off." In fact, the actual letter did not read anything like Wynkoop described it.[2]

John Smith, who served as interpreter for the participants, repeated a similar statement in his deposition to a Congressional Committee in 1865, namely, that the Indians "never desired to be at war." Sam Colley, in his sworn deposition on January 15, 1865, added a twist. According to the agent, One Eye and Minimic came to the post claiming they "had several white prisoners among them that they had purchased, and were desirous of giving them up and making peace with the whites." The Bent–Guerrier peace letters, however, said nothing about purchasing Indians. Sam Colley knew this and indicated so in his letter to Governor Evans written the same day the Indians arrived at the fort. The stories were changing.[3]

Wynkoop's questioning of One Eye evolved in the officer's autobiography into a fanciful rationalization for his later actions. According to Wynkoop, he asked One Eye if he knew it was certain death for an Indian to come to the post.

"I knew it," One Eye supposedly replied.

"How was it then, you dared approach as you did?"

By this time One Eye was surely puzzled and perhaps exasperated at such questioning because both he and Wynkoop knew the Indian was a government employee and was being paid to do the very thing Wynkoop was questioning him about. According to Wynkoop, however, One Eye replied as if reciting pages of Longfellow's "The Song of Hiawatha," or Cooper's *The Last of the Mohicans*. The soliloquy goes on for a page or more, speaking of the Indians' golden days, hunting buffalo, past wars, Great Fathers, suffering Red Children,

2 This contradiction offers a good example of an eyewitness "memory" problem. Did Wynkoop misremember the details, or did subsequent events cloud his recollection? Did a later suggestion introduce a false memory, or did he rationalize what he thought he remembered into a new schemata that eased his conscience? Did he purposely lie? This and other related memory issues will be discussed in detail in Section III of this book.

3 "Sand Creek Massacre," 84; "Massacre of Cheyenne Indians," 14, 81, 84, 91, 116; Edward W. Wynkoop, *The Tall Chief: The Autobiography of Edward W. Wynkoop* (Denver, CO, 1994), 86-87; Colley to Evans, September 4, 1864, OR 41, pt. 3, 196.

being unafraid to die, and communicating with the Great Spirit, who told him "you must try and save your people."

After all that, Wynkoop supposedly replied, "But did you not fear you would be killed when you endeavored to get into the Fort?"

"I thought I would be killed," One Eye is said to have answered, "but I knew that paper would be found on my dead body, that you would see it, and it might give peace to my people once more."

"And how about him?" Wynkoop asked, pointing to Minimic.

Old Minimic would not let One Eye come alone, he replied, "and was willing to go with him to the Happy Hunting Grounds satisfied if he could look down and see his people happy once more."

Wynkoop claimed these answers flabbergasted him, and the he had never experienced an "exhibition of such patriotism on the part of two savages," and felt himself "in the presence of superior beings."[4]

One Eye was quite a prize, for in 1864 not all superior beings could earn $125 a month as an Indian spy for the white man. One might also marvel at the superb interpretation job done by John Smith, who somehow managed to capture all the nuance and flavor of One Eye's grand oration, and at how superbly Wynkoop remembered it all 12 years later. Wynkoop's autobiographical flight of fancy is merely a justification of his conduct couched in terms of Victorian romance literature—a prime example of a memoir subject to psychological forces that controlled and warped his recall and twisted it into something far removed from historical accuracy.

John Smith, in his aforementioned deposition, however, indicated that there was no such involved conversation. According to Smith, the the major asked One Eye "whether he thought the Indians were sincere, and whether they would deliver the white prisoners," to which One Eye replied that the Indians were sincere. Wynkoop (in his autobiography) wrote, "One Eye assured me that if I would accompany him to the Camp of the Indians they would deliver to me the white captives, two women and three children."

Wynkoop decided to take the matter to Black Kettle. He had to justify his poor decision-making in his later writings by altering truth when the need arose. First, the peace proposal he held in his hand did not say the Indians wanted to see anyone in person; they wanted "true news from you in return, that is a letter." Second, Wynkoop was under orders of Gen. James G. Blunt to "confine

4 Wynkoop, *Tall Chief*, 87-89.

your operations to the defense of your post and give such protection to the road and mail coaches as you can afford." Third, both Blunt and Curtis had issued orders that the Indians were not to be negotiated with, but punished. Fourth, Wynkoop had been chastised previously for going outside district lines, for not asking permission for his actions, and for not keeping his own superiors informed of his movements. It seemed not to matter. Wynkoop marched out, failing to inform Blunt or Curtis that he was doing so.[5]

If Wynkoop's intentions were good, then no good deed goes unpunished. Perhaps he was hoping to free the prisoners and end the war. If so, that may explain why he ignored orders again and went to treat with the enemy (and later tried to justify it all by embellishing his memoir).

And so Wynkoop and elements of the First Colorado rode to the Smoky Hill River near the Kansas-Colorado line. When about 600 warriors appeared, many of the troopers wished they were elsewhere, but One Eye intervened and arranged a meeting. On the morning of September 10, about 60 Indians rode into Wynkoop's camp. They included chiefs Black Kettle, White Antelope, Bull Bear, Big Mouth, Left Hand, Neva, and Little Raven. Wynkoop, Capt. Silas Soule, Lt. Joseph Cramer, and a few other officers were present. John Smith and George Bent interpreted the often tense meeting. The Indians affirmed they sought peace; Wynkoop explained that although he was not authorized to make a peace agreement, if the prisoners were turned over, he would take a delegation of chiefs to Denver to talk peace.

The Indians complained that they had many grievances and it would be foolish to give up their captives without firm assurances. The argument grew dangerously overheated to the point that John Smith said to Lieutenant Cramer, "I have now got to talk for my life." Wynkoop's autobiography paints a dramatic scene of "dusky faces" with "dark eyes flashing" and the Indians acting "like snarling wolves." Two Indians calmed the situation: One Eye, "with brandished Tomahawk and his one eye gleaming," and Black Kettle, with a "brightness upon his face." One Eye supposedly faced down the horde of growling savages and said that he would fight alongside the whites if they were harmed. Black Kettle arose for another oration that would make the best noble savage of Victorian literature blush with envy. Soule and Cramer testified about

5   John Smith, deposition, January 15, 1865, OR 41, pt. 3, 195-96; Blunt to Wynkoop, August 26, 1864, OR 41, pt. 2, 881-82; Wynkoop, Tall Chief, 17, 89; "Massacre of Cheyenne Indians," 84-85; "Sand Creek Massacre," 84.

this council, but did not recall such a dramatic scene. Cramer acknowledged that One Eye stood up for the white men, while Black Kettle, after a monologue of grievances, indicated he would get the captives and go to Denver. Wynkoop gave it more flourish, claiming that when Black Kettle finished his speech, he told Wynkoop to move his men a dozen miles toward the fort, "Until the sun has kissed the Prairie," and wait for further word.[6]

Black Kettle wisely moved Wynkoop away because many of his warriors who were not pleased with a peace deal, and because they were having second thoughts about giving up all their bargaining chips. Bull Bear argued that they would be fools to give up all their captives, so they concocted a story that they didn't have seven captives. According to Lieutenant Cramer, Black Kettle indicated "that they would give up what prisoners they had and try to get them all, most of which were with the Sioux." Not only that, but Black Kettle "would have to buy part of these prisoners . . . and he could make no pledges." This was a strange turn of events and the officers should have been suspicious of foul play. The peace letters claimed the Indians had seven prisoners, but now Black Kettle was saying the Sioux had some of them, and they would have to buy them back. The tale was a lie, as the captives (who were hidden in the camp) would themselves later testify.

Wynkoop's command waited out a tense night. Some of the men even talked of mutiny, wanting desperately to get out of what they considered a very dangerous situation. Officers approached Wynkoop to demand that they leave immediately and make a forced march for the fort. Wynkoop, with his reputation on the line for disobeying orders and leading his small command into a situation where they might be massacred, testified in his 1865 Congressional testimony, "they did not threaten in my presence to return to Fort Lyon." He changed his story in his 1876 autobiography, admitting that "a large number of my men . . . demanded to be immediately led back to Fort Lyon." "These demands," he added, "assumed the shape of a mutiny, which required extreme measures to quell." Wynkoop either had a memory lapse or consciously changed his stories to suit his needs. He was either telling the truth to the Congressional inquiry and lying in his autobiography, or vice versa. The issue creates a real dilemma for students of Sand Creek.

The next morning, Black Kettle turned over four captives taken from the Little Blue and Plum Creek raids in August: Laura Roper, Isabelle Eubank,

---

6 "Sand Creek Massacre," 29-31, 56; Wynkoop, *Tall Chief*, 91-93.

Ambrose Asher, and Danny Marble. They kept Lucinda Eubank, Willie Eubank, Jr., and Nancy Morton, all of whom had been hidden under buffalo robes while the soldiers were in camp and threatened with death if they revealed themselves. Wynkoop was ecstatic about their return. "Such happiness I never experienced before, never since, and do not expect to in this world," he wrote in his autobiography. "Wellington surveying the victorious field [Waterloo] that changed the destinies of a world had no greater feeling of triumph, than I the humble instrument of a Divine Providence experienced in accomplishing the object of my mission." Divine providence works in mysterious ways, for in addition to allowing Wynkoop to know what Wellington felt, it enabled him to forget that the object of his mission was to rescue seven captives, not four.

The soldiers marched back to Fort Lyon and then on to Denver. Riding with them were Black Kettle, White Antelope, and Bull Bear of the Cheyenne, and Neva, Bosse, Notanee, and Heap of Buffalo of the Arapaho. About 50 members of their families accompanied them. On September 19, Wynkoop wrote to Chivington to explain what he had done and that he was bringing in the Indians. The news did not please Colonel Chivington or Governor Evans.[7]

As the procession approached Denver, Wynkoop rode ahead to prepare Evans for their arrival, but the governor avoided him. On September 26, Colonel Chivington wired General Curtis: "I have been informed by E. W. Wynkoop, commanding Fort Lyon, that he is on his way here with Cheyenne and Arapaho chiefs and four white prisoners they gave up. Winter approaches. Third Regiment is full, and they know they will be chastised for their outrages and now want peace. I hope that the major-general will direct that they make full restitution and then go on their reserve and stay there." Curtis's reply arrived on the day of the conference (September 28): "I shall require the bad Indians delivered up; restoration of equal numbers of stock; also hostages to secure. I want no peace till the Indians suffer more. . . . I fear agent of Interior Department will be ready to make presents too soon. It is better to chastise before giving anything but a little tobacco to talk over," he added. "No peace must be made without my directions."[8]

Curtis did not want peace without chastising the Indians, but Wynkoop's coup was Governor Evans's *fait accompli*. He had no choice but to meet the

---

7   Michno, *Battle at Sand Creek*, 156-59.

8   Chivington to Charlot, September 26, 1864, Curtis to Chivington, September 28, 1864, *OR* 41, pt. 3, 399, 462.

delegation. Evans finally stopped avoiding Wynkoop and, according to the major, said he was sorry Wynkoop had brought the Indians to Denver. They were at war, explained the governor, and he had gone through hell trying to raise the Third Colorado and could not allow the men to be mustered out without seeing some action. At least, that is what Wynkoop wrote in his autobiography. His account changed several times.

In his letter to General Curtis on October 8, 1864, Wynkoop explained that the governor thought the Indians should be referred to the military authorities. On January 16, 1865, Wynkoop was apologetic, admitting that taking the Indians to Denver was "a mistake of which I have since become painfully aware." At the military tribunal two months later on March 21, 1865, Wynkoop claimed Evans grumbled about who had authority to make peace and of the necessity of using the Third Colorado troops, but gave Wynkoop credit for rescuing the captives. Three months later on June 9, 1865, Wynkoop testified to the Doolittle Commission that Evans wanted nothing to do with the Indians and that he could not make peace. He and Wynkoop argued over the need for using the Third Colorado, with the major getting a bit flippant, and Evans protesting several times that he could not dismiss the regiment without a fight or he would be blamed for wasting government money. Evans supposedly said that the troops "had been raised to kill Indians, and they must kill Indians." In Wynkoop's autobiography, the events become biblical in proportion. He said that certain parties had condemned him, mostly contractors who would make more money if the Indian war continued. He claimed that Evans and Chivington were in league with these schemers and crooks. "The Monster Chivington" had heedlessly brought on the war in the interest of the contractors and for his own ends. Wynkoop and the chiefs were threatened with death by "Indian killers" and "frothy speculators," but his sturdy veteran soldiers protected them. Wynkoop's hatred of Chivington and Evans grew the further removed in time he was from the initial meeting.

Which of the versions is true? By the time he wrote his autobiography, the former major was jousting with imaginary demons—in one hand an ax of mendacity and in the other a sword of justification.[9]

The council was held outside Denver at Camp Weld on September 28, 1864. In addition to Wynkoop and the Indians, attendees were Evans,

9 "Chivington Massacre," 62-63, 77; "Sand Creek Massacre," 90, 121; Wynkoop, *Tall Chief*, 99; Harry E. Kelsey, Jr., *Frontier Capitalist*, 146, 149-50, 296n59.

Chivington, Capt. Silas Soule, Lt. Joseph Cramer, Capt. Samuel Robbins, Capt. George Sanborn, Lt. Charles Hawley, Col. George L. Shoup, Sam Colley, John Smith, Denver attorney Amos Steck, Ute Agent Simeon Whiteley, who recorded the proceedings, and several other civilians. Evans began by asking what the chiefs had to say, and Black Kettle answered that they were there because of Evans's June announcement telling the friendly Indians to come to the forts. That may not have been true, for he had had the proclamation for a month and a half before William Bent wrote him a personal message, delivered by One Eye, which convinced Black Kettle to sue for peace; and, he came in only after Wynkoop forced his hand.

Evans said he was sorry that the Indians did not respond earlier, that they had allied themselves with the Sioux and had made war all summer. Evans was indignant because the previous year, he had gone out on the plains to meet with the tribes to make peace, but had been snubbed. "I sent messengers out to tell you that I had presents, and would make you a feast," he said, "but you sent word to me that you did not want to have anything to do with me, and to the Great Father in Washington that you could get along without him."

"That is true," Black Kettle admitted.

Perhaps Evans savored the irony of the moment. In 1863 when he had asked for peace, the Indians had replied, "The white man's hands are dripping with our people's blood, and now he calls for us to make a treaty!" Twelve months later the tables were turned—the Indians's hands were dripping with the white man's blood, and now they called for him to make a treaty. It was not to be.

"Your young men are on the warpath," Evans explained. "My soldiers are preparing for the fight. You, so far, have had the advantage, but the time is near at hand when the plains will swarm with United States soldiers." Evans added that he believed the Indians only wanted peace for the winter, but they would make war again when the grass was fresh in the spring. The governor added a dark, prophetic observation: "The time when you can make war best, is in the summer time; when I can make war best, is in the winter . . . my time is just coming."

Evans went on, telling the Indians that they must show friendship by making arrangements with the soldiers. White Antelope said that he understood, but wanted to know how they could protect themselves. He feared that other soldiers would kill some of his people while he was here.

"There is great danger of it," admitted Evans, who added that whatever peace was made must be made with the soldiers and not with him. The conference broke down into rapid-fire questions about past depredations. Neva admitted that Arapahos had killed the Hungate family. He said Comanche and Kiowa killed people at the head of Cherry Creek, and that Cheyenne under Powder Face and Whirlwind stole horses at Jimmy's Camp near Colorado City. When Evans asked about the fight at Fremont's Orchard, White Antelope replied that Fool Badger's son had led the Cheyenne, but the fight was all a mistake. He said, "this was the beginning of war," but "a soldier fired first." Evans then asked about the raids along the Little Blue, to which White Antelope answered, "We took two prisoners, west of Fort Kearny, and destroyed the trains." White Antelope blamed the raids at Cottonwood on the Lakota. Bull Bear broke in to add that it was the Sioux who "plan to clean out all this country."

Neva expressed what may have been the real reasons for the Indians coming to Denver: "I know the value of the presents which we receive from Washington. We cannot live without them. That is why I try so hard to keep peace with the whites." Evans refused to discuss gifts.

Colonel Chivington spoke last. He told the Indians that he was not the big war chief, but that all the soldiers in the territory were under his command. That was not accurate, for the men at Fort Lyon were now under General Blunt's command. Chivington ended by stating, "My rule of fighting white men or Indians is to fight them until they lay down their arms and submit to military authority. They are nearer to Major Wynkoop than anyone else, and they can go to him when they get ready to do that." With the conference ended, the chiefs shook hands with everyone and Black Kettle embraced Governor Evans.[10]

Was peace made? It all depends on one's perspective. According to historian Stan Hoig, "The inference is crystal clear—if the Indians turned themselves over to the Fort Lyon military they would be safe from attack by soldiers."[11] It also seems clear that the Indians were still in extreme jeopardy, for Evans had all but promised them that they would be attacked during the winter.

The Indians were certainly not assured that peace was at hand. After the council Black Kettle and One Eye, whose daughter Amache Ochinee was married to the white rancher John Prowers, told Prowers of the meeting. According to the rancher's later testimony, his wife had told him that "Black

10 "Sand Creek Massacre," 39; John M. Carroll, ed., *The Sand Creek Massacre: A Documentary History* (New York, NY, 1973), iv-vii.

11 Stan Hoig, *The Sand Creek Massacre* (Norman, OK, 1961), 120n13.

Kettle had been to Denver; had seen Governor Evans and Colonel Chivington; that they could not make any treaty of peace with them."[12]

What the Indians (and the whites) understood at the time was filtered through nuance and implication via their own memory processes and preconceptions; they all heard what they wanted to hear and filtered out the non-confirmatory information. Only Neva had a rudimentary understanding of English, and all the Indians relied on translations from a man who had earned the sobriquet of "Lying John" Smith.

Whites and Indians alike exited the conference understanding just what they wanted to understand—with disastrous implications.

<hr>

12 "Sand Creek Massacre," 104.

Chapter 4

The March to Fort Lyon

John Chivington had finally shaken free of General Connor to hurry south to join his troops, who had spent weeks struggling through snow and frigid temperatures. Major Sayr had moved several companies across the divide from the South Platte to the Arkansas watershed. "The snow was so deep on the north side of the divide," recalled Private Shaw of Company A, "that it took all of one day for the company to plow its way through the snow and out of the timber." At dark they threw their blankets on the snow and waited for morning. One soldier died. Sayr marched south through snow of "unknown depths" in the gulches, where, he wrote, "horses and riders would go nearly out of sight." A number of animals died while others were abandoned.

On November 15 at Fountain Creek, the cold and snowy weather of the past two weeks finally broke. The temperature now got so warm it became uncomfortable. More horses broke down. A day later the weather turned cold once more with a bitter west wind, and more animals had to be abandoned. The weary troops headed east along the Arkansas River about 15 miles to the new Camp Fillmore, just above Boone's Ranch. Albert Boone, a grandson of frontiersman Daniel Boone, was enjoying retirement from his former job as Indian agent. He was less than pleased when the soldiers made their sudden appearance, and would later file claims with the government for damages they inflicted to his ranch.

Colonel Shoup finally caught up five miles east of Pueblo and gathered Company G of the Third Colorado, whose members had just been recalled after being sent home weeks earlier. Only a day after Irving Howbert returned from Colorado City, the company finally received its arms, ammunition, and equipment. It had taken nearly three months to get the munitions. "The guns were old, out-of-date Austrian muskets of large bore with paper cartridges from which we had to bite off the end when loading," grumbled Howbert. "Their accuracy was atrocious. One could never tell where it would hit." When the horses arrived, Howbert's spirits dropped again. " They were a motley looking group, composed of every kind of an equine animal from a pony to a plow horse," he observed. "I had the misfortune to draw a rawboned, square-built old plow horse, upon which thereafter I spent a good many uncomfortable hours . . . our equipment, as to arms and mounts, was of the poorest kind." Ready or not, Company G joined Shoup as he continued down the Arkansas "From that time on," recalled Howbert, "our real hardships began."[1]

The troops rested at Camp Fillmore for two days under clear and cold weather. On November 23, Colonel Chivington, Maj. Jacob Downing, and acting adjutant Lt. John S. Maynard rode into camp. As district commander, Chivington outranked Colonel Shoup and assumed command. While Chivington was still the hero of the fighting at Glorieta Pass and the ideal of a dashing and fearless commander, his image had tarnished of late. He may have been seen as something of a usurper. His assuming command, wrote Sayr, "gives pretty general dissatisfaction."

Under his direction the force moved downriver, making 15 miles on the 24th. Courier Billy Breakenridge camped with the scouts and seemed to be enjoying their company. "They were splendid fellows and knew their duties," recalled Breakenridge. Alexander F. Safely of the Third Colorado's Company H was one of the scouts, as was Antoine Janis. A third, Duncan Kerr of Company C, First Colorado, had scalped some Indians in a battle at Buffalo Springs the month previous. Charles Autobees, a 52-year-old ex-mountain man and trader, was riding along for his expertise. (Autobees' 27-year-old son, Mariano, was the earlier mentioned lieutenant in Company H, Third Colorado.) The most famous of the scouts was old James P. Beckwourth, a mulatto born in Virginia in 1798, an ex-mountain man, trapper, trader, and Crow Indian "chief." For the past few years, Beckwourth had operated a store in Denver for Vasquez and Company. He was never that comfortable with city life, however, and had

---

1 Perrigo, "Sayr's Diary," 53-54; Howbert, *Indians of Pike's Peak*, 97-98; Roberts, "Sand Creek," 833n49; Shaw, *Pioneers of Colorado*, 65.

recently ran afoul of the law after blasting a man with a shotgun during a barroom brawl. Beckwourth was probably more than happy to accept Colonel Shoup's offer to scout for the regiment.

The weather warmed as the men rode down the Arkansas River. The scouts caught 11 antelope unfortunate enough to have gotten stuck after breaking through the crust of the deep snow. Breakenridge and Kerr rode on either side of the struggling animals, catching each by the horns and lifting them up so Kerr could cut its throat with his Bowie knife. They killed them all without firing a shot and loaded them on to the supply train when it passed by. Kerr's partiality for the free use of his Bowie knife was becoming more evident.[2]

Twelve miles of marching the next day under warm clearing skies brought the column to Spring Bottom, a stage station on the river and a good site with plenty of wood and water. Here, another troop joined Chivington's command when Lt. Clark Dunn and the available men of Company E, First Colorado, came down from Camp Fillmore.

On Friday night, November 25, Chivington and some of his officers were warming themselves at the station when James M. Combs entered the room. Combs, who resided at Fort Lyon and had left there five days earlier to do business in Pueblo, was astonished to come across all the soldiers.

"They don't expect me down there, do they?" Chivington inquired, beginning a line of inquiry that would aptly demonstrate how little he knew about the situation into which he was riding. When Combs answered that no one at Fort Lyon knew he was coming, the colonel replied, "No sir, they won't know it till they see me there."

Major Downing joined the conversation and asked Combs about the Indians and the commander at the fort. Combs replied that when he left, Major Anthony was in command. When Chivington asked who was in command before Anthony, Combs replied "Major Wynkoop." At that, Chivington offered a hearty laugh "Oh! You must be mistaken. I think that Left Hand was in command before Major Anthony came here."

By this time Combs was convinced they were making sport of him. When asked about Wynkoop's location, Combs offered that he had heard the major had been ordered to Fort Larned (he knew not why), and he believed that he had left there the same day Combs left for Pueblo. At this, Chivington

---

2 Perrigo, "Sayr's Diary," 54; Elinor Wilson, *Jim Beckwourth: Black Mountain Man and War Chief of the Crows* (Norman, OK, 1972), 172-75; Breakenridge, *Helldorado*, 43-44.

Fort Lyon (top center) was built in 1860 and was originally named Fort Wise. It was erected on the left bank of the Arkansas River above Bent's New Fort. *Denver Public Library*

straightened in his chair and replied, "I know what he has gone there for; it is to take command of that post." The facetious manner in which Chivington replied convinced Combs such was in fact not the case. Wynkoop "is a nice commander, and an honor to the Colorado first," continued Chivington.

Changing the subject, the colonel asked, "How do the Indians like Major Anthony down there?"

Not very well, Combs answered, for they gave him "hard names, calling him the red-eyed chief, and other names." In reply to another inquiry Combs said he had no idea if Anthony fed the Indians as well as Wynkoop did, but confirmed both had given the Indians supplies.

When Chivington asked how far the Indians were from the post, Combs confirmed a large party was within a mile and a half of it, but that most had permission to be there.

"Are they troublesome?" asked the colonel.

Combs replied they were at the post almost every day, "begging and troubling us in that way."

"Have they been in as much since Major Anthony has been in command?" Chivington asked.

On some days the major had allowed them in, explained Combs, and on some days he had not, but none were allowed in after Anthony gave express orders forbidding them. He went on to explain that soldiers and officers, including Major Wynkoop, Captain Soule, and Lt. Charles E. Phillips, visited the Indian camp, for Combs had been there often and had seen them there many times.

Chivington next inquired as to their numbers. There were some 200 warriors, replied Combs. He had seen them mounted all at the same time, with weapons ready about to go out to meet what was thought was a party of Ute

© Colorado Historical Society

Major Scott J. Anthony,
First Colorado

He pretended peace,
but led his troops to war.

Colorado Historical Society

raisers. When Chivington followed up with the question of whether the Indians were friendly, Combs confirmed that they were.[3]

Anxious for information, Chivington and his officers continued pumping Combs with questions. According to Dunn, Combs told Chivington that when Major Anthony took over, he did not approve of Wynkoop's actions and ordered the Indians away from the post. He also ordered them to give up their arms, but the Indians only turned in a few bows and some broken rifles. Anthony also told the guard to fire on Indians who approached the fort without permission. When the Arapaho moved to Sand Creek, added Combs, warriors occasionally came to the fort to demand rations, but were refused. The soldiers at Fort Lyn "were daily expecting the post to be attacked."

After digesting all this news, Chivington declared that "scalps are what we are after." Combs would later relate that the conversation became "promiscuous" about scalps, with almost all of the officers engaging in the talk. Some wanted Neva's hair, while others wanted Left Hand's, and so on. Combs fed the fire by adding that he thought they could get nearly 500 scalps within

---

3 "Sand Creek Massacre," 115, 116-117, 133. Combs was mistaken for Wynkoop had not yet left for Larned on the 20th. Wynkoop was not even sure when he left: he testified to two different days, either the 25th or 26th. "Massacre of Cheyenne Indians," 82; "Sand Creek Massacre," 87, 123.

one day's march of the fort. "I thought he ought to do it with that party," Combs admitted, adding that the Indians had given up their weapons and could probably be taken with 50 men, but Anthony had returned some weapons to let them go out on a buffalo hunt.

"Have they all gone?" asked Chivington.

"Left Hand is very sick," Combs replied, and most of his band was still at the post with him. Combs did not know where the rest had headed. After the colonel remarked that he would soon give them a lively buffalo hunt, the conversation died down. According to Combs, when he finished his supper and walked out, Chivington remarked, "Well, I long to be wading in gore."[4]

* * *

Probably the same day Chivington and Combs conversed at Spring Bottom, Major Wynkoop left Fort Lyon for Fort Riley. Since November 2, when Major Anthony rode in with orders for his relief, Wynkoop had had plenty of time to reflect on the events that brought him to such dire straits.

When news of Wynkoop's peace-making excursion had reached headquarters, the response was rapid. On October 17, Maj. Benjamin S. Henning, temporarily commanding the District of the Upper Arkansas, ordered Major Anthony to replace Wynkoop and ordered him to Fort Riley. The reason given for the change was because "certain officers have issued stores, goods, or supplies to hostile Indians, in direct violation of orders from the general commanding the department." In his letter to Anthony, Major Henning added, "I am very desirous to have an officer of judgment at Fort Lyon, and especially one that will not commit any such foolish acts as are reported to have occurred there."

Henning also cited a number of general and special orders, adding that Anthony was to obey "not only the letter of the order but the spirit." Wynkoop's actions met with "disapproval and censure," he noted, and it could only have arisen from two causes: a total lack of knowledge "requisite to make a good and efficient officer, or an intentional disobedience of orders and almost

4 "Sand Creek Massacre," 117-18, 179, 182. Combs's memory was confused. He met Chivington on November 25, and could not have known the Arapaho had vacated the post for they were doing so that very day. Combs told Chivington that he could attack "that party"—the Arapaho who had been hanging around the post—but intentionally or not, Chivington did not go after that Arapaho band.

criminal mismanagement of the affairs of his command." Henning hoped that Anthony would not "have occasion to again refer to this subject." General Curtis, the commander of the Department of Kansas (including the Colorado Territory), was also incensed that Major Wynkoop had broken almost every order he had been issued. Curtis warned Anthony not to make the same mistakes.

Anthony's orders included the observation that "Major E. W. Wynkoop has laid himself liable to arrest and dismissal for absence without leave, and the Officer [Soule] who went with him liable for being absent without proper authority." Henning stressed that the districts had been restructured in July, so they must follow orders from the District of the Upper Arkansas, and that all orders from the District of Colorado should have been returned. Supplies were to be kept under strict control. Captain Soule, explained Henning, had given a destitute emigrant a suit of clothes from the commissary when he should have given the man a suit of his own clothes, "as the issue on the order will be charged up to him."

No commissary or ordnance would be allowed out of the district (the commanding officer "had as much right to turn them over . . . to the Confederate forces in Texas, as to send them from the district"), continued Henning. The looseness that existed at Fort Lyon would be dismissed as "more to ignorance than intentional insult"—at least up to September. Thereafter, it was simply considered intolerable for officers and men to have left their posts and imperiled government property, marching from their districts with large commands "seeking and assisting to make treaties between a hostile force, and parties that had no authority to make peace." In a final admonition to Major Anthony, Henning reiterated that post commanders and their subordinates "will not inaugurate or send out military expeditions without orders from these Head Quarters."[5]

Wynkoop had broken a series of rules, and Henning did all in his power to make it clear to Anthony that he could not commit the same errors. Unfortunately, the major did not get Henning's directive until after Sand Creek.

*   *   *

---

5   Henning to Anthony, October 17, 1864, *OR* 41, pt. 4, 62; Scott J. Anthony Papers, Colorado Historical Society.

Before Major Anthony arrived, Major Wynkoop had to deal with the 600 Arapaho who arrived on October 18. Governor Evans and General Curtis had ordered that no rations or other annuities should be given to the Indians, but Wynkoop fed them.

William H. Valentine, veterinary surgeon with the First Colorado, was disturbed by the menagerie of soldiers, civilians, traders, and Indians mingling freely. Some of the Arapaho involved in the Snyder killings were within the grounds of the fort. Valentine spoke with Left Hand and asked him if they were the ones who had attacked the Snyder wagon. "They are the Indians," Left Hand affirmed. They still had eight of the mules that pulled the wagon and ambulance, claimed Valentine, but Major Wynkoop did nothing to arrest them. The slayers of the Snyders had the cheek to come in to Valentine's office, but he immediately threw them out. Valentine was glad when Anthony arrived and ejected the Indians from the post. Later, at the military tribunal held to investigate the Sand Creek affair, Captain Soule testified that no one at the fort at the time knew that these Indians were the murderers of the Snyders. Who was telling the truth is difficult to discern.

Wynkoop believed his actions would be exonerated—until the westbound stage brought Major Anthony with orders for Wynkoop's relief. Wynkoop was flabbergasted at his ouster, while Anthony was appalled to see Arapaho wandering around the post trading robes and receiving rations. "I immediately gave instructions to arrest all Indians coming within the post until I could learn something more about them," explained Anthony. The Arapaho chiefs told him "that they had always been on peaceable terms with the whites, had never desired any other than peace." They blamed other tribes for the war.

Anthony remained unconvinced and ordered them to give up all their weapons and stolen stock. The Arapaho agreed, but they only handed over 10 mules, four horses, and a few old useless firearms. Anthony warned them that if he learned any of them had taken part in the depredations of the past summer, he would promptly arrest them.

On November 6, nine Cheyenne arrived claiming that 600 of their tribe were 35 miles north of the post and wished to come in. "I shall not permit them to come in, even as prisoners," replied Anthony. "They pretend that they want peace, and I think they do now, as they cannot fight during the winter." The major concluded that 1,000 cavalrymen could catch them and punish them severely, but with the force at hand, he could only hope to defend the post he now commanded. In any case, he would not let the Cheyenne camp anywhere near the fort. Black Kettle disregarded Anthony's orders and about 50 men arrived at the fort in mid-November. Wynkoop, who was allowed to speak to them, explained that he was no longer in command and they should listen to Major Anthony.[6]

Anthony was playing for time. He would rather fight them, but he knew he was not yet strong enough to do so. "I have been trying to let the Indians that I have talked with think that I have no desire for trouble with them," he reported to General Curtis, "but that I could not agree upon a permanent peace until I was authorized by you, thus keeping matters quiet for the present, and until troops enough are sent out to enforce any demand we may choose to make."

When the Cheyenne once more asked to move to the fort with winter upon them, Anthony flatly rejected the request. "I would not permit this," he explained, "but told them that they might camp on Sand Creek." They could go there "or between there and the headwaters of the Smoky Hill." Neither the Cheyenne or the Arapaho were "satisfied" with the new commander "for not permitting them to visit the post and cannot understand why I will not make peace with them. My intention, however," continued Anthony, "is to let matters remain dormant until troops can be sent out to take the field against all the tribes."

Indeed they were not "satisfied." The Cheyenne were especially displeased Major Wynkoop, the "tall chief," had been removed. The Arapaho called Major Anthony the "red-eye chief"—a name related to the residual effects of his scurvy from which he had suffered—and thought he wanted to fight them. Matters, as far as the Arapaho were concerned "looked dark." Interpreter John Prowers tried to reassure the Indians by telling them "everything [was] favorable," but few if any believed him.[7]

About November 25, Wynkoop boarded the eastbound stage for Fort Riley. Did the major fully understand why he had been removed from command? In his March 1865 testimony to the Doolittle Commission, as well as in his autobiography, Wynkoop claimed he left Fort Lyon because he had received orders to go to Fort Riley to take command of that post![8]

Wynkoop's version of events deeply influenced historians. He later insisted the Indians had been peaceful since his conference with them on Smoky Hill on

---

6   "Sand Creek Massacre," 27, 225-26; *OR* 41, pt. 1, 912-13.

7   Anthony to Helliwell, November 16, 1864, *OR* 41, pt. 1, 914; "Sand Creek Massacre," 105; "Massacre of Cheyenne Indians," 19-20, 28.

8   "Sand Creek Massacre," 92; Wynkoop, *Tall Chief*, 100.

September 10 until after the Sand Creek fight on November 29. That contention is inaccurate in both fact and implication. If the Plains were suddenly peaceful after the Smoky Hill talk, then it was these Indians who were the ones causing all the trouble. If the region was so peaceful, why was his stage protected by an escort force of 28 soldiers?

When Wynkoop was in command, the Indians, who had usually gone into their annual autumn peace mode by then, had been engaged in at least nine fights along the trails leading to Colorado—more that year (1864) than than in any other year. Since the Smoky Hill council, there had been many fights between whites and Indians:

At Cottonwood Canyon on September 20;

A major confrontation between Gen. James Blunt and a few hundred Cheyenne at Pawnee Fork on September 25 (some of these warriors belonged to the bands of the same chiefs who were then arriving in Denver for a peace council);

Fights at White Butte Creek on October 10 and at Mullahla's Station on the 12th; Hay cutters were attacked at Midway Station on the Platte River on October 28;

On November 13 at Ash Creek east of Fort Larned, Indians attacked a wagon train, killed two men, and stole the stock;

On November 19, Indians attacked an ox train four miles west of Plum Creek, Nebraska. Captain T. J. Majors and Capt. Thomas Weatherwax, with men of the First Nebraska Volunteer Cavalry, chased them to no avail;

On November 20, Capt. Henry Booth and Lt. A. Helliwell (the latter of whom had drafted the orders to remove Wynkoop from command) were jumped by Indians near Fort Zarah and raced back to the post, both having received several non-fatal arrow wounds;

On November 26, Indians attacked a coach five miles east of Plum Creek Station, killing two and wounding six among the drivers and passengers. Captain Majors and his men chased the raiders for 16 miles to Spring Creek before the horses became too exhausted to continue. The Indians made a stand in a ravine, and a sharp fight ensued that resulted in a draw. Majors recovered two scalps of the men murdered on the coach. One trooper was wounded and Majors claimed he killed three Indians.[9]

Clearly, the Indians had continued raiding into late fall. Whether or not they had a just cause is endlessly debatable. By 1864, both sides had been fighting a war that had flared off and on for a decade, and the conflict would continue for another 25 years. Wynkoop's assertion that he had single-handedly stopped the fighting with his talk on the Smoky Hill was nonsense, and most likely a rationalization to save himself by trying to show that his peace initiative was justified. By insisting the fighting did not re-kindle until after Sand Creek, Wynkoop could place the onus of the Indian war at Chivington's feet. His ploy was at least partially successful, for after more than a century, the popular conception is that Chivington started the Indian wars.

When Wynkoop left Fort Lyon, Captain Soule returned the weapons to the Arapaho and told to leave the post. Once they realized their sojourn at the fort was over, the Indians grew somewhat surly. Only a few days before Colonel Chivington arrived, Anthony had fired on some Cheyenne to keep them away. The Indians sent word to Anthony: "if that little G—d d—d red-eyed chief wanted a fight out of them, if he would go up to their camp they would give him all he wanted."[10]

Little Raven expected trouble and had already gone to Sand Creek two weeks before. He camped south of the junction with Rush Creek only 25 miles from Fort Lyon, as did Neva and about 600 more Arapaho. Left Hand, however, took his family and some others and moved to Black Kettle's camp farther up Sand Creek. Most of the Arapaho who had been fed, had surrendered their arms, and who likely considered themselves under army protection, were not later attacked. Some of the Arapaho who initially followed Left Hand later moved farther south to join Little Raven and Neva, a move that also would save them. Even Chivington's critic, Lieutenant Cramer, understood the salient point that "but very few" of the protected Indians were targets—those who were struck were the Arapaho who chose to camp with Black Kettle.[11]

---

9   Michno, *Battle at Sand Creek*, 188-89; Michno, *Encyclopedia of Indian Wars*, 153-56.

10   "The Chivington Massacre," 91.

11   "Sand Creek Massacre," 24, 63; *Sand Creek Massacre Project, Volume I: Site Location Study* (Denver, CO, 2000), 213-14.

On November 26 the last few Indians vacated Fort Lyon and Chivington left Spring Bottom. That same day a Cheyenne named War Bonnet returned to the fort to ask Major Anthony if John Smith could go to the village to trade with them. Agent Sam Colley believed it was a good idea, and asked Smith if he "was able and willing to go out and pay a visit to these Indians, ascertain their numbers, their general disposition toward the whites, and the points where other bands might be located in the interior." Colley's trader son named Dexter could also go and use the opportunity to make a little money for both of them.

Governor Evans had sent Colley a letter on November 10 to cease trading, but Colley simply ignored it and Major Anthony sanctioned it. One Eye, who worked for the US Army, was already in Black Kettle's village gathering intelligence. According to Anthony, "He [One Eye] was to remain in this Cheyenne camp as a spy, and give me information from time to time of the movements of this particular band." In addition, Dexter Colley's hired man, R. Watson Clarke, went along as teamster and laborer. Smith asked Anthony if trooper David H. Louderback from Company G, First Colorado, could accompany them. Louderback, explained Smith, understood they were to go to the camp "and see what the Indians were doing." At the same time, they could also take along some goods to trade. As Louderback explained it, "Major Anthony gave me his permission to go out with him."

The little party camped out on the open plains the evening of the 26th, and pulled into the Cheyenne village the next afternoon. They were not given a hearty welcome. Some of the warriors were angry. Louderback did not think Smith was in danger, but "they threatened to injure me." The Cheyenne took their weapons, but when they saw the trade items they cooled down. Smith unpacked his goods in War Bonnet's lodge, the mules were turned loose to graze, and they sat for an uneasy supper. The entire affair was stressful. "They thought I was a spy," wrote Louderback—which was in fact a correct divination of his purpose—"sent out there by Major Anthony to see what they were doing." The wary warriors, he concluded, believed the white men had come to "leave marks to show the soldiers the way out."[12]

*   *   *

12 "Sand Creek Massacre," 27-28, 134-35, 141; "Massacre of Cheyenne Indians," 5, 21, 87, 93.

While Louderback passed the long anxious hours, Chivington drew closer to Fort Lyon. The colonel, trying to ensure that no word of his approach leaked out, enveloped William Bent's ranch along the Arkansas. It was a sound preemptive move because William's son, George, had been moving regularly between his father's house and Black Kettle's village. At that moment, William Bent's son Charlie, his daughter Julia, and her husband, Edmund Guerrier, were living in camp with their mother's Indian relations. Bent felt uneasy, for he likely discerned the reason for the soldiers' presence; three of his children and his son-in-law were with Black Kettle. Trouble was brewing.

Other soldiers continued downriver to Caddo Creek, where they circled John Prowers's ranch as he was herding government cattle, horses, and mules. Prowers was a son-in-law of One Eye and well acquainted with several chiefs. "I was taken prisoner one Sunday evening, about sundown," recalled Prowers, "by men of Company E [First Colorado]." He and seven of his employees were disarmed and not allowed to leave his place for three days. "The colonel commanding thought I might communicate some news to the Indians encamped on Sand Creek."[13]

No one at Fort Lyon knew of Chivington's approach. No mail from Denver had arrived in three weeks, and Agent Colley assumed the Indians had cut off the settlements. At night someone thought he saw campfires upriver, and at sunrise on November 28, Captain Soule and 20 troopers rode to investigate. At Big Bottom, about a dozen miles above the fort, Soule met Chivington.

When the colonel inquired if anyone knew he was coming, "I told him they did not," said Soule, who told Chivington that there were some Indians camped below the fort, but they were not dangerous because they were considered prisoners. Someone in Chivington's entourage remarked "that they wouldn't be prisoners after they got there." Soule rode in with the regiment, but Chivington hurried on ahead.[14]

The colonel and his staff arrived about 9:00 a.m. and immediately set a guard around the fort. Adjutant Lt. John Maynard penned General Field Order No. 2:

---

13 David Lavender, *Bent's Fort* (Lincoln, NE, 1972), 374, 383; "Sand Creek Massacre," 51, 107.

14 "Chivington Massacre," 27-28; "Sand Creek Massacre," 10, 24.

I. Hereafter, no officer will be allowed to leave his command without the consent of the colonel commanding, and no soldier without a written pass from his company commander, approved by the commander of his battalion.

II. No fires will be allowed to burn after dark, unless specially directed from these headquarters.

III. Any person giving the Indians information of the movements of troops will be deemed a spy and shot to death.

Chivington was determined that no one would spoil his surprise. "A picket guard was thrown around the fort to turn away any Indians that might be coming in," recalled Private Howbert, "and also to prevent any of the trappers or Indian traders who generally hung around there from notifying the savages of our presence." How effective his order was in keeping men on the grounds is uncertain. Lieutenant Luther Wilson, for example, seems not to have even been aware of it. "No pickets were thrown around the post by the command," he explained, "and nothing done to prevent anyone from passing out.[15]

As the command rode in, a surprised Scott Anthony went out to greet it. The first people he met were Capt. Presley Talbot, Lt. Harry Richmond, and Captain Soule. Before Anthony could say anything Richmond asked, "Where are the Indians?"

"I am damned glad you have come," Anthony replied, reaching out to shake Richmond's hand. "I have got them over here about twenty-five miles until I could send to Denver for assistance." According to Talbot. Anthony expressed gratitude that they had come to attack the Indians, and "that he would have attacked them before this time if he had had force enough at his command."[16]

Chivington rode upon the scene and told Anthony that he would ride for Sand Creek that night. Anthony volunteered to accompany him with a battalion of the First Colorado, and suggested that they also strike the larger camp of Indians on Smoky Hill. Chivington agreed, but figured the decision would depend on the outcome of the first attack. Anthony mentioned the three white

15 "Chivington Massacre," 67; "Sand Creek Massacre," 46, 165; Howbert, *Indians of Pike's Peak*, 99. Historians have consistently misstated this order, saying that the penalty for leaving the post was death.

16 "Sand Creek Massacre," 208, 212.

men in the camp, as well as Black Kettle, One Eye, and Left Hand before pointing out that if a battle broke out, "all means to save those parties," and that "if he did fight them he should give notice beforehand in order to get them out."[17]

Word of the impending attack spread quickly. "I was indignant," grumbled Captain Soule, who immediately went to Lt. James D. Cannon's room (Company K, First New Mexico) and found there a congregation of officers. According to Soule, he "told them that any man who would take part in the murders, knowing the circumstances as we did, was a low lived cowardly son of a bitch." Captain Jay J. Johnson reported Soule's comments to Chivington. "You bet hell was to pay in camp," wrote Soule. His position and name-calling were guaranteed to elicit a reaction, and "all hands swore they would hang me before they would move camp."

The angry Soule next visited Major Anthony, where his protest was offered in vain: Anthony had already decided on a course of action. According to Soule, "He told me that we were going on the Smoky Hill to fight the hostile Indians; he also said that he was in for killing all Indians, and that he was only acting or had been only acting friendly with them until he could get a force large enough to go out and kill all of them."

Soule reminded Anthony of the pledges he had made to some of the Indians, to which Anthony replied that Chivington had also pledged those particular Indians and the white men in camp would not be killed, "and that the object of the expedition was to go out [to] the Smoky Hill and follow the Indians up." The reply failed to satisfy Soule. Both Anthony and Cramer warned Soule to stay away from Chivington because the colonel was upset over his remarks in Lieutenant Cannon's room. Soule instead penned an explanation of his actions and gave it to Captain Talbot to present to Chivington. It was returned unopened.[18]

* * *

---

17 "Massacre of Cheyenne Indians," 29.

18 Anthony to Helliwell, November 28, 1864, *OR* 41, pt. 4, 708; "Sand Creek Massacre," 13, 21, 25; Gary L. Roberts and David Fridtjof Halaas, "Written in Blood The Soule-Cramer Sand Creek Massacre Letters," *Colorado Heritage* (Winter 2001), 25.

The Sand Creek affair is generally viewed as an operation carried out by the Third Colorado, but the First Colorado Regiment also played a major part. The troops of the First Colorado posted at Fort Lyon were no longer part of Chivington's district, and so were not under his command. Chivington did not order these men to accompany him. As Lieutenant Cramer later testified, Chivington "did not order" Anthony to fight the Cheyenne. The colonel, he continued, "did not feel authorized to issue any orders" to the soldiers at Fort Lyon. Chivington wished Anthony would help them, and he ended up doing so on his own accord.[19]

The march to Sand Creek was originally scheduled to begin at 8:00 p.m. on November 28. With time running out, Lieutenant Cramer attempted to lodge a protest of his own and met Chivington in the company of several others. The conversation included a briefing of the upcoming operation. Sam Colley complained to Chivington that had had been unable to accomplish anything with the Indians for about six months, and that only a sound whipping would bring peace. According to Andrew Gill, one of Chivington's aides, Colley went on to say that "the Indians were hard to manage, and the only thing to do any good was to chastise them severely." Colonel Shoup had heard the same story from Colley: "He stated to me that these Indians had violated their treaty; that there were a few Indians that he would not like to see punished, but as long as they affiliated with the hostile Indians we could not discriminate; that no treaty could be made that would be lasting till they were all severely chastised. . . . and also told me where these Indians were camped." Later, with the investigations in play and anti-Chivington fever running high, Colley changed his story and claimed he was a peace advocate and that he never wanted to go after the Indians. Self-preservation trumped truth.

Cramer also made his feelings known, stating openly that it would be murder to attack the camp because of "obligations that we of Major Wynkoop's command were under to those Indians." Wynkoop had pledged his word, he continued, and that meant all officers under him were at least indirectly pledged in the same manner. Fighting the Indians "was placing us in very embarrassing circumstances."

Cramer's plea enraged Chivington, who approached him to thunder, "The Cheyenne nation has been waging bloody war against the whites all spring, summer, and fall, and Black Kettle is their principal chief! They have been guilty

19 "Sand Creek Massacre," 62.

of robbery, arson, murder, rape, and fiendish torture, not even sparing women and little children. I believe it right and honorable to use any means under God's heaven to kill Indians who kill and torture women and children." Chivington raised his fist close to Cramer's face and added, "Damn any man who sympathizes with Indians."[20] The meeting ended.

Before long, the officers had their units formed on the parade ground. Each man, recalled Private Howbert, was to take "two or three pounds of raw bacon and sufficient hardtack to last three or four days, which he was to carry in his saddlebags." The supply train would follow along with another twenty days' rations. Taking more than three weeks of foodstuffs is firm evidence that Chivington planned to honor his promise for a thorough campaign.

One of William Bent's sons was not in the Sand Creek village—but he soon would be. Chivington may have been unsure of Jim Beckwourth's ability or willingness to take them to the camp, so he sought out Robert Bent. The 24-year-old mixed-blood son of William Bent and Owl Woman was employed as a guide and interpreter at Fort Lyon. "Colonel Chivington ordered me to accompany him on his way to Sand Creek," remembered Bent. It was his job to do so.

"Boots and Saddles" was sounded about 8:00 p.m. The long lines of troopers made an imposing sight. Sergeant Morse H. Coffin of Company D, Third Colorado, estimated the column to number between 650 and 675 men of all ranks. "Our regiment," explained Private Breakenridge, "had about five hundred men, as, when we got orders to move, a lot of soldiers were home on leave of absence and were not notified in time to join us."

Chivington's troops, comprised from two regiments, were divided into five battalions. Colonel Shoup's Third Colorado Regiment included: Lieutenant Colonel Leavitt L. Bowen's First Battalion, which consisted of Companies A, C, H, L, and M; Maj. Hal Sayr's Second Battalion, which consisted of Companies B, G, I, and K; and Capt. Theodore Cree's Third Battalion, which consisted of Companies D, E, and F. From troops of the First Colorado, Major Anthony's First Battalion consisted of Companies D, G, K, and Lt. Luther Wilson's Second Battalion consisted of Companies C, E, and H. Portions of all 12 companies of the Third Regiment were represented, although the majority of Companies K and L were still guarding the South Platte. Portions of seven

20 "Massacre of Cheyenne Indians," 104-05; "Sand Creek Massacre," 47, 156, 178, 180; U.S. Congress, Senate, "Chivington Massacre," 74.

companies of the First Colorado participated, as did some of Company K of the First New Mexico, which was overdue to return to its assigned post at Fort Union. Company F of the First Colorado, which had only a handful of men, joined Anthony's First Battalion. The fact that the ranks were depleted was specifically mentioned by several officers. Neither regiment was at full strength, and some companies were merely skeletons of their usual roster.

One officer who did not go on the expedition had been out of the regimental mainstream for some time. Lieutenant Colonel Samuel F. Tappan of the First Colorado had been away for some months at Fort Leavenworth on court-martial duty. He had returned to Fort Lyon only two days before Chivington's appearance. Tappan and Chivington had never gotten along. The hard feelings began in 1862 when Chivington, then a major, had been promoted to colonel of the regiment above Tappan, who was its second-in-command. Tappan's chance to join his regiment and participate in the action ended when a horse-riding accident left him with a broken foot. He watched as the troops rode off without him.[21]

21 Michno, *Battle at Sand Creek*, 198-200.

Chapter 5

The Last Night of Peace

Colonel Chivington and elements of the First and Third Colorado regiments walked out of Fort Lyon on the evening of November 28, heading into the darkness and into the history books.

"Our course was almost exactly under the north star most of the time," recalled Sergeant Coffin. The First Colorado was on the right and the Third Colorado was on the left. Each company was formed into fours, and steadily pushed on. It was walk, trot, gallop, dismount, and lead, at hour intervals, throughout the night. The pace exhausted Private Howbert. "I would willingly have run the risk of being scalped by the Indians for a half-hour's sleep," he declared. In order to stay awake, Howbert and others nibbled on their hardtack, unaware it was infested with weevils. The surprise at what they were eating arrived with the dawn. "Much to our disgust," grumbled Howbert, "we found [it] to be very much alive." Some managed to nap in their saddles, but Coffin admitted "it is a poor way to get sleep." When an occasional halt was made, many troopers dropped off their mounts, fell to the ground, and fell quickly to sleep, only to be jostled awake a short time later when the march resumed.

About midnight, the column passed through an area dotted with several shallow lakes about a dozen miles north of the fort. Guides Robert Bent and Jim Beckwourth were doing their best, but there was no moon that cool starlit night. When the leading artillery and caissons began splashing through icy water, many troopers believed they were being purposely led into a like to get the ammunition wet. The officers, however, were well aware of these small lakes. Lieutenant Horace W. Baldwin had taken his command there to water the horses back in August. The course was adjusted and no further problems occurred.

Sometime during the night, James E. DuBois of Company D, Third Colorado, dropped back when his horse went lame. With his horse barely able to walk, DuBois hailed one of the last passing troopers and asked him to relay a message to Capt. Jay Johnston, acting provost marshal, to whom DuBois was attached. DuBois knew Johnson had some fresh horses just for this purpose. The soldier rode off, but no one came back with a spare mount. DuBois led his horse another mile or so when the animal refused to take another step. The soldier stripped his mount, turned him loose, hoisted all of his ammunition and rations, and continued to follow the trail north on foot.

Billy Breakenridge rode ahead with the scouts. He was tired and slept fitfully in the saddle half the night. About three in the morning, the scouts came upon a number of ponies far out on the plain. Breakenridge rode back to inform Chivington while the rest of the scouts rounded up the small herd. A detachment of men from the First New Mexico drove the ponies back to Fort Lyon and Chivington appointed Breakenridge as courier for the day between himself and Colonel Shoup. He was waiting in the darkness for orders when Breakenridge heard scout Beckwourth tell Chivington that the Indian camp would be about six miles ahead. As soon as the New Mexico troops departed, the command veered to the right, north by northeast.

As they drew closer to where they believed the village was located, Robert Bent drew his horse up and listened. Chivington rode closer to hear what Bent had to say. According to one account, the scout said: "Wolf he howl. Injun dog he hear wolf, he howl too. Injun, he hear dog and listen; hear something, and run off." Chivington glared at Bent and ominously tapped his revolver. "I haven't had an Indian to eat for a long time," he said. "If you fool with me, and don't lead us to that camp, I'll have you for breakfast."[1]

*   *   *

---

1   Morse H. Coffin, *The Battle of Sand Creek* (Waco, TX, 1965), 18, 30; "Sand Creek Massacre," 176; Howbert, *Indians of Pike's Peak*, 99–100; Breakenridge, *Helldorado*, 43, 47–48; J. P. Dunn, Jr., *Massacres of the Mountains: A History of the Indian Wars of the Far West, 1815-1875* (New York, NY, 1886), 342. This conversation is almost surely apocryphal. Dunn indicates Chivington spoke with Jack Smith, but Smith was in the Indian camp, and Bent was better versed in English.

In Black Kettle's village, meanwhile, the embers of the campfires were dying. The lodges cooled, and everyone snuggled into their buffalo robes and blankets. Hours earlier, about the time Chivington made his surprise appearance at Fort Lyon, business was booming in the village.

David Louderback of Company G, First Colorado, arose from his uneasy sleep, and when John Smith broke out his trade goods, the tension of the previous evening seemed to vanish. Louderback and Dexter Colley's hired man, R. Watson Clarke, assisted Smith in a rousing business, which was surprising considering what many Indians thought of Smith and Colley. Old John Smith—"Gray Blanket" or "Lying John"—had been known (and distrusted by) the Indians for some 25 years. He and his partner Colley had been cheating the Indians for years. William Bent was aware of their shady dealings. Government goods, meant as annuities for the Indians, were withheld until the Indians traded something of value for them, most often in the form of ponies or buffalo robes.

"The son of Major [Sam] Colley, the Indian agent of the Cheyennes and Arapahoes, was an Indian trader," remembered Bent, who continued:

> He [Dexter] came to this country the fall after his father was appointed agent. When he first came he could not have had property of the value to exceed fifteen hundred dollars . . . From what he said to me he must have made twenty-five or thirty thousand dollars in the two or three years he was trading with the Indians. John Smith acted as the Indian trader, and was considered a partner in the business. It is hard to identify Indian goods, but I am satisfied that a portion of the goods traded with the Indians were annuity goods.[2]

When Dexter Colley was not using annuity goods to trade, Sam Colley was distributing them improperly. Bent explained that the goods would be "piled in a heap on the prairie, the Indians sit round in a large circle, and the agent tells them, 'There are your annuity goods—divide them among yourselves.'" The agent then gets a few chiefs to put their marks on the vouchers. "As a matter of course," he continued, "the Indians do not know what or how much they are signing for." Still, some Cheyenne told Bent "that they had no confidence in Major Colley, knowing he was swindling them out of their goods."

---

2 Coel, *Chief Left Hand*, 118; "Chivington Massacre," 95.

Nevertheless, winter was upon them and the Cheyenne needed their annuities and so traded freely with Smith—especially when part of the trade goods may have included powder, lead, and caps. During the transactions and while moving about the village, Louderback made a specific count of the tipis: 115, with about eight lodges of Arapaho one-half mile below the main village. Before dark on Monday, November 28, Smith had traded and sold most of his and Dexter Colley's goods, possibly some of the very items Sam Colley was supposed to hand over to the Indians for free. In return, Smith collected three ponies, one mule, and 104 buffalo robes, property he would assess at $12,000. The robes were bundled that evening, and with business completed the three white men went to the lodge to rest. They expected to head back to Fort Lyon the next morning.[3]

Eyewitnesses and participants in catastrophic events who later take up the pen to record their experiences often look back and decide that the warning signs that something was coming were there all along, but they had failed to heed them. The were plenty of swirling currents gathered in proximity that evening at Black Kettle's village.

There were warriors present who had stolen horses the past summer. Since there were peace talks of late, however, they contemplated returning the horses in a show of good faith. Perhaps they would discuss the matter more the next day. There were also warriors in the camp who had participated in the recent raiding and killing. Some of these same Cheyenne had destroyed civilian wagons at Plum Creek and captured Nancy Morton and Danny Marble in August. War Bonnet and his men had fought against General Blunt and Major Anthony in September. Their plunder, including white scalps from many raids, filled some of the lodges. Although some Indians felt at ease in the camp, a significant number of others were wary. The warriors who had threatened to kill Louderback earlier that day were concerned that he left a trail for the soldiers from Fort Lyon to follow to their camp. They were smart enough to realize that a pledge of safety was no guarantee.[4]

---

3   "Chivington Massacre," 95; "Sand Creek Massacre," 135, 138, 208.

4   Monahan, *Denver City*, 165; "Massacre of Cheyenne Indians," 29; Roberts, "Sand Creek," 421; Michno, *Encyclopedia of Indian Wars*, 147–49, 153–55, 356; Thomas T. Smith, *The Old Army in Texas A Research Guide to the U.S. Army in Nineteenth-Century Texas* (Austin, TX, 2000), 32. Some have made the point that the Cheyenne didn't post sentries because they were assured they were at peace and that no harm would come. Such declarations show a lack of understanding of Indian warfare. Even while at war, Indians did not "defend" a village in the

Some of the Indians in the village on Sand Creek had peaceful inclinations. A significant number, however, still considered themselves at war. Black Kettle often said he could do nothing with his uncontrollable young men. The US military had heard that sentiment so often that it once prompted Gen. William T. Sherman to retort, "Tell the rascals so are mine; and if another white man is scalped in all this region, it will be impossible to hold mine in." Now, several hundred possibly uncontrollable young white men were riding hard to catch some of the uncontrollable young Indians who had been making war for much of the year. The fact that many young men on both sides may have been more or less peaceably inclined was immaterial at this point. The past was both prologue and irrelevant.[5]

These temporary villages also contained innocent Indian women and children who had never been on raids and who had never harmed any whites. These families, however, were also manning the home bases of warriors who did engage in those acts. They aided and abetted their men in their warlike actions. Likewise, the settler homes on the frontier were filled with women and children who had never harmed any Indians, but they too supported the militia and the soldiers. The noncombatants on both sides shared similar roles. The best of the scenarios would be to leave all of them out of the fighting, but if one was looked upon as a legitimate target, so was the other. It was in the Indian villages and the settler homesteads where the real tragedy of the Indian wars took place.

That evening, a group of young people stayed up late playing games. They did not return to their lodges until well after dark. One of the girls spotted a light moving on the distant prairie. Several others also saw a light that flashed, disappeared, and then flashed again. The news was reported to War Bonnet, who also saw the light. He passed the word on to others and became uneasy,

---

conventional sense of the word. They did not entrench, or put out skirmish lines or pickets. They rarely had more than a token number of boys as herd guards. For all the Indians' ability to attack suddenly, to maneuver, to move quickly, to disperse and disappear, their lack of military discipline was nearly always fatal after pitching camp. They invariably let their guard down. One study shows that the military surprised Indians in their camps on 205 occasions, while another concludes, "The fact that Indians were so often surprised is a reflection of their notoriously lax security."

5   Robert G. Athearn, *William Tecumseh Sherman and the Settlement of the West* (Norman, OK, 1995), 69.

wondering what it meant. He thought that it would be a good idea to get the horses in before daylight.

The Cheyenne chief Cometsevah sat in his lodge that evening. His little sister, 14-year-old Tallow Woman, had gone to visit her aunt. She was on horseback, moving along in the moonless night when she heard strange voices and whistling sounds in the darkness. She slowed and turned her head from side to side, but could not see anyone. Suddenly, objects that might have been sticks went flying past her. She heard what sounded like whistling, but could see nothing. Frightened, she put her heels to the pony and hurried home. When she told all this to her older brother, Cometsevah brought it up with other chiefs, who laughed and said it was just some young men trying to get her attention.

Cometsevah was not so sure and and argued that the camp should be moved. "No, maybe tomorrow," came the reply. There would be plenty of time to move the camp once the morning sun rose.[6]

6 *Sand Creek Massacre Project*, 203.

Chapter 6

The Approach

The last few miles of the march of the Colorado volunteers crossed a gently rolling plain. After a long and cold night, the sun was finally beginning to peek above the eastern horizon.

Chivington had ridden hard to get in position, but he was close to losing his quarry. He had promised Major Anthony that he would surround the camp and deliver an ultimatum, but now the sun was coming up—Major Sayr recorded the time as 6:00 a.m.—and his command had still not come upon the village. Morse Coffin commented that "they made an awful din and clatter, which must have been heard for several miles away, as the morning was clear, cool, and calm." The soldiers in the ranks were not privy to Anthony's and Chivington's plans to extricate the white men from the camp. "Some men remarked at the time that this was a queer way to surprise the Indians," recalled Coffin, "and we wondered that we were not timed to reach the enemy's camp at dawn, provided we were to attack them."[1]

Before they set eyes on the village, the troops spotted the Indian pony herd of about 1,000 horses being driven away. Anthony's Battalion, with Companies D, G, and K, First Colorado, and a detachment of Company K, First New Mexico, was sent after the nearest bunch. When Anthony rode to the edge of a bluff, he finally spotted the village—still about two miles north. Major Sayr's Battalion, Companies B, G, I, and K, Third Colorado, was behind Anthony.

---

1   Coffin, *The Battle of Sand Creek*, 18-19.

Colonel Chivington's approach led him to these bluffs about one mile
south of the village. *Author*

When Sayr and his troopers reached the edge of the bluffs above Sand Creek,
they also spotted more horses off to the northwest. Captain Oliver H. P.
Baxter's Company G was sent after them. Private Irving Howbert recalled they
immediately went on a run to get between the ponies and the camp. They had
barely set out when Howbert saw a half-dozen Indians coming out from the
village toward the ponies, "but, on seeing our large force, they hesitated a
moment and started back as fast as their ponies could take them." The soldiers
secured about 500 horses.[2]

Billy Breakenridge rode to the edge of the bluffs and looked out upon the
creek and a wide valley with scattered brush and bunch grass. The streambed
had little water running through it, and beyond were the Indian tipis, with
smoke issuing from some of the tops. "It is rather hard to express the sensation
I felt as we came in sight of the battlefield," Breakenridge explained. "While I
had been close to several Indian skirmishes I had never been in a real fight with
them, but my feeling of antipathy toward the Indians was so strong that I forgot

2 "Massacre of Cheyenne Indians," 17; Howbert, *Indians of Pike's Peak*, 100.

all fear and was only anxious to get into a fight with them. The idea I might get hurt never entered my head." The troops snaked down the bluffs in several columns and moved into the sandy valley.

Lieutenant Clark Dunn of Company E, First Colorado, recalled first spotting the village when it was "nearly two miles north of us." The majority of the command rode down the bluffs. About one-half mile south of the village, they halted to discard extra baggage. During the halt, an agitated Colonel Chivington turned to his men to make a statement. Riding nearby, Robert Bent heard him say, "Remember our wives and children murdered on the Platte and Arkansas."

Jim Beckwourth also recalled Chivington saying, "Men, strip for action. I don't tell you to kill all ages and sex, but look back on the plains of the Platte, where your mothers, fathers, brothers, sisters have been slain, and their blood saturating the sands on the Platte." Morse Coffin also remembered something similar: "Boys, I shall not tell you what you are to kill, but remember our slaughtered women and children." As Coffin would later write, "I think the above to be correct, nearly word for word." Three witnesses, three slightly different recollections, but all along the same lines.

Colonel Shoup also had some words for them. According to Alston Shaw, Company A, and John Patterson, Company C, both of the Third Colorado, Shoup said, "Boys, you have been anticipating that you would have no opportunity to fight, but your chances look good."

As they hastily shed their saddle blankets, overcoats, food, and any items that would hinder them, Breakenridge heard it said that the First Colorado "should go ahead and clean up the village." The men of the Third were incensed. "This meant that we would not get into it at all," Breakenridge complained, "and we should still be known as 'The Bloodless Third.'"[3]

*   *   *

The village along Sand Creek was about 34 air miles northeast of Fort Lyon, a little more than a mile north of the existing marker on the bluffs above what is today called Dawson's South Bend. Here, Sand Creek runs generally northwest

---

3 Breakenridge, *Helldorado*, 48-49; "Chivington Massacre," 96; "Sand Creek Massacre," 13, 68-69; Shaw, *Pioneers of Colorado*, 81; Coffin, *The Battle of Sand Creek*, 19; Dunn to Chivington, November 30, 1864, *OR* 41, pt. 1, 951, 955.

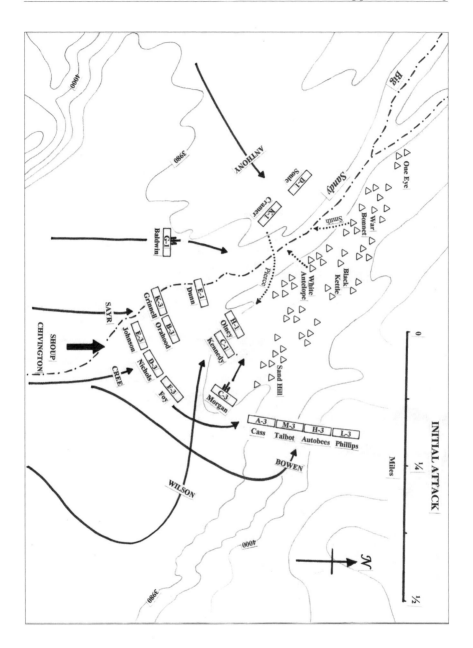

to southeast, and the village of about 115 lodges and 500 men, women, and children stretched about 500 yards along the left (north or east) bank, generally conforming to the meandering course of the creek. One Eye's band camped at the northwestern end, followed downstream by War Bonnet, White Antelope, Black Kettle, and a small number of Arapahos. Yellow Wolf, Bear Man, and Spotted Crow were in the mix near this point. According to George Bent, Sand Hill's band was camped at the southeast end, slightly separated from the other lodges.

The village Chivington rode upon that morning was in a loose configuration, not the tighter circle usually drawn during a more formal tribal gathering. According to George Bent, "each band was camped by itself with its lodges grouped together and separated by a little open space from the camps of the other bands." As a result, the sprawling camp covered some 15 acres, with a tipi dispersion of about eight per acre. Because of its length of more than one-quarter mile, it would be very difficult to see what was occurring at one end of the camp from the other.

Some controversy exists as to whether or not Arapaho were camping within the Cheyenne circle. Traditionally, Arapaho did not camp with Cheyenne because at some point in the past the tribes had commingled and a lethal illness had spread from the former to the latter. Since then, the Arapaho always camped downstream of the Cheyenne. On this November morning, the Arapaho Left Hand was going to move south to Little Raven's camp on Rush Creek, a 20-mile trip. His eight lodges were downstream of the main village, but there were a few Arapaho lodges within the Cheyenne circle. About two-thirds of the village consisted of women and children. According to David Louderback, there were not any more women and children in the village than are usually found in any village.[4]

John Smith and Edmund Guerrier both estimated the male warrior population to number some 200, which would mean that about 40 percent of the village population was male. If the Sand Creek village contained two-thirds

---

4 Many contemporary accounts stressed the number of women and children as if it were an extraordinarily large proportion, apparently to place a greater stigma on the soldiers. However, if one couple had only two children, then three-fourths of the family would consist of women and children. If they had three children, then four-fifths of the camp would be woman and children. Families with several children were common, while some were very large with eight or ten offspring. One old man named Half Bear had four wives and 30 children. In such situations one might expect a village to consist of 90 percent women and children.

women and children like many insist—meaning that it was about one-third adult male, or even 40 percent as Smith and Guerrier claimed—then there was an extraordinarily large percentage of men available to fight.[5]

On the cold Tuesday morning of November 29, the Indians awoke to begin their day, which required the retrieval of water. The Cheyenne call Sand Creek "Ponoeohe," or "Dry Creek," and the waterway certainly lived up to its name. At that time of year there were pools of water and muddy banks, but in most places there was no running water. The pools were good for the horses, but the Cheyenne would not drink from standing water. It was against their beliefs to drink water that sat overnight even in containers, for spirits might have drunk from the same receptacles. Thus, a small spring flowing into Sand Creek near the lower end of the camp provided the necessary running water.

Cheyenne chief Cometsevah awoke, perhaps thinking about the odd things his sister, Tallow Woman, had reported the night before. Other early risers included Kingfisher and Little Bear, the latter the son of Bear Tongue and Yellow Woman. Both of the young men set out to care for the horses grazing in several places in the valley. "I got up before daylight to go out to where my brother-in-law Tomahawk had left our pony herd the evening before," reported Little Bear. He crossed the creek to the southwest and was climbing the bluffs when he met Kingfisher, who had already been farther south. Kingfisher was running toward camp shouting that white men were driving off the ponies. "I looked toward the Fort Lyon Trail and saw a long line of little black objects to the south, moving toward the camp across the bare brown plain," said Little Bear. He and Kingfisher ran to the village.[6]

They were not the first ones to bring the warning. Left Hand had already broken camp and was on his way to Little Raven when he saw soldiers moving toward them from the south. He could have circled out of harm's way, but instead raced back to the Cheyenne camp. Left Hand stopped short to sound the danger signal by howling the wolf's call. The cries alerted some of the sleepy Cheyenne, warnings from the herders awakened others, and the hooves of 600

5 *Sand Creek Massacre Project*, 20, 36, 38, 134, 162, 210, 213-14, 243; "Chivington Massacre," 28, 41, 65; "Sand Creek Massacre," 139; George Bird Grinnell, *The Cheyenne Indians: Their History and Ways of Life*, 2 Vols. (Lincoln, NE, 1972), vol. 1, 149; Hyde, *George Bent*, 149-51; Powell, *Sacred Mountain*, Vol. 1, 299.

6 Hyde, *George Bent*, 151, 153; *Sand Creek Massacre Project*, 17, 200, 201, 204.

US Army horses stirred the remainder into action. Before any troopers were near enough to open fire, the Indians were awake and preparing to fight or run.

George Bent had been back in the camp only a few days since visiting his father. He was still in bed when shouts startled him awake. He ran out of the lodge and recalled a fearsome sight: "From down the creek a large body of troops was advancing at a rapid trot, some to the east of the camps, and others on the opposite side of the creek, to the west. More soldiers could be seen making for the Indian pony herds to the south of the camps," he added. "In the camps themselves all was confusion and noise." Men, women, and children rushed out partly dressed. Some men ran back to the lodges for their arms, while others, with weapons, lassos, and bridles, ran for the pony herds. The village was now on full alert, if not fully prepared for what was transpiring.[7]

David Louderback, Watson Clarke, John Smith, and his son Jack were in one of War Bonnet's lodges eating breakfast when an Indian woman stormed into the lodge to announce "there was a heap of buffaloes coming." A few minutes later, War Bonnet came in with a correction: they were not buffaloes, but soldiers. War Bonnet asked John Smith if he would go out and see who they were and what they wanted. Smith and Louderback agreed and left the lodge. Louderback searched about unsuccessfully for a horse to ride out and investigate, but the women had already driven away all the nearby ponies.

Edmund Guerrier was sleeping in another tipi when disaster struck. The son of a Frenchman and a Cheyenne woman, Guerrier had spent a lot of time with the Cheyenne. One of the first things he heard was women excitedly talking about buffalo before one of them told him to get up because "there were a lot of soldiers coming."

Guerrier ran out of his tipi and into Smith and Louderback. All three decided to find out what was happening. From Guerrier's perspective, the soldiers were unlimbering artillery. "I struck out," he said. "I left the soldier and Smith; I went to the northeast; I ran about five miles." There, he met a cousin driving a herd of ponies, grabbed one of the animals, and together the men continued riding toward the Smoky Hill River.[8]

---

7 *Sand Creek Massacre Project*, 211, 213; Hyde, *George Bent*, 151-52. Left Hand did not die in front of his lodge as some reports claim. He was already very sick and had some injuries. He died three days later in camp on the Smoky Hill.

8 "Chivington Massacre," 66; "Sand Creek Massacre," 135.

Although the soldiers had reached the village with surprise in their favor, they did not charge through the camp, and it was not the Indians who suffered first. After discarding their excess baggage, Chivington split his other battalions. Lieutenant Luther Wilson, commanding Companies C, E, and H, First Colorado, went after ponies east of the village. Wilson swept them up and drove them toward the Indian camping ground, which he reached before Major Anthony's First Colorado companies finished their roundup to the southwest. Colonel Shoup, meanwhile, brought the Third Colorado in from the southeast, between and slightly behind the two battalions of the First Colorado.

When the advance stalled without warning, the soldiers moving toward the village had no idea why. Only a select few knew of the plan to first extricate some of the whites and Indians before engaging in open war. Theodore Chubbuck of Company M, Third Colorado, believed the pause was made to send an interpreter into the camp "to tell the Indians what was coming." Before they could engage, George W. Pierce of Company F, First Colorado, lost control of his horse. When the animal and rider ran through the lower end of the village, Indians there opened fire at them. Horse and rider went down in a heap, but the uninjured Pierce jumped on his feet and ran a short distance before stopping to assess his predicament. Private Alexander F. Safely, Company H, who was acting as a scout and so well in front of the rest of the troops, watched what happened next: "I saw the smoke rise from an Indian gun, and also saw George Pierce drop." Actually, two Cheyenne fired at him: Big Head and Big Baby.

Another witness, Major Downing, also recalled Pierce being killed because his runaway horse took him to the edge of the camp. "This was the first shot fired, to my knowledge," explained Downing. The Colorado volunteers had taken the first casualty.[9]

9 "Chivington Massacre," 70; "Sand Creek Massacre," 49, 135, 220; Theodore L. Chubbuck, "Dictation. Battle of Sand Creek," P-L 135, Bancroft Library, University of California, 1; *Sand Creek Massacre Project,* 60; Powell, *Sacred Mountain* , vol. 1, 302; Hoig, *Sand Creek Massacre,* 149. There are many guesses as to why Pierce died as he did. Hoig thinks Pierce died while trying to save John Smith; Powell claims Pierce died while trying to save One Eye; Morse Coffin believed Pierce might have been trying to save Louderback. Most thought it was simply a runaway horse incident. The confusion arises because there were two similar incidents. Pierce's runaway horse carried him in front of Wilson's battalion, where he was killed, while another man from Lieutenant Cramer's Company K was killed shortly thereafter riding in front of Major Anthony's Battalion. Many authors have combined these two events into one incident.

Chapter 7

Flags and Friendlies

John Smith and David Louderback made their way through the village to the southeast end toward the nearest troops they could see. Private Louderback placed a white handkerchief on a stick, which he waved vigorously when they reached the edge of the camp. He and Smith were still 150 yards from the troops, however, and they retreated when bullets began flying in their direction. Lieutenant Cramer of Company K, part of Anthony's Battalion, witnessed the event: "I saw someone with a white flag approaching our lines, and the troops fired upon it."

In the village, teamster Watson Clarke also tried to signal the troops. "When the attack was made I got up on a wagon and waved a white skin—a flag of truce," he said. "When I was waving it three or four bullets went through it. Then I got down and lay under a wagon, as I had nothing to fight with." According to an eyewitness at least two of the whites in the village were waving white flags but the firing continued. "I staid outside, sitting on the wagon tongue, until they commenced firing the howitzers," explained Louderback.[1]

Whether or not an American flag was flying over the camp has been hotly debated. Only two soldiers claimed they saw one. Private Naman D. Snyder of Company D, First Colorado, said the banner was flying at the west end, and he also claimed he saw a soldier (Louderback) "place the white flag."

---

1 "Chivington Massacre," 41, 74, 96; "Sand Creek Massacre," 135; "Massacre of Cheyenne Indians," 5; Roberts, "Sand Creek," 843n43.

The historical Sand Creek Indian village was located here, more than one mile north of the traditional site. *NPS*

The only other soldier who told a similar story was Pvt. George M. Roan, Company G, First Colorado. "I saw a camp of Indians, and the stars and stripes waving over the camp," reported the private. Roan said Chivington had not yet reached the village when he first saw the flag, because he (Roan) "was on the right of the battalion and in front." His statement conflicts with that of Cpl. James J. Adams, who was in the same company with Roan. Adams testified that the mules had broken down and so the battery was late getting to the village. Company G was not in front as Roan claimed, and Roan later admitted that there were men three-fourths of a mile in advance of the battalion. Captain Soule recalled that the battery prepared for action in the rear of Anthony's Battalion. The only two soldiers who claimed to see an American flag were in Anthony's Battalion, and one of those could not have been up front as he first claimed. A flag, pennant, robe, or rag, may have been waving near the west end of the village—the end closest to Anthony's Battalion—and farthest from the main command under Chivington. No other soldier left a record of a waving American flag, although Lieutenant Cramer said he saw a folded one in the camp late that night.

Others outside the ranks of the soldier also claim they saw a flag. John Smith said he saw Black Kettle raise one, although he was in War Bonnet's lodge at the west end of the camp. The flag was one purportedly given to Black

Kettle by Commissioner A. B. Greenwood years earlier. Some oral history alleges that the flag was always waving, but Smith testified it was raised a few minutes before the troops began firing. Robert Bent was riding far away near Chivington, but made the absurd declaration that he "saw the American flag waving and *heard* [emphasis added] Black Kettle tell the Indians to stand round the flag."[2]

George Bent was in the village. In a letter to George Hyde he wrote, "I looked towards Black Kettle's Lodge and he had [a] Flag on [a] Lodge pole in front of his Lodge. Just than the Soldiers opened fire from all sides of the Village." Bent also gave Hyde Little Bear's story as that Cheyenne had related it to him. Little Bear had been out to get the ponies that morning. When he returned, he saw women and children running away, and "as I ran by Black Kettle's Lodge he had [a] Flag tied to [a] Lodge Pole and was holding it."[3]

Taken together, about six people claimed to have seen an American flag flying. As might be expected, others adamantly denied it. Milo H. Slater of Company H, First Colorado, was in the forefront of the advance with Wilson. When he heard people claim after the event that an American flag was flying over the camp, he adamantly disagreed: "Permit me to say that these statements are unqualifiedly false. When I say that my battalion made the attack (precisely at sunrise), that I saw the first gun fired, and that I was in the engagement until its close, I will be pardoned for believing myself in a position to know whereof I speak."[4]

It is common for eyewitnesses to witness the same general event and yet report different things (as will be discussed in more detail in Section Three), but it is also sensible to believe that enough people saw a flag of some kind to conclude that one was flying. In addition, the white flags seen waving by several people may simply have been those held aloft by the few white men in the village. In any case, flags proved to be of no deterrence to the advancing troopers. Smith and Louderback sought the dubious protection of a buffalo hide tipi, but Louderback could not contain his curiosity and peered out. He spotted an officer approaching who he later identified as Colonel Chivington.

2   "Chivington Massacre," 96; "Sand Creek Massacre," 13, 50, 77, 80, 128, 142.

3   George Bent, "The Letters of George Bent to George E. Hyde, 1904–1918," March 15, 1905, April 14, 1906. Coe Collection, Beinecke Manuscript Library, Yale University.

4   Milo H. Slater, "Indian Troubles in the Early Days of Colorado," P-L 169, Bancroft Library, University of California, 4.

When he got within 50 yards Louderback emerged and hollered. The officer waved him forward.

"He told me to come on, that I was all right, calling me by name," Louderback recalled. When he got closer a soldier fired at him, a move that enraged the private. Chivington ordered everyone to hold their fire and ordered the private to fall in with the rear. Louderback informed the colone that the lodge in front of them was filled with white men. Just then, John Smith popped his head out, and Lieutenant Cramer saw him at the same time he heard someone shout, "shoot the damned old son of a bitch." The firing at Smith, Louderback, and Clarke incensed the officer. "Well I got so mad," he said, "I swore I would not burn powder, and I did not."

Captain Soule had a similar reaction. "Poor old John Smith and Louderback ran out with white flags but they paid no attention to them, and they ran back into the tents. . . . I refused to fire and swore that none but a coward would."

Smith heard words similar to those reported by Louderback: "Run here, Uncle John; you are all right." Smith thought it was Lieutenant Wilson's Battalion, but it was Major Anthony's men he spotted. Chivington may have been nearby, but it was Major Anthony who waved at him to approach.

"As I came up with my command, my men formed in line very close to the Indian camp; among the first persons I saw was John Smith," reported Anthony. He did not want to "open the ball," but wished Chivington to do so, and soon enough, Chivington's men commenced firing on both sides of him. Anthony did not instruct his men to fire right away, as he was concerned with getting Smith out safely. The old trader looked frightened. "I rode out in front of my men and called out to him to come to me. I held up my hands, called him by name, and swung my hat at him."[5]

Smith advanced, but hesitated when the bullets whizzed by him. Just then, one of Lieutenant Cramer's attached men of Company F, Pvt. Joseph W. Aldrich, rode to Anthony and said, "Major, let me bring him out." Aldrich rode a short distance toward Smith through a hail of flying bullets before slumping in the saddle. Aldrich's horse circled around before both horse and rider fell. The private tried to rise, but an Indian ran up to him, "snatched his gun from him,

---

5 "Massacre of Cheyenne Indians," 5, 24; "Chivington Massacre," 73; "Sand Creek Massacre," 48, 65, 135; Roberts and Halaas, "Written in Blood," 25, 27. Cramer and Soule were both lauded for not firing at the Indians, but in their letters to Wynkoop, it is clear they were talking about not firing at Smith, Louderback, and Clarke.

and beat him over the head and killed him." The Coloradans had suffered their second casualty.[6]

Things were not working out as planned. Chivington had promised Anthony that he would surround the village and give the whites a chance to escape, and possibly even get out the chiefs who had been inclined toward peace. Instead, the Cheyenne were shooting at them. The situation was deteriorating by the minute, but still Chivington did not order a charge through the village.

When John Smith reached Anthony's men, he spotted Lt. Horace W. Baldwin of Company G, the commander of the two-gun battery. "Catch hold of the caisson and keep up with us," Baldwin told Smith.

Teamster Clarke joined them, and the firing picked up considerably. Up until that time, it had been strangely quiet. Major Anthony saw most of Wilson's Battalion to the right (east) as he approached the camp from the southwest, where he "was attacked by a small force of Indians posted behind the bank of the creek, who commenced firing upon me with arrows."

Major Downing rode up when an Indian fired at him from below the creek bank. He pulled back, looked at the arrangement of the village, and rode over to Major Anthony. "Under the supposition that he was going to charge the village with his cavalry," recalled Downing, "I advised him not to do it, believing that the horses would become entangled among the ropes and fall." Anthony agreed and most of the command dismounted and led their horses at a walk.

Contrary to popular belief, the traditionally depicted hell-for-leather saber charge by Colonel Chivington and his Coloradans did not happen, for they had no sabers and most walked into the Indian village. According to Lieutenant Cramer, Wilson arrived first at the northeast side of the village, Anthony came up from the south, and Chivington with the Third Colorado "took position in our rear, dismounted, and after the fight had been commenced by Major Anthony and Lieutenant Wilson, mounted, and commenced firing through us and over our heads."[7]

6 "Massacre of Cheyenne Indians," 24; M. S. Elswick, Colorado Historical Society, correspondence November 18, 2001.

7 "Massacre of Cheyenne Indians," 5; "Chivington Massacre," 70, 73; "Sand Creek Massacre," 35, 139; Anthony to Chivington, December 1, 1864, *OR* 41, pt. 1, 951. The ordnance record shows only seven sabers were issued to the entire Third Regiment.

Just as the soldiers did not barrel into the village, neither did the Indians hang around waiting for them to arrive. Cheyenne Chief White Antelope, Stand in the Water, and a few others, however, offered some resistance. After Lieutenant Wilson cut off some horses to the east, he detached Company H to continue the advance, and it became engaged about five minutes before the other units. Wilson saw the Indians, "who had approached me under a bank as if they were going to fight." Louderback saw them also, but he believed they initially did not want to fight, and did so only after being fired upon. "The Indians returned our first fire almost instantaneously," reported Wilson.

Exactly what happened next depends on who you believe. Black Kettle stayed back, testified Louderback, but White Antelope and Stand In The Water "got their guns, came back, and commenced firing at the troops. Both of them were killed within fifty yards of each other. White Antelope," he continued, "was killed in the bed of the creek and Stand In The Water was killed right opposite to him, on the left hand side of the creek." Several who either witnessed or participated in the event have described the deaths.

Private Safely, who knew White Antelope by sight, assisted in his demise. He saw three Indians come out of the village firing arrows to contest Company H's advance. One of the Indians was killed on the spot. Another, on the same bank as Safely, was White Antelope. "He came running directly towards Company H," Safely explained. "[H]e had a pistol in his left hand, and a bow with some arrows in his right. He got within about fifty yards of the company; he commenced shooting his pistol, still in his left hand."

The company was now about 100 yards from the village, with White Antelope in between. The soldiers took many shots at him, but their bucking horses ruined their aim. Exasperated, one soldier asked if there was any one who could hit that Indian? Private Safely announced that he could, and another trooper held his horse steady while he took aim.

"I got off and fired at the Indian," Safely said, "the ball taking effect in the groin. He turned then and ran back towards the village, and Billy Henderson, of H Company, shot the Indian through the head when he was about the middle of the creek. That was the commencement of the fight, as near as I can recollect."

Lieutenant Andrew J. Templeton, Company G, Third Colorado, saw White Antelope lead the fight until he was killed. Templeton, however, thought the Cheyenne's demise came at the hands of one of his privates, Hugh H. Melrose. Among the first to reach White Antelope's body was Pvt. Henry Mull, one of a handful of men at the battle from Company F, First Colorado. Mull hurried in to claim the fine Navajo blanket wrapped around the dead chief.

John Smith, now comparatively safe with Major Anthony's men, also witnessed White Antelope's death. He was the first Indian killed, believed Smith, "within a hundred yards of where I was in camp at the time." This occurred, recalled Louderback, "opposite the lower end of the main village, "and opposite to War Bonnet's lodge."[8]

The discrepancies in this body of testimony over this episode are remarkable. "Black Kettle and his wife," wrote George Bent in a letter to George Hyde, "were [the] last ones to leave their Lodge at Sand Creek. White Antelope, his Chief Lieutenant who always stayed with him never left his Lodge and was Killed in front of his Lodge. Black Kettle ask[ed] him to come on with him but [he] said he would not leave and sung [his] death song." Bent, however, was not an eyewitness and heard the story later from Black Kettle. If Bent had been close enough to see and hear all this for himself, he would also have likely been killed.[9]

Another divergent tale comes from Jim Beckwourth. The scout claimed he saw White Antelope run out to the troops with his hands up, saying, "Stop!" in English. He said Chivington and Shoup could not hear him because of all the noise, but Beckwourth apparently could hear him just fine. "He stopped and folded his arms until shot down."[10]

Another variation comes from Lieutenant Cramer, who argued the Indian was not White Antelope but Left Hand. The Arapaho, explained the officer, "stood with his hands folded across his breast, until he was shot saying: 'Soldiers no hurt me—soldiers my friends.'" Cramer was not in earshot, it is doubtful whether he could understand Arapaho, and Left Hand was not shot and killed. Cramer's statement is nonsense.[11]

Several white soldiers witnessed White Antelope fighting and being killed in the creek bed, which is where his body was found. Bent, Beckwourth, and Cramer used variations of the story that White Antelope (or Left Hand) died stoically in front of his lodge. How could people witnessing the same general episode tell such conflicting tales? Did any of them see White Antelope's death at all? Did they hear of it from others? Were they simply speculating? Did they

---

8 "Chivington Massacre," 41, 67; "Sand Creek Massacre," 137–40, 220–22; Roberts, "Sand Creek," 435, 843n39.

9   Bent, "Letters of George Bent to George Hyde," April 25, 1906.

10 "Sand Creek Massacre," 70.

11 "Chivington Massacre," 73; Roberts and Halaas, "Written in Blood," 27.

Sgt. Morse H. Coffin, Company D, Third Colorado, participated in much of the action and later wrote a book about his experience.

History Colorado, Denver, CO

make it up from whole cloth, or did their unconscious memory construct it from expectations either of a tenacious warrior or a peace-loving friend of the white man? Are there any facts evident at all, or is all of this a figment of our fallible memories and biases?

Colonel Shoup's men, behind and to the left of Wilson's battalion, had not yet gotten into the action. "[I] kept my men in column of fours till I arrived at the village, when I formed them in line of battle," explained Shoup. Both Wilson to his right and Anthony to his left were lightly engaged, but, per Chivington's agreement with Anthony, he did not charge through the village. "I did not allow my men to fire when I formed my first line: the battalion on my right was firing," said Shoup. "I wheeled my men into column of fours and marched to the rear of the battalion on my right, to the right of that battalion, to obtain a better position."

Morse Coffin rode behind Colonels Shoup and Chivington, who were a few rods in advance and separated slightly. They rode to the right, then formed again into line and moved forward. "While we were passing the village," Coffin said, "and before a gun was fired by the soldiers, so far as I can recall, we passed a dead soldier, and his horse, also dead, a little distance from him. This man was a Mr. Pierce." According to Coffin, there was no furious charge on horseback. "We proceeded through the village on a walk," he testified. "I think the town at this time was entirely deserted by the Indians, as not one was to be seen thereabouts, though plenty were not far away."

Forced by Chivington to guide the soldiers to a village containing his own relatives, Robert Bent claimed that some Indians ran away at the first fire, while others dove into their lodges to get their arms. "They had time to get away if they had wanted to," Bent later testified. Right in the village, Private Louderback saw the exodus close-up. "I was in such a position that I could see when they got away, as a large number started before the troops commenced firing."[12]

It is obvious from several perspectives there was no galloping charge through the village at Sand Creek. Yet many illustrations, novels, movies, and published histories depict crazed troopers on horseback charging through a crowded village wielding sabers to cut down fleeing women and screaming children. Why? How can eyewitnesses tell such diametrically opposed accounts?

Major Anthony's request to Colonel Chivington that they attempt to surround the village and get certain people out had been partially fulfilled. The civilians and soldiers were safe, but the few Indians that Anthony, Soule, and Cramer sought to save either fled or fought. Regardless of what precisely took place during the opening stages of the fighting (charge or slow approach), it was a no-win situation for the Indians because the soldiers were not aware of any arrangements made among the officers. It would not have mattered whether the villagers approached shooting weapons or with their hands up—they would have been fired upon by the soldiers. A private deal between Chivington and Anthony, an uncertain battle plan, a lack of communication among the officers and men, and poor command control led to a hesitant, uncoordinated opening advance. In some sense the Indians were beneficiaries of this clumsy plan because it could have been much worse. As Bent explained, "They had time to get away if they had wanted to."

When the first warnings earlier described alerted the village, the sleepy morning turned immediately chaotic. Ten-year-old Singing Under Water was one of a small number of Arapaho in the village. She awoke to the sound of the camp crier yelling, "Wake up Arapahos, the soldiers are attacking, the soldiers are attacking us. Run, scatter, run, scatter, we will all meet again in two moons where we had our last Sun Dance."

Singing Under Water pulled on her moccasins. She recalled an "awful lot of noise. As I went outside of the teepee I saw people running in every direction and I saw people falling down and teepees falling apart." The destruction

12 Coffin, *Sand Creek*, 19; "Chivington Massacre," 96; "Sand Creek Massacre," 135, 139, 176.

among the lodges was from the howitzers that had just opened fire. "I was terrified," she confessed. "Then I ran and ran, north."

When the Cheyenne Braided Hair heard the commotion, the first thing he went for was his rawhide rope. He knew he had to catch a horse to get his pregnant wife out of the village. Once outside the lodge, he saw ponies running past and roped one. Rushing back, he told his wife to ride out of the area. When she told told him that she did not know where to go, Braided Hair ordered her to follow the rest of the horses and slapped the pony on the side.

A 13-year-old Arapaho girl who later took the white name "Lizzie" recalled running along the creek bed with a group of boys and girls when one of her moccasins slipped off in the water. They were good moccasins, and she didn't want to lose one. While the others ran, Lizzie stopped to hunt for the footwear. Her sisters, however, grabbed her by the arms and made her keep running. They finally found a safe place in the sandy banks and hid from the troopers.[13]

The situation was no less harrowing for the warriors. Little Bear returned to camp to find people running up the creek. He made it to his lodge to get his bow, quiver, shield, and war bonnet. "By this time the soldiers were shooting into the camp from two sides," he recalled, "the bullets hitting the lodge cover with heavy thumps like big hailstones." Little Bear hid among the lodges before jumping into the creek bed, where he found Big Head, Crow Neck, Cut-Lip-Bear, and Smoke hiding under the bank. The soldiers were on both banks firing into the camp, said Little Bear, "but they soon saw that the lodges were nearly empty, so they began to advance up the creek, firing on the fleeing people."

According to George Bent, he looked toward Black Kettle's lodge and saw a flag on a lodge pole when the soldiers started firing. He and about 10 others started across Sand Creek west of the camp to make a stand, but the firing became so hot they traveled upstream about two miles to where some old men and women were digging holes in the banks for cover.[14]

Lone Wolf, a grandson of Black Kettle, was one of the lucky ones to get a horse. He rode out of the camp toward the sand pits where others were gathering, but his pony threw him off while trying to scale one of the high sandy banks. Lone Wolf jumped up and ran "as fast as my legs could carry me." He hid in the breastworks the Indians had dug in the sand.

13 *Sand Creek Massacre Project*, 160, 163, 164, 177, 181, 244.

14 Bent, "Letters of George Bent to George Hyde," March 15, 1905.

After Braided Hair got his wife on a horse and out of the camp, he retrieved his weapons from the tipi and fought his way out of the area. North of the village he came across an old blind man guided by a boy hurrying away on foot. Braided Hair stopped to help, but took a bullet in the elbow as he did so. With blood coursing down his arm, he left the pair and hurried on.

With nearly everyone else was fleeing the village, and the soldiers firing into the Indians and their lodges, Black Kettle finally realized he had no immunity from Chivington and his men. He and his wife Medicine Woman started up the streambed, following the main body of the fleeing Indians. Medicine Woman was struck by a bullet and fell. She was bleeding badly and appeared to be dead. Black Kettle ran on alone to the sheltering sand pits.[15]

The Cheyenne escaped the battle area in any way they could. The Tallbird family members ran up the creek. When one mother, carrying her little girl, could not run any farther, she dropped to the sand and dug a hole. She placed the little girl into the pit, covered her with sand and brush, and told her not to move and that she would come back for her later. The Cheyenne Man On Cloud also hid a young girl in the sand and brush. Another woman managed to get a horse and was riding away when she saw a little girl running alone. The girl stopped and held out her arm, and with hardly a break in the pony's stride, the woman scooped up the child and continued riding. Another little girl lost her parents in the confusion. She ran and hid in a hollow log, where she watched from a knothole. She remained inside the log for two days.

Soon after the fight began, Charles Autobees and Oscar Pixley, Company D, Third Colorado, together with three more men, took some captured ponies to the main herd about a mile south of the village. When the five soldiers headed back to the camp, they noticed that the sand in the creek bed had been disturbed in a peculiar way. One of them suggested that maybe Indians were buried there. When they poked around, one jumped up and Autobees shot him. Two more wiggled out of the sand and ran, but both were killed. Morse Coffin thought that many escaped in this manner because, he explained, "cases were related where Indians or squaws would be seen to drop down, and after making the sand fly lively for a minute or two, be out of sight."[16]

The fighting was just beginning.

---

15 *Sand Creek Massacre Project*, 197, 199, 245; Powell, *Sacred Mountain* I, 304.

16 *Sand Creek Massacre Project*, 201; Coffin, *Sand Creek*, 29.

Chapter 8

A Battle

The Colorado volunteers moved through the village on a southeast to northwest axis. Only a few Indian dead were found at the northwest end of the main village, and only a few soldiers had been killed. So far, the fighting had been light.

Thaddeus P. Bell of Company M, Third Colorado, was passing among the tipis when he peeked into an Indian lodge. Lying on the ground was the fresh scalp of a red-haired man.[1] In the abandoned camp, Chivington changed his troop formation from line to column, which he would not have done in the face of a resisting enemy, and continued up the left and right banks of the creek.

Company G of the First Colorado unlimbered its guns near the creek on the south side, while Company C of the Third Colorado unlimbered nearby on the north side. Company G had been left behind in the run toward the village, said Cpl. James J. Adams, because the mules drawing the artillery gave out. They caught up after the cavalrymen were already firing and, according to Sgt. Lucien Palmer, the Indians had already moved up the creek several hundred yards. "We threw several shells, which did not reach them," he testified. Hauling the pieces all the way out to Sand Creek seemed to be a wasted effort, for the men only carried with them 16 rounds of ammunition per gun.

Up ahead of them, Morse Coffin saw an artillery shell burst about 100 feet above some Indians who had taken refuge along the banks. Baldwin's battery

1 "Sand Creek Massacre," 151, 223.

fired several times before moving upstream to a new position. After unlimbering again, related Palmer, "We threw several rounds of grape and canister at them when they were entrenching themselves on the opposite side of the creek." The artillery ammunition was quickly exhausted.[2]

The main command, meanwhile, approached the village from the southeast. But when Irving Howbert's company secured the ponies, they approached out of the south, which allowed the Indians to retreat to the west and north. Those were not the only avenues of escape. Some also slipped away to the south, in the same direction from which the soldiers had just come.

Jim DuBois was still walking north after his horse played out. At daybreak, alone on the open plains, he heard the sound of guns and forced his tired legs to keep moving. After another hour, and now within two or three miles of the battlefield, he spotted a large party of Indians about one mile to the west, heading south. As they drew near, he took cover and counted 75 Indians and nine horses. When DuBois reached the village, he told his story to Morse Coffin; both concurred this was the largest party of Indians to escape in one body.

By the time Howbert approached the field the action was rather heavy. "[T]he firing had become general," he remembered, "and it made some of us— myself among the number—feel pretty queer. I am sure, speaking for myself, if I hadn't been too proud, I should have stayed out of the fight altogether."

To the north, Indians were riding away on ponies taken from another herd grazing on the far side of the village. Down in the creek bed, however, the fight was a hot one. "The Indian warriors concentrated along Sand Creek," testified Howbert, "using the high banks on either side as a means of defense. At this point Sand Creek is about 200 yards wide, the banks on each side being almost perpendicular and from six to twelve feet high."

The sight of the Indians running from the village was more than most of the volunteers could handle. They had kept in some semblance of order until then, but now the Indians were getting away, and the officers could no longer restrain the soldiers. According to Privates Shaw and Patterson, the left wing of the command broke after the Indians first. Colonel Shoup tried to check them, but as he did so the soldiers on the right side picked up the chase. "The officers lost control over them," testified the privates, "for the volunteers, at sight of the Indians, remembered the crimes committed by their hands and were

2 "Sand Creek Massacre," 143, 149-51; Coffin, *Battle of Sand Creek*, 20.

determined to wreak vengeance." Private Chubbuck took note of the loss of discipline. "Colonel Shoup tried to keep the soldiers in line," he said, "but he could not control them. They broke ranks and began firing as fast as possible. Some of them fought the Indians in the pits, some chased Indians out on the plains, and some chased Indians up the creek."

Morse Coffin of Company D, Third Colorado, took in the chaotic scene unfolding along the creek bed: "From nearly opposite the village, and extending up the creek in a northwest direction, for, say, a half mile or more, the bed of the creek was dotted more or less thickly with moving humanity. I think a majority of these were women and children, and who seemed to be going away in a sort of listless, or dazed, or abandoned manner, as though they knew not what to do, nor where to go." The village was deserted, but the Indians were waiting for the soldiers one-half mile upstream where the creek changed course abruptly from east to south.[3]

Captain Theodore G. Cree led a battalion consisting of Companies D, E, and F of the Third Colorado. They formed to the southeast of the village, moved forward along the north bank about one-half mile, and dismounted. The bank where Sergeant Coffin dismounted was four to six feet high, and the Indians made good use of the bluffs for defense. Some of the volunteers rushed to the creek bank without orders, and Coffin thought them foolhardy. An arrow hit Jim Arbuthnot's horse. Hiram J. "Hi" Lockhart of Company D was thrown from his mount. As he tried to follow on foot, an Indian rose from the bank and shot at him. Lockhart went to ground and returned fire, but also missed. The Indian shot again before Lockhart could reload. The soldier dropped flat, for it was difficult to reload his old infantry musket while lying down. Finally, some of his company came up and killed the Indian that had him pinned down.

Coffin watched as many women and children took shelter in the creek bed. "I am of the opinion that no special attack was made on these women and others," he later testified, "from the fact that comparatively few were found in that locality after the battle." But when the artillery opened up, continued the

---

3 Howbert, *Indians of Pike's Peak*, 101–02; Shaw, *Pioneers of Colorado*, 81–82; Chubbuck, "Dictation. Sand Creek," 2; Coffin, *Battle of Sand Creek*, 19–20, 30; *Sand Creek Massacre Project*, 130–34. Archaeological investigations showed little evidence of Indian resistance in the village, which confirms observations that it was nearly deserted before the soldiers got into it. The soldiers found few weapons there. This does not mean the Indians were unarmed; it means, as the narratives tell us, that they had plenty of time to gather their weapons before leaving.

Company D sergeant, they scattered up the creek and to the west bank, which was ten to fifteen feet high about a mile upstream.[4]

Lieutenant Colonel Bowen took his battalion of Companies A, H, L, and M of the Third Colorado through the deserted village and along the north side of the creek. Company M, under Capt. Presley Talbot, was in the advance. Its members emerged from the camp to find another cluster of tipis near the creek, defended by more Indians than they had faced before. Colonel Shoup described this as "the main body." Most of the adult warriors of these families were said to be out hunting. A Cheyenne girl named Man Stand said that all who were left to protect them were teenage boys, but if so, they bravely took on the job. The oldest ones, armed only with bows and arrows, rode their ponies straight into Talbot's oncoming soldiers. When they were scattered or killed, the younger boys went in, with the same result. Whether adult warriors or teenagers, they put up a good fight.

Irving Howbert described this part of the action: "I saw a line of about one hundred Indians receive a charge from one of our companies as steadily as veterans, and their shooting was so effective that our men were forced to fall back." The troopers counter-charged and forced the Indians behind the banks of the creek, which they effectively used as breastworks. They retired in a "leisurely manner," said Howbert, but they left "a large number of their dead on the field." The remaining men and boys fled. One boy rode by Man Stand, grabbed her by the hair, and hoisted her on his pony. They rode away and survived.

John Smith, traveling with Lieutenant Baldwin's battery, was near that spot where "about a hundred" Indians were cornered. The soldiers nearly destroyed them, although, Smith added, "Four or five soldiers had been killed, some with arrows and some with bullets." The companies were scattered. "There were not over two hundred troops in the main fight, engaged in killing this body of Indians under the bank," concluded Smith.

Jim Beckwourth claimed the Indians did not fight in the village and didn't form up in a line of battle "until they had been run out of their village." Once out in the open, they formed up and fought "until the shells were thrown among them," at which time they broke and "fought all over the country."

Major Anthony figured there were between 75 and 100 male warriors firing at them. He briefly described the confrontation: "Quite a party of Indians took

4 Coffin, *Battle of Sand Creek*, 20–21.

position under the bank, in the bed of the creek, and returned fire upon us. We fought them about seven hours, I should think, there being firing on both sides."

Many defenders lined the creek on the east side. "My company was permitted to charge the banks and ditches," Captain Talbot recalled. "There I received so very galling a fire from the Indians under the bank and from ditches dug out just above the bank that I ordered my company to advance, to prepare to dismount and fight on foot." As they moved in, the Indians fired a volley. Talbot's orderly, Sgt. Louis P. Orleans, moved too near the bank and was hit with an arrow in the arm and a bullet in the side. He staggered and fell. Talbot spurred his horse toward Orleans to assist him, and as he did so, thought he recognized one of the warriors firing from only 75 feet away. "At the command to fight on foot I was shot," he said, "with a ball about fifty to the pound, from the rifle of a chief known by the name of One Eye." The projectile went through his groin on the right side. He dragged his right leg over his horse and tried to ease off, but fell to the ground. If the Indian was One Eye, he assuredly felt both anger and satisfaction when his ball plunked into a blue-clad officer.

With Talbot and Orleans down in front of the command, some warriors rushed forward but were met by soldiers determined not to let the wounded men be captured alive. "Indians," said Talbot, "twenty-five or thirty in number, (bucks) made [a] charge, [and] were repulsed, some of my men clubbing their guns on account of [the] guns refusing to discharge, and forced [the] Indians to seek shelter under the banks, and in holes dug out for concealment."

Theodore Chubbuck saw his captain go down along with two or three other volunteers who tried to go to his assistance. After the wild melee, a five-minute lull in the fighting allowed Chubbuck and another soldier to rush forward. While his companion placed a blanket under Talbot's right leg to ease his pain, the captain asked Chubbuck to fetch the doctor, who was thought to be riding with Capt. John McCannon's Company I. Chubbuck hunched over and hurried back to his horse. Talbot spotted an Indian he recognized as Big Head stand up and wave a buffalo robe as if to draw their fire. When scattered shots rang out, the prone and wounded captain cautioned his men "to be guarded, hold their fire, and be very particular what they fired at, and to be sure it was an Indian." While Talbot was being carried away, "The Indians," he recalled, "en masse, at least thirty in number, made a charge, which was repulsed by eight of Company M" and two men of the First Colorado. The Indians, Talbot added, "acted with desperation and bravery." He estimated that 30

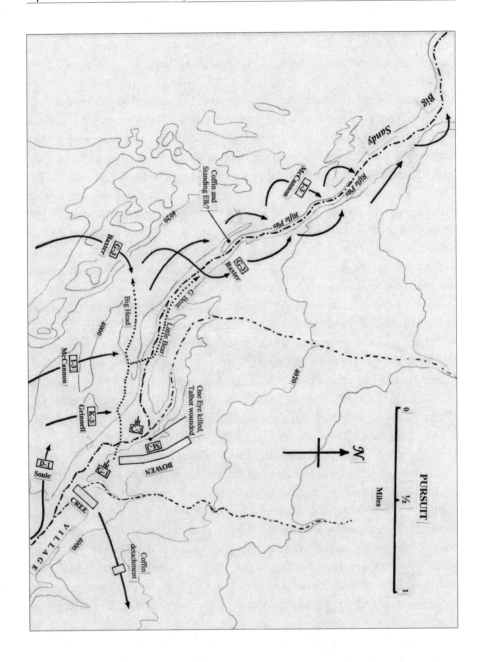

Indians were killed within 75 feet of where his company fought. Big Head got away to head west across the prairie, only to run into McCannon and Baxter.

Colonel Shoup reported the same action. "Here a terrible hand-to-hand encounter ensued between the Indians and Captain Talbot's men and others who had rushed forward to their aid, the Indians trying to secure the scalp of Captain Talbot," testified Shoup. "I think the hardest fighting of the day occurred at this point, some of our men fighting with clubbed muskets, the First and Third Colorado Regiments fighting side by side, each trying to excel in bravery and each ambitious to kill at least one Indian."

Privates Shaw and Patterson remembered the Indians being scattered over hundreds of acres, but there in the sand pits "was the principal scene of the fight. Some fought from ambush, some stood in the open and exchanged shot for shot; some struggled in hand-to-hand fights, using knives for weapons; squaws would take their bow and arrows and at every opportunity would down a soldier. No discipline was used; the soldiers had to fight in the savage fashion."

Lieutenant Cramer, who was opposed to the fighting and often expressed it as a massacre, said the "warriors, about one hundred in number, fought desperately." Billy Breakenridge believed that the Indians "were much better armed than the soldiers and they put up a desperate fight. . . . Although they put up a stubborn resistance and contested every inch of the ground, they were slowly driven back from one position to another for about four miles."[5]

When the Coloradans broke through this defensive position, a slight lull ensued, as if both sides stopped to catch their breath. Scout Duncan Kerr, ever ready to wield his Bowie knife, advanced to the creek bed and searched around for more trophies. There, he found the body of One Eye. "Some of the boys had scalped him," Kerr recalled, "but they either did not understand how to take a scalp, or their knives were very dull, for they had commenced to take the scalp off at the top of the head, and torn a strip down the middle of the neck." Kerr continued beyond the creek and a short distance away found One Eye's wife sitting alone in a buffalo wallow. He recognized her; for she had been with One Eye and Minimic when they carried the message from the chiefs to Fort

5 "Chivington Massacre," 68, 73; "Sand Creek Massacre," 70, 207-08; Howbert, *Indians of Pike's Peak*, 103; "Massacre of Cheyenne Indians," 6, 17; *Sand Creek Project*, 234; Williams, *Through the News*, 274; Cree to Shoup, December 6, 1864, Sayr to Shoup, December 6, 1864, Shoup to Chivington, December 7, 1864, OR 41, pt. 1, 956-59; Chubbuck, "Dictation. Sand Creek," 2; Shaw, *Pioneers of Colorado*, 82; Breakenridge, *Helldorado*, 49-50.

Lyon. He described her as "a lively, sprightly, mischievous, little thing, that fairly worshipped her Chief One Eye." He walked up and put his hand on her head.

"How de do Dunk," she said, "me heap dry. Give me some water."

They spoke in Cheyenne, and Kerr asked if she were seriously hurt. She pulled back her blanket and showed him "a ghastly wound in her side, through which the entrails were protruding. The wound must have been caused by the fragment of a shell," concluded Kerr. "I gave her a drink of water, and left my canteen. As I turned to leave, she took my hand to detain me, and begged me to shoot her with my gun." Kerr couldn't do it, he said, "for I had known her a long time." He walked away while she covered up her head and began singing her death song. The scout met another soldier nearby and pointed her out to him. He told the man that he had just wounded an Indian but had fired his last shot and could not finish the job. Kerr asked him to "creep up behind the Indian and shoot him in the back of the head." The crash of the gunshot echoed in the crisp air as Kerr strode away.[6]

When Private Chubbuck left the wounded Captain Talbot, he rode off "between two fires," dodging bullets from Indians and soldiers. He failed to find the doctor. When he was returning across the dry creek bed, an Indian rose and shot his horse from under him. Chubbuck tumbled to the ground and sought shelter. He fished for his cartridges, but found to his horror that his pouch was empty. He had been so excited, he "could not tell when he had shot his eighty rounds of ammunition." He extricated himself from that tight spot and made his way downstream to the camp. Somehow the sun had already traversed the sky and it was getting dark when he stumbled in, so overwrought that he "could not remember what he did afterwards."

The battle upriver unfolded in a staccato series of starts and stalls. Lieutenant James D. Cannon, accompanying Major Anthony as adjutant, rode along the north side of the creek and described the haphazard nature of the battle. One company would ride up to the bluffs above the creek, dismount, fire, and dodge along the banks until the Indians got out of its reach. "Then the dismounted cavalry would be ordered to mount and renew their charge. In the

---

6 Roberts, "Sand Creek," 430.

meantime another company would often pass them and get in ahead and dismount to commence their fire the same as before."[7]

Little direction was given the men, and the battalion commanders appeared less involved in the decision-making than the company commanders. All of this would have implications for what happened at Sand Creek.

---

7 Chubbuck, "Dictation. Sand Creek," 2; "Sand Creek Massacre," 110–11.

Chapter 9

A Massacre

Major Hal Sayr's Battalion scattered during the opening stages of the fighting at Sand Creek. At the beginning of the action, Colonel Shoup sent John McCannon's Company I, Third Colorado, to the southwest to cut off another herd of horses. Company I, wrote Shoup, "captured about 200 ponies at the first dash." McCannon's pony gathering was interrupted, however, when a large number of fleeing warriors ran right into him in a sandy valley west of the creek. McCannon "sent the ponies to the rear and opened a terrible and withering fire on the Indians, completely checking them, killing many, and causing them to retreat up Sand Creek."

This group of Indians is the same one that vacated the village before the soldiers entered it from the east. This retreating throng included George Bent, Little Bear, Big Head, and Crow Neck. The Indians hurried beyond the west end of the camp for about 100 yards to where the creek made a bend from the north to the southeast. The warriors joined up with a larger group of Indians and fought Captain Talbot to a standstill before continuing their retreat. When they crossed the creek, they figured they were out of harm's way, only to run into McCannon and Lt. William E. Grinnell's Company K of the Third Colorado.

"We hardly knew what way to turn," Little Bear later explained, fortunate to have survived the action, "but Big Head and the rest soon decided to go on. They ran on toward the west, but passing over a hill," continued Little Bear, "they ran into another body of troops just beyond and were surrounded and all killed."[1]

Big Head's party moved across the prairie about a mile, trying desperately to reach an area of sand hills and make a stand there. Unfortunately, it had the misfortune to collide with Capt. Oliver Baxter's Company G, Third Colorado. Baxter had been rounding up horses west of the creek and rode to reinforce McCannon. Panicking, the Indians turned about and ran back east to the creek bed. Another company of cavalry came upon them from the east bank and opened fire.

Little Bear chose not to follow Big Head's group out onto the prairie. Instead, he left them and ran off on his own up the creek in the direction most of the villagers had taken. He did not get far before about 20 cavalrymen got in the streambed behind him and chased him for about two miles.

"Nearly all the feathers were shot out of my war bonnet, and some balls passed through my shield." reported Little Bear, "but I was not touched. I passed many women and children, dead and dying, lying in the creek bed." He ran until he found "the place where a large party of the people had taken refuge in holes dug in the sand up against the sides of the high banks." The soldiers fired at them from both banks, "but not many of us were killed. All who failed to reach these pits in the sand were shot down."

George Bent was in the same predicament. Shunning the dash out to the prairie, Bent later explained what happened: "We ran up the creek with the cavalry following us, one company on each bank, keeping right after us and firing all the time."

The dry streambed was a terrible sight with men, women, and children lying scattered in the sand. The carnage in front of Little Bear and Bent is evidence that they had spent considerable time west of the stream before returning to it, for fleeing Indians and pursuing soldiers had already swept beyond them. Bent ran north about two miles until he came to a place where the banks were high and steep. "Here a large body of Indians had stopped under the shelter of the banks," related Bent, "and the older men and the women had dug holes or pits under the banks, in which the people were now hiding." Just as he reached that point, Bent said, "I was struck in the hip by a bullet and knocked down; but I

1   Coffin, *Sand Creek*, 34.

managed to tumble into one of the holes and lay there among the warriors, women, and children."[2]

A young baby boy named Three Fingers and his mother were in one of the pits. Strapped in a cradle board on her back, she held her youngster's hand and ran for the creek. Bullets whizzed by and she one slammed into her shoulder. Somehow she kept running. They made it below the bank, where it was safer for her to pull her baby off her back. To her sadness, he was dead—shot through the body, which had stopped the bullet that would have gone into her back.

As soldiers chased the Indians up the creek, individual acts of bravery, cowardice, and savagery took place. Duncan Kerr saw one soldier dismount from his horse to better his aim, but when he fired, his horse ran off and left him. A woman sprang up from hiding not far in front of the soldier and caught his horse, apparently thinking that if she caught it and held it for him, he would spare her. As the soldier approached the nameless woman, she held out the reins to him. He took them, but pulled the trigger on his carbine anyway. Nothing happened because he had forgotten to reload his weapon. The woman fell to his feet in supplication, but the heartless soldier, recalled an eyewitness, "coolly reloaded his gun and blew her brains out."

An old Cheyenne named Yellow Fingernails was shot and fell to the sand badly wounded. A soldier jumped on him and cut away his scalp while the old man feigned death. The soldier got away with the hair, but the old Indian crawled away still alive.

David C. Mansell of Company A, Third Colorado, spied what appeared to be a dead Indian who wore a headdress ornamented with small Mexican coins and "a queue about four feet long platted out of the shaggy mane of buffalo hair, platted into his own hair." Mansell had to have such a prize. He dismounted and straddled the fallen brave, but when Mansell touched the knife to the Indian's scalp, he sprang up and tried to run. Mansell grabbed the warrior's hair and as they dashed about, yelled "Boys, shoot! Shoot! Shoot!" The action frightened the horses into a near-stampede, and the nearby soldiers could not get a shot off. "I held on to the queue until it pulled loose from his head," recalled Mansell. "He saved his scalp, and I saved the ornaments. . . . I fired two or three shots while he was running but they had no effects."[3]

---

2 Hyde, *George Bent*, 152-54; Shoup to Chivington, December 7, 1864, *OR* 41, pt. 1, 956-58.

3 Margot Liberty and John Stands in Timber, *Cheyenne Memories* (Lincoln, NE, 1972), 169; Roberts, "Sand Creek," 430, 435; *Sand Creek Massacre Project*, 190.

Capt. Silas S. Soule,
Company D, First Colorado,
contended that he would not
shoot at the Indians.

*The Denver Public Library,
Western History Collection*

One troop not heavily engaged was Captain Soule's Company D. Soule was ordered to open fire when within about 100 yards of the lodges, and his men commenced desultory shooting after Smith, Louderback, and Clarke had been rescued. When the battery opened fire behind him, Major Anthony ordered Lieutenant Cramer to take his company to the left to the edge of Sand Creek, and Soule to take his company down into the creek bed and then move upstream "for the purpose of killing Indians which were under the banks." Soule complied and went into action, firing and advancing. Before he could go far, however, troops moved along both sides of the banks and were spitting out a crossfire above him. This unnerved the captain. "It was unsafe for me to take my command up the creek," explained Soule. "I crossed over to the other side and moved up the creek."[4]

At some point before he crossed the Sand Creek, Soule, in the words of one of his men, Jesse S. Haire, asked his soldiers, "Boys, do you know who you are fighting today?"

"No," an unidentified man replied.

"Well," Soule supposedly shot back, "We are fighting Left Hand and his band."

Someone identified as simply "Mr. Lynch" answered, "Well, we won't fire a shot today." The others shouted much the same thing.

---

4 "Sand Creek Massacre," 11, 13, 21, 22, 48.

It was then that Soule decided, "I don't ask you to shoot, but follow me and we will mix in this fuss and go through it. So, come on boys." The soldiers galloped through the cross fire of "both sides to [the] north end."[5]

Soule moved his men out of the line of fire and in doing so, became separated from Anthony's battalion. From that point on, he was effectively out of the fight. Watching the battle unfold, Soule slowly moved two miles upstream, maintaining a safe distance below the south bank. It has been argued Soule stayed out of the fight because of moral principles, but he had been fighting, if only desultorily. He followed Anthony's orders to fire, and he continued to do so until too many bullets from hostile and friendly sources forced him to hightail it out of the creek bed. He pulled out of harm's way and never returned until the battle was nearly over.

While Soule cut out, Major Anthony had Lieutenant Cramer moved to the north bank of the creek to await further orders. Half an hour later, Andrew Gill arrived with orders to burn the village. Cramer's men did little fighting, perhaps from a moral stance or perhaps from a lack of opportunity. Had Cramer been face-to-face with Indians firing at him, he would have had no choice but to fight harder. As it was, he only fired intermittently and then quit altogether when orders sent him back to the village. The circumstances of the one-sided fight gave Soule and Cramer excuses for their non-belligerence. Their sudden scruples against killing Indians may have been legitimate—which was good for humanity's sake, but not so good considering they were under military orders to fight—or, other factors may have influenced the testimony about what they did that day.

Riding near Chivington, Breakenridge saw the Indians dispersing. He believed the women and children must have escaped while the men made a "desperate fight, as I saw very few squaws and no children." After Chivington sent Gill back with orders for Cramer to burn the village, Chivington had a slightly different idea. He turned to Breakenridge and ordered him to catch up with Gill "to tell them to save some of the largest tepees for hospital use for our wounded." As Breakenridge rode downstream, the battle moved upstream. Along the creek he saw "a good many dead Indians, all of them scalped." The stretch above the camp was comparatively quiet, but still dangerous. "About a

---

5   Pam Milavec, "Jesse S. Haire: Unwilling Indian Fighter," *Prologue* (Summer 2011), vol. 43, No. 2, accessed March 30, 2014, www.archives.gov/publications/prologue/2011/summer/hair.html and www.archives.gov/publications/prologue/2011/summer/haire.html.

mile from the village," Breakenridge recalled, "an Indian arose from behind a tuft of bunch grass, when I was about thirty feet from him and shot at me with an arrow; he missed me but slightly wounded my horse on the rump. I had my Sharps carbine across my lap, and before the Indian could dodge I fired and hit him. I was so close I knew I killed him, and I did not stop, but kept on to camp."

After Breakenridge delivered the message, the first assistant surgeon, Dr. Caleb S. Burdsal, picked out the tipis he wanted and ordered them cleaned out. The camp included many buffalo robes and plenty of dried buffalo meat, flour, bacon, and other foodstuffs and supplies. Breakenridge entered some of the tipis and noticed wearing apparel that he believed was taken from looted ranches and wagon trains. Much of the contraband was confiscated.[6]

While Dr. Burdsal set up a hospital and the ambulance began bringing in the wounded, the main command moved northwest up the creek right behind the Indians. Some of Anthony's battalion and a portion of the Third Colorado, including Company I and the color-bearer with the flag, moved up the south bank. There was little order to the pursuit, with companies and groups of men and even individuals engaged piecemeal, fighting their own actions as they followed close on the Indians' heels.

In several locations above the village and the banks of the creek, the Indians defended themselves and enhanced their positions by digging hasty entrenchments in the sand, which, said Coffin, "gave them a strong position." Artillery fire "was the only way they could be reached except to our disadvantage," he added. "It was along the banks of the creek, but more especially the west bank, that most of the fighting took place, and where several of our men were killed."

One of the unlucky soldiers, Henry C. Foster of Company D, Third Colorado, did not make it as far as the west bank. Foster had been on the sick list for some time, but did not feel that he could let his comrades down by missing the fight. Two days prior, he rejoined his company. He got as far as the edge of the east bank of Sand Creek when he was shot in the neck and chest. He died almost instantly.

As the fighting intensified, Irving Howbert's nervousness dissipated. "After the first few shots I had no fear whatever," he said, "nor did I see any others displaying the least concern as to their own safety." His Company G moved up the south bank, while the fight "became general all up and down the

6 Breakenridge, *Helldorado*, 50, 53; "Sand Creek Massacre," 203.

valley." The Indians put up "a constant fusillade" from the banks of the creek while the soldiers shot at every Indian who appeared. "I think it was in this way that a good many of the squaws were killed," Howbert said. "It was utterly impossible, at a distance of two hundred yards, to discern between the sexes on account of their similarity of dress."[7]

Captain Cree's battalion fought dismounted for about one hour. The men, he boasted, "behaved like veterans." During the maneuvering, however, Company F became separated and moved off with Lieutenant Colonel Bowen's battalion. Cree took the remaining companies of D and E eastward away from the bluffs by the creek "for the purpose of killing Indians that were making their escape to the right of the command."

Sergeant Coffin noticed Indians and about 20 ponies in that direction and appealed to Capt. David H. Nichols of his Company D and to Captain Cree to be allowed to take some men and go after them. Cree agreed, and Coffin and 15 men rode out with instructions to remain together. The advice was soon forgotten, however, as the men on faster horses pulled ahead. Coffin was mounted on a slow horse and, "not wishing to run him to death, was soon left alone in the rear."

The lead soldiers caught up with a couple of Indians and promptly shot them down. When Coffin rode up, James Cox was already scalping one. Farther on, Coffin spotted two Indian women lying in the dirt, one face down and writhing in agony. Coffin went up to her and saw that "in her efforts to breathe the blood was expelled from a wound which must have been through the lungs. After thinking it over a minute or so," he said, "and believing it an act of mercy, I drew my revolver and shot [her] through the head."

Coffin thought the other woman was already dead, but when Cox arrived, she sat up to look around and he shot her. While this was taking place, an Indian sped by on foot and the Coloradans sprinted after him, firing several shots to no effect. In an effort to run faster, the Indian snatched off his ill-fitting moccasins as he ran. Coffin mounted and tried to cut him off. The chase was about six miles from the village. When the Indian saw Coffin riding in on his flank, "[he] seemed to realize his situation though not a word or sign escaped him; but in the most deliberate manner possible he faced about and laid down, but with his head raised and eyeing us. I dismounted and fired at him and his head fell,"

---

7   Coffin, *Sand Creek*, 21, 26; "Sand Creek Massacre," 23, 63-64, 67; Howbert, *Indians of Pike's Peak*, 103-04.

explained Coffin. "[The] boys took several shots to be certain he should not play us." When they walked closer, they found a rifle bullet had gone through his left eye, which, Coffin noted, "was presumed to be mine." Hank Farrar took hold of his hair, asked for Coffin's pocketknife, and cut off his scalp lock. "He was brave," Coffin concluded, "but we showed him no mercy."[8]

The other half of Coffin's small command, consisting of Cpl. Steve Phillips, Robert McFarland, Hi Lockhart, William Elliott, Franklin Montgomery, and David Ripley, an aged veteran of the War of 1812, had veered off east of the village after some horses. They rode farther out than Coffin's party and finally succeeded in catching the herd. Hi Lockhart, who had been earlier thrown from his horse, was on foot again when his mount played out. When they captured the animals, Lockhart found a mule complete with saddle and riding gear. Mounted once more, he and his fellow soldiers drove the animals back toward the village.

On the prairie about four miles east of the village, Phillips and McFarland discovered a buffalo robe lying in the grass. Phillips thought there might be an Indian hiding under it, and McFarland rode up and dismounted. Suddenly, a warrior threw back the robe and jumped up with a yell. When both soldiers fired and missed, McFarland dodged behind his horse. The Indian shot two arrows into the animal's side, which bucked wildly in pain. The adversaries rushed together, and McFarland, using his carbine as a club, dealt the warrior a blow that splintered the gunstock. Somehow the warrior mananged to fire another arrow that stuck in McFarland's exposed side.

Lockhart, meanwhile, rode up on his recalcitrant mule and found the men wrestling in the grass. To Lockhart, who was still about 75 yards away, it looked like the warrior took an arrow in his hand and, using it as a dagger, plunged it into McFarland's heart.

"Oh God, boys I'm killed!" McFarland exclaimed as he fell to the ground.

Phillips, who was nearby, jumped on the Indian. It was all he could do to hold one arm, while the man struck at him with his free hand, using the arrow like a knife as he had with McFarland. Phillips took several wounds to the head and neck before Elliott and Ripley arrived and dispatched the warrior with their pistols. The considerably shaken Corporal Phillips ordered the soldiers to mount and get out of there, lest they encounter more warriors. None of them

8 Cree to Shoup, December 6, 1864, *OR* 41, pt. 1, 958; Coffin, *Sand Creek*, 21-22.

thought to remove McFarland's body or gather his carbine, pistol, and other valuables.

As Phillips and Coffin returned to the village on their own tangents, Coffin came across an ambulance containing the badly wounded Cpl. Andrew J. Maxwell of Company D, who had taken a bullet in the chest as the company attacked along Sand Creek. Although grievously wounded, Maxwell's iron constitution helped him pull through, but the wound would cause him problems for the rest of his life. While Coffin comforted Maxwell, Phillips and his party galloped in from the northeast.

"Mac is dead," Phillips exclaimed to Coffin as they drew together, showing the sergeant his own chopped and torn hat and shirt. When Coffin asked Phillips if he was sure McFarland had been killed, and received repeated assurances there was nothing that could be done for him and it was more important to care for the wounded, the men fell in with the ambulance. "This news made many of us feel sad and half sick," admitted Coffin.

Just then, a soldier rode up and told them to turn the ambulance back upstream toward the creek. There were more Coloradans being killed and wounded. The fight was proving to be no easy affair.[9]

Coffin, Phillips, and the remnant of the party rode with the ambulance holding the suffering Corporal Maxwell back to the battle that was inexorably moving away from them to the northwest. The soldier who had ridden up to the ambulance gave Sergeant Coffin directions to where another wounded man was located. As Coffin rode out, the soldier warned him to be careful because Indians were still hiding in the tall grass.

Coffin approached Sand Creek northwest of the village where the creek made a big bend. On the west bank was a ridge slopping down to the creek, and in front of it was a tangle of bushes and small cottonwoods. From the directions he was given, Coffin expected to find the wounded man on the ridge. As he crossed the dry creek bed, he saw another soldier apparently headed for the same ridge. Part way across the creek Coffin spotted a puff of smoke rise above the brush, heard the crack of a rifle a second later, caught a glimpse of an Indian, and watched as the nameless soldier fell to the sand. The man rose and scrambled back to cover. The Indian was out of sight before Coffin could take aim and fire.

9   Coffin, *Sand Creek*, 22-23, 26-27.

The Indian was probably Cheyenne warrior Standing Elk, who had become separated from the other Indians while fleeing the village. Dodging the soldiers, he ran west to where the creek turned from north to southeast but stopped to fight on the bluffs west of the creek when he found a good defensive spot on a little hill. He dug in there, but when he saw that most of the soldiers had bypassed him, he moved down closer to the creek where he might pick off a lone soldier. His weapon was poor, however, and he had only a few rounds of ammunition. Even so, he wounded a "ve'ho'e" (whiteman) in the creek bed before crawling back to the ridge. He would have to rely on his bow, which was no match for a Spencer.

Coffin beat back and forth along the creek, trying to find a spot where he could draw a bead on the warrior. He did his best to stay at least 100 yards away, sometimes shooting from behind his horse, sometimes lying flat behind a sand drift. Coffin played this game for about an hour, "but a fair shot I could not get. He was cautious."

Finally, another man from the Third Colorado armed with a Garibaldi musket "with an awful bore" joined him. The weapon made a tremendous noise when fired. Although Standing Elk had no weapon but a bow and arrows, other Indians were also nearby, for an occasional shot whizzed by the soldiers. Coffin was sure his horse would be hit, for it spend the time calmly munching grass.

After a few hours of hide and seek, Coffin concluded they were being fooled and shooting at a rag or other object displayed only to draw their fire. Still, they had plenty of ammunition and doggedly hung on. Standing Elk finally decided to abandon his hiding place and crept over the top of the ridge. Coffin eventually discovered him a few rods beyond the spot they had been targeting, crawling away on his hands and knees through the weeds. The distance was considerable, explained Coffin, but "Three to five shots were sent after him before he disappeared, and we were very sure he was hit."[10]

Coffin's partner decided to leave, so Coffin covered him as he hurried along the creek bed and over the bank. When he caught sight of some men about one mile up the creek, Coffin presumed they might be from his company and headed northwest toward them. All along the route, there were isolated groups of Indians, some of whom would jump up to take a pot shot at him. He fired several more times while riding until his Smith and Wesson rifle became so

---

10 Coffin, *Sand Creek*, 23-24; *Sand Creek Massacre Project*, 206-07. Coffin returned the next day and located the dead warrior, who proved to be Standing Elk. His body was never recovered.

fouled that an empty cartridge stuck fast in it. Coffin switched to his revolver, but after a few shots a piece of gun cap got stuck in the lock, and he could not cock the gun or remove the obstruction. While trying to free the mechanism, Coffin spied an Indian rise up in full view from his hiding place. "I thought him bold," he recalled, "as he could not know my arms were out of fix." Coffin turned to see another Indian sitting calmly on a pony watching him. Another glance off to the side found yet another Indian riding in at full speed. It was then he realized he had not seen a group of soldiers, but Indians. Coffin spun around, bent low in his saddle, and headed his horse in a zigzag course through the sandy creek bed. A couple of bullets whizzed by his head, but he never looked back.

Farther downstream, Coffin wheeled right and went up the west bank, where he happily found fellow soldier Melanthon Williams. His comrade had tied his horse on the east bank, crossed over to help a wounded man, and had stayed by his side for about three hours before the ambulance arrived. Once the man was safely in the wagon together with the other man Standing Elk had wounded, Williams went in search of his horse. Groups of Indians were still shooting from isolated pockets along the creek however, and Williams could not get across. Eventually he abandoned the hope of getting his horse back, and he was walking downstream when Coffin rode up. The two soldiers joined up. It was late afternoon, and the Colorado cavalry was nowhere to be seen.[11]

The main fighting along the creek had been heavy. After Private Louderback got to comparative safety out of the tipis, he hooked up with his Company G and helped Lieutenant Baldwin work the battery. The mountain howitzers were not immune to Indian fire. Baldwin narrowly escaped injury when a bullet slammed into his horse, Poker. By then, Louderback had had enough fighting. He decided to head back to the village "to get my boots and overcoat." John Smith, after witnessing what he believed to be the main action, also returned with the first body of soldiers who went back to the camp. There, he met Colonel Chivington, who questioned him about his son Jack, about who the Indians were, about which chiefs were there, and whether he could recognize them. Smith replied that he could, so Chivington directed him to survey the field after the battle.[12]

---

11 Coffin, *Sand Creek*, 24-25.

12 "Sand Creek Massacre," 135; "Massacre of Cheyenne Indians," 8-9.

While Coffin and Williams fought in isolated actions, larger groups were still doing battle along the creek. As Company A, Third Colorado, moved upstream, Joseph H. Connor got into a duel with a young warrior, exchanging shot for shot. After a few rounds, one of Connor's bullets hit home and the Indian fell. Connor stood out in the open, where he failed to heed the warnings of his comrades. The men hiding in the grass behind him saw a woman rise up out of the tall weeds where the warrior had fallen. They raised their rifles, but before they could fire, she fired an arrow that pierced Connor's right lung. As Connor went down, several shots rang out and the woman spun and fell dead.

The seriousness of Connor's wound meant it would be very dangerous to move him. Nearby, a bullet slammed into the left leg of Pvt. Ed Frank Parks, also of Company A, Third Colorado. Connor and Parks waited together for the ambulance, but it did not come. Alston Shaw had seen both men go down and he tried to make them as comfortable as possible. Hours later, the sun was dropping low and most of the soldiers had returned to the village. Shaw was worried because there was not an ambulance in sight, but he refused to leave the wounded men. He finally saw another man of his company, David G. Cobb, and talked him into standing guard over them. Shaw was not gone long before he found the ambulance on its way to pick up McFarland's body and turned it back to the creek, where he and Cobb helped the two injured men board. On their way back to camp, they watched as four Indians jumped up from the opposite bank and ran off onto the prairie.[13]

Captain Baxter's Company G fought along the south and west bank throughout the morning, slowly moving upstream. By noon the Indians were fully under cover in sand pits and along the banks where they could fire with little exposure to themselves. Company G joined another unit that was carrying on a brisk fight with a group of Indians shooting from behind a pile of driftwood along the creek banks, while another group fired from a similar driftwood pile in the middle of the dry bed. Baxter's men crept up in a depression on the edge of the north bank and tried to shoot over the bank and down into the driftwood. Howbert arrived just in time to see a man from the other company step out "a little too far." When he turned around to speak, he "was shot in the back, the bullet going straight through his lungs and chest."

Howbert thought it was a fatal wound. The man asked to be taken back to his company, and Howbert volunteered. He helped him on his horse, and they

13 Shaw, *Pioneers of Colorado*, 89, 93-94.

Sand Creek about two miles upstream of the village. This is the location of some of the rifle pits used by the Indians for defense. *Author*

started across the prairie. "With every breath, bubbles of blood were coming from his lungs," recalled Howbert, "and I had little hope that he would reach his comrades alive." Just when they met some of his mates, he fainted, but was caught by his captain as he fell from Howbert's horse. Howbert returned to his own unit.

It was dangerous for Indian or soldier to show himself for long, but when one spot got too hot, somebody had to make a run for it. Howbert saw one small group of warriors jump up from a sand pit. "They ran in a zigzag manner, jumping from one side to the other, evidently hoping by so doing that we would be unable to hit them—but, by taking deliberate aim, we dropped every one before they reached the other bank."[14]

After being wounded in the hip, George Bent remained in one sand pit for a time. Many of the Indians with him were wounded. Even though the sun was bright, the day was bitterly cold to those trapped in holes and barely able to move. The troops surrounded them and kept up a nearly constant fire, but Bent was contemptuous of their fortitude. "If they had been real soldiers they would

14 Howbert, *Indians of Pike's Peak*, 104-06.

have come in and finished it," he said, "but they were nothing but a mob, and anxious as they were to kill they did not dare to come in close."

Little Bear remained in the pits throughout the day, but he was actively firing back at the soldiers whenever he had an opportunity. The soldiers took positions on both sides of the creek and fired down into it, but few bullets struck home for the sand and deep pits gave them good protection. Many soldiers commented about the rifle pits. Most likely these were natural depressions in the sandy banks that the Indians scooped to greater depths during the fight, but some insisted they had been dug before the battle. According to Private Slater, "the camp was surrounded by rifle pits and the fact of the snow lying in the bottom of these pits was evidence that they had been dug some time previously, as snow had not fallen for some ten days before."[15]

According to Morning Star, a Cheyenne, most of the Indian deaths were caused by cannon fire, especially those firing from the south bank at Indians fleeing up the creek. The entrenched Indians, however, were given respite when the howitzers ran out of ammunition. Just after Morgan's battery ceased firing, a moment of silence gave Sgt. Stephen D. Decatur, Company C, Third Colorado, an opportunity to strike up a conversation with a companion sheltering along the creek bed. The soldier told him that in a hole up ahead was an Indian who could speak English. Decatur started to go forward, but the soldier warned him not to go closer or the Indian would shoot him. Decatur hesitated, and a voice called out from under the bank, "Come on, you God damn white sons of bitches, and kill me if you are a brave man." It is quite possible that the man calling to Decatur was George Bent.

Private John Patterson described one Indian as a "medicine man" because he placed what looked to be "bags of medicine" around the pit from which he fought. The Indian would pop up, shoot an arrow, and duck before anyone could get a shot at him. Lieutenant John F. Wymond, Company C, Third Colorado, sat on his horse in direct range of the Indian in the sand pit. When Private Patterson saw the Indian rise up to shoot an arrow, Patterson shouted a warning to the lieutenant. Wymond turned his mount and the arrow buried itself into the horse's leg. The animal jumped in pain before acting as if it was paralyzed. Patterson surmised he arrow had been poisoned, and the horse

---

15 Hyde, *George Bent*, 155-56; Slater, "Indian Troubles," 4. Some soldiers insisted the rifle pits were already there, while most historians reject that notion as nonsense. Yet, Cheyenne oral history occasionally supports the soldiers. Blanche White Shield, for one, claimed the Indians "already made like fox holes in case the soldiers really came." *Sand Creek Massacre Project*, 193.

killed. The next day, the private found the "medicine man" dead in his hole with several bullet wounds.

Later in the afternoon, the Cheyenne Red Owl called out the names of five men to join him, asking them to move to some pits farther upstream to defend about 30 people trapped there. Little Bear, Spotted Horse, Big Bear, Bear Shield, and George Bent (who was apparently not too badly wounded) joined him and they made their way up the creek. They reached the upper pit and prepared a defense, but more soldiers were moving up from the south.[16]

As Morse Coffin and Melanthon Williams hid by the creek, both wondered how they would get out alive since Coffin's weapons were useless and Williams only had an old dragoon revolver. When Coffin spotted soldiers of Company I, Third Colorado, carrying the regimental flag about a mile to the south, they moved toward them. McCannon, however, was still on the offensive, and the two men had to join in and continue the hunt for Indians. As McCannon moved up the creek, he was "much of the time sustaining a heavy fire" from a group of well-armed Indians, reported Major Sayr, "who were secreted under a high bank on the south side of Sand Creek."

Company I dismounted and surrounded the area, where, said Coffin, "a lively fire was kept up for some time." Still, McCannon could make little headway without taking casualties. He called for artillery support, but there was no more ammunition. In the pits during a slackening in the shooting, Spotted Horse noticed soldiers circling around to vantage points from where they would be able to get the Indians in a crossfire. Even so, the Indians' fire had been good, for he saw a few of the soldiers fall. At the last moment, Spotted Horse called to the warriors to move out. Several of them, including Bent and Little Bear, abandoned the position, left the women and children behind, and fell back to the lower pits. It was well for the warriors that they did so for the soldiers eventually closed in and killed those who had remained behind. When the last warriors were killed, the women sent out a little girl of about six years old with a white rag on a stick. She advanced only a few yards before the volunteers shot her down. McCannon's men moved in for the finish. In his report, Colonel Shoup wrote, "His brave company killed 26 Indians in one pit."

Coffin figured it was about four in the afternoon when Company I headed back to the village. They came out of the fight at the upper pits with one dead

16 *Sand Creek Massacre Project*, 207; "Sand Creek Massacre," 195; Shaw, *Pioneers of Colorado*, 93; Powell, *Sacred Mountain* I, 305-06.

man tied across his horse. McCannon did not follow along the creek bed, which Coffin was thankful for, for there were still Indians in pits between them and the camp. They swung wide to the southwest, then back east to the village.

When Baxter's Company G received orders to return to the village, hidden Indians took pot shots at the men. Irving Howbert saw one child, perhaps four years old, run out of a pit toward the soldiers, crying, with arms extended as if he wanted to be picked up. "At first I was inclined to do so," admitted Howbert, "but changed my mind when it occurred to me that I should have no means of taking care of the little fellow." He knew that the Indians, within a few hundred yards of them, would come to get the boy as soon as the soldiers cleared out. "No one dreamed of harming him," Howbert said. Unfortunately, many of the other volunteers were not so kind-hearted.[17]

Lieutenant Luther Wilson recalled that "the ears were cut off the body of White Antelope." Wilson didn't see it, but he heard that White Antelope's "privates" were cut off "to make a tobacco bag out of." He also heard men say that "the privates of one of the squaws had been cut out and put on a stick."[18] There were a number of similar atrocious actions.

Soldiers had been straggling back to the village since noon, but the fighting didn't die out until three in the afternoon when ammunition ran low. As the attack slowed and dispersed, Indians individually and in small groups began to extricate themselves from the creek bed and head for safety. Some were seen, but Colonel Shoup declined to pursue them. "The fact was," Morse Coffin explained, "men and horses were very tired and hungry, and the boys were glad for an opportunity to rest and look around camp."[19]

One unit safe in camp for the past three hours was Soule's Company D. After cutting out of the fight early, Soule and his men stayed far to the west for the rest of the morning. Having moved only about two miles in the intervening time span, Soule found a quiet place to cross and moved to the east bank around noon. Soule did not reestablish communications with a superior officer until about 1:00 p.m., when Major Anthony found him. Soule asked him what he should do with his command. Although Anthony might have had a caustic

17 Michno, *Battle at Sand Creek*, 236-38.

18   "Chivington Massacre," 67.

19   Coffin, *Sand Creek*, 26.

comment in mind, he simply told Soule to go to the village and guard the wounded men and the baggage.[20]

Among the prisoners taken early in the day was Charlie Bent, the youngest son of William Bent. He hid in a lodge for a time with an Indian woman, but was luckily recognized by Charles Autobees, a friend of his father's. Bent and the woman were taken to scout Jim Beckwourth. Charlie had pronounced Indian features, and so was fearful for his life and begged Beckwourth to save him. The scout took him under his wing, and later in the day placed Charlie in the ambulance that carried the wounded Captain Talbot. He told him to stay there. Beckwourth also took the woman and the wounded James A. Metcalf to the hospital area.[21]

An old woman and two children were also found in one of the lodges that evening. Elsewhere, two more girls and a little boy were taken, and John Smith's Indian wife, Zerepta, and his child, four-year-old William Gilpin Smith, were unharmed. Amache, the wife of John Prowers and daughter of One Eye, was saved with her two children, as were an old Arapaho woman and her grandson, both found hiding in a ravine. The wife of Charlie Windsor, the sutler at Fort Lyon, was also brought in. They were fed and cared for while in the camp. A lady named Spanish Woman was stabbed by a soldier, but other soldiers brought her to the hospital tipi in an effort to save her. She had also lost her little girl. They tried to take care of her, but she was obviously dying. When she asked for her child, a soldier told her she had escaped. For that at least, she was happy.[22]

Before 3:00 p.m. Major Anthony was ready to return to Fort Lyon with the prisoners and return to Sand Creek with supplies. Since Captain Soule was only guarding the baggage, he was ordered to accompany Anthony. Concerned with the white men and mixed-bloods who were prisoners in the village, Soule sought out Chivington and asked if he could take Charlie Bent back home to his father. Chivington replied that Charlie's brother, Robert, did not much care

20 "Sand Creek Massacre," 22-23.

21 Silas Soule later claimed that he had "saved little Charley Bent," but this does not appear to be the case. Bent was about 17 years old, and hardly "little," and he was taken by Autobees and Beckwourth. Soule was west of the creek avoiding Indian bullets at the time of Charlie's rescue.

22 "Sand Creek Massacre," 71, 107; Stan Hoig, *The Western Odyssey of John Simpson Smith Frontiersman, Trapper, Trader, and Interpreter* (Glendale, CA, 1974), 116, 156, 158; *Sand Creek Massacre Project*, 193.

about having his wild younger brother sent back home, so Soule had better not. Chivington had a change of heart, perhaps realizing that the move would placate the influential William Bent, and told Soule that he had no objections either way. Soule prepared for the ride back to Fort Lyon, his participation in the battle was over. Perhaps this is what prompted him to later declare that he "saved" Charlie Bent.[23]

Others at Sand Creek were not so lucky.

---

23 Monahan, *Denver City*, 196; "Sand Creek Massacre," 22-23.

Chapter 10

Scalp Dance

When the main action was over, some of the ghoulish deeds that made the "battle" at Sand Creek infamous occurred. Stories circulated among the Indians and soldiers of instances where fingers, ears, hearts, and genitals were mutilated or cut out—from both men and women. White Antelope had been maimed. Jim Beckwourth, no friend of Colonel Chivington, claimed that Indians were scalped, but "White Antelope was the only one I saw that was otherwise mutilated." The Indians argued that the vengeance was worse than was done by the Pawnees, the bittere enemies of the Cheyenne. John Smith claimed to seen Indian bodies "worse mutilated than I ever saw before." They were cut "with knives; scalped; their brains knocked out."[1]

Major Anthony recalled several scalped Indians, but did not see any additional mutilations. Bodies with "their privates cut off and all that kind of thing—I never saw anything of that, and I never heard it until I saw it in those affidavits at Fort Lyon, two months after the fight." Anthony did see a child walking in the sand trying to catch up to those who had abandoned him. "I saw one man get off his horse, at a distance of about seventy-five yards, and draw up

---

1 "Sand Creek Massacre," 70; "Massacre of Cheyenne Indians," 9. Smith's shock at seeing scalped Indians was likely posturing for the benefit of the Congressional Committee. Smith once poisoned five Indians with laudanum, shot two more, than scalped all seven, taking care to get all the trinkets and shells tied in their hair. See Hoig, *Odyssey of John Smith*, 31-33.

his rifle and fire—he missed the child. Another man came up and said, 'Let me try the son of a bitch; I can hit him.' He got down off his horse, kneeled down and fired at the little child, but missed him. A third man came up and made a similar remark, and fired, and the little fellow dropped." Anthony also saw one mortally wounded Indian woman escaping with two children. When she could run no farther, she "gathered her two children near her, and cut both of their throats," testified Anthony. "That was not done by our men."[2]

Lieutenant Cramer verified these incidents. He wrote to Major Wynkoop that "squaws were known to kill their own children, and then themselves, rather than to have them taken prisoner." Captain Soule said much the same thing, although the fact that he hid out for most of the battle makes it likely that he was repeating only what he had heard. According to Soule, one woman "took a knife and cut the throats of both children, and then killed herself. One old squaw hung herself in the lodges." Red Dust Woman told of Arapaho women who were with the soldiers and aided in some of the mutilations, while one took an Arapaho child off one of the wagons two days after the fight and left it by the roadside to die.[3]

Soldiers committed atrocities, but a disposition to commit murder and mayhem was not a characteristic unique to any one people. Robert McFarland was abandoned on the prairie when Coffin's detachment fled without him. When his body was found, a squad under Sgt. William M. Barney returned with it. McFarland's scalp could not be taken because his hair was so short that he was virtually bald, but his chest had been chopped open, and his splintered gun shoved into the open wound. Only one other soldier fell into the hands of the Indians, and he was scalped. The warrior who did it, however, was chased off and dropped the hair. "The fact was," concluded Coffin, "our men were nearly all killed where the enemy could not safely get to them, or where they had no time to spare for it." That night, all the soldier dead that could be found were gathered and laid in a row. Coffin counted nine bodies, Howbert recalled 10, and Chubbuck thought there was a dozen. "The number of our dead and wounded showed that the Indians had offered a vigorous defense," Howbert said, "and . . . if they had been mounted, it is questionable whether the result would have been the same—had they remained to fight." Coffin concluded, "It

2   "Massacre of Cheyenne Indians," 26-27.

3   Roberts and Halaas, "Written in Blood," 26, 27; *Sand Creek Massacre Project*, 209-10.

was a rather hard sight, to those of us who were unused to war and its accompanying horrors."[4]

John Smith reported that 70 to 80 Indians had been killed, including 25 to 30 warriors. Major Wynkoop testified that 60 to 70 Indians were killed. Silas Soule said he counted 69 Indian bodies a month after the fight. Coffin thought maybe 125 Indians fell. Sergeant Stephen Decatur said he counted 450 dead warriors, and Chivington later claimed about 500 Indians had been killed. Numbers ranging from 70 to 500 makes one wonder if these witnesses were at the same battle.

Initial reports indicate that some 10 soldiers had been killed and 38 wounded—numbers that would increase during the fighting the next day. By December 4, as the chase continued, adjutant Samuel Lorah reported 11 killed and 47 wounded. Major Anthony buried more than a dozen. He wrote from Fort Lyon in December 1864: "This makes, now, thirteen men that I have buried here out of that command . . . besides some of whom are yet in danger." Morse Coffin was introspective after seeing the dead soldiers: "I then fully realized that our battle had been dearly won."

The final numbers were higher still. The Third Regiment lost 20 killed or mortally wounded and 31 wounded, and the First Regiment lost four killed and 21 wounded.[5]

The village revealed plenty of evidence that the Indians had been collecting white scalps. About four in the afternoon, Doctor Burdsal was busy in a large tipi doubling as a field hospital. "I was in the lodge dressing the wounded," he recalled, "when some man came to the opening of the lodge and hallooed to me to look at five or six scalps he had in his hand." Burdsal took a minute to inspect the objects. They were Caucasian scalps. Some were very light, almost white, and some were sandy brown. When was asked how fresh he thought they were, the doctore replied, "My impression is that one or two of them were not more

---

4   Howbert, *Indians of Pike's Peak*, 107-8; Coffin, *Sand Creek*, 27, 32, 36.

5   "Chivington Massacre," 42; "Sand Creek Massacre," 195, 198; Wynkoop to J. E. Tappan, January 15, 1865, *OR* 41, pt. 1, 962; Williams, *Through the News*, 272-74, 284-88, 309-310; Scott J. Anthony Papers; Coffin, *Sand Creek*, 32; Colorado State Archives, Civil War Casualty Index. Historians consistently under-count the soldier casualties. The names of the killed and wounded, with types of wounds, if known, are in Appendix B. The full list of soldiers engaged, killed, and wounded appear in Michno, *Battle at Sand Creek*, 291-304.

than ten days off the head. The skin and flesh attached to the hair appeared to be yet quite moist."[6]

On the afternoon of the first day's fighting, the Coloradans spent time rummaging through the abandoned tipis. They remembered Governor Evans's proclamation that they could have all the Indian property they captured, and they were determined to help themselves. Private Howbert discovered flour, sugar, bacon, and coffee, as well as "articles of wearing apparel and other things that had been taken from wagon-trains which the Indians had robbed during the previous summer." But the thing that most angered them and allowed them to rationalize the treatment they had meted out were the scalps. "In these same tents," Howbert testified, "we found a dozen or more scalps of white people, some of them being from the heads of women and children, as was evidenced by the color and fineness of the hair, which could not be mistaken for that of any other race. One of the scalps showed plainly from its condition that it had been taken only recently." Lieutenant Wilson "saw one new scalp, a white man's, and two old ones. Some clothing was found, women's shoes and dresses, and officers' uniforms and other articles."

Sergeant Coffin believed that of all the Indian camps he had seen, this one had the most wealth. Even after much was burned, he saw tons of dried buffalo meat, many packages of coffee, sugar, dried cherries, saddles, bridles, axes, lariats, and robes. It was the general opinion among the soldiers, explained Coffin, "that if Uncle Sam furnished the commissary supplies for that camp, they were rather better looked after than were his own boys." In one lodge they found an old woman who had hanged herself. Coffin recalled a number of white scalps and "also daguerreotypes, children and women's wearing apparel," and similar items.

Private Milo Slater figured the battle was justified retribution. "With the history of the previous six months fresh in their minds," he concluded, "our soldiers were ready to fight. If an additional incentive had been needed, it was presented in the sight of a white woman's scalp, with long, beautiful blonde hair, which hung in one of the lodges. It was not intended that Colonel Black Kettle should cast any further reflections upon the inferiority of the white man's method of fighting Indians."

As Sergeant Decatur was gathering lodge poles for the night's campfires, he saw soldiers break open some bundles. Inside they found white scalps, "part of

6   "Sand Creek Massacre," 203-04.

a lady's toilet and one box of rouge, also a box containing a powder puff." One scalp particularly affected him. "The head had been skinned, taking all the hair; the scalp had been tanned to preserve it; the hair was auburn and hung in ringlets; it was very long hair. There were two holes in the scalp in front, for the purpose of tying it on their [the Indians'] heads when they appeared in the scalp dance." The sight infuriated Decatur, who wanted to go across the battlefield right then to see how many Indians they had killed.[7]

The presence of white scalps in the village elicits an argument similar to the American flag controversy. About six people claimed to have seen an American flag waving in the village. Others vehemently denied it. Likewise, about six people recalled seeing white scalps in the captured village. Many others, however, denied seeing any. The supporters and detractors of these claims were eyewitnesses, contemporaries, and later on, historians. It seems reasonable to accept the statements of those who saw flags and scalps. In fairness, we cannot believe one claim and dismiss the other without exposing our own biases or at least the limitations on our analysis and judgment by the disparate testimony.

Were those who claimed to have seen the American flag and scalps telling the truth? Did they see these things themselves? Did they hear it from others? Were they victims of leading suggestions, false memories, traumatic memory distortion, or were they outright fabricators?

After the day's momentous events, there was a good deal of mental confusion swirling about Chivington's camp that night.

---

7   "Sand Creek Massacre," 195; "Chivington Massacre," 67; Howbert, *Indians of Pike's Peak*, 109-11; Coffin, *Sand Creek*, 31-32; Slater, "Indian Troubles," 5.

Chapter 11

Night of Phantoms

The hospital tipis overflowed with wounded that evening. Assistant surgeon Caleb S. Burdsal and surgeon-in-chief of the volunteers, T. J. Leas, had their hands full as they busily worked by campfire light, taking care of more than 60 injured men, several with mortal wounds.[1]

While the surgeons tirelessly worked, the widely scattered soldiers returned from the battle and were ordered to form in a hollow square. Horses were picketed inside the formation, and on the outside the remaining lodges were set afire and burned brightly against the dark plains. Theodore Chubbuck and his friend Frank Bartholf, both members of Company M, took turns torching a number of tipis. Some soldiers walked to the creek in search of water, but believed the few trickles they found tainted with blood. Some dug holes in the sand to let the water seep through in an effort to filter the bloody liquid so that by morning, they would have what they hoped was clean drinkable water to satiate their thirst.

"I was so utterly exhausted," said Howbert, "for want of sleep and food . . . that I hunted up a buffalo robe, of which there were large numbers scattered around, threw myself down on it, and was asleep almost as soon as I touched the ground." Howbert was jostled awake at dusk to eat supper and once he finished, wanted nothing more than to sleep again. The soldiers were instructed,

---

1 "Sand Creek Massacre," 165.

however, that they must sleep "with our guns in our hands, ready for use at any moment."[2]

Alston Shaw and John Patterson visited the badly wounded Joe Connor in one of the hospital tipis. There was talk that Little Raven would attack them that night. Connor told Shaw that if the Indians attacked and it looked like the soldiers would be overrun, he wanted Shaw to shoot him. It would be a hard thing to do, but Shaw agreed. He did not have to think about it long, however, for that night "between nine and ten," recalled Shaw, "the Angel of Death relieved him of his promise." Connor's passing did not relieve them of other troubles. The men were unable to sleep "on account of the horrible nerve-racking noise that lasted throughout the night." The barking of dogs combined with the yipping of coyotes, they explained, "had the heinous sound of a fiend's chuckle when he is tormenting a victim." The neighing of the horses and the groans of the wounded all served to numb the soldiers, who were already battling exhaustion, hunger, anxiety, and fear.[3]

Morse Coffin also remembered the howling dogs. He was certain sleep would find him, but "a hundred or two Indian dogs were scattered over the plains and making the night hideous by their dismal wailing cry." It was no use trying to sleep, he explained, for it was "like a night among the wolves."

Another disruption occurred at midnight when nervous pickets fired in the darkness and came running back toward camp crying out that Indians were coming. "Third battalion, turn out!" shouted Captain Cree. The order, repeated by Captain Nichols, shook Coffin awake. The exhausted soldiers stumbled about, bewildered by the order and unsure where to go. It made for "a confusion not readily described," wrote Coffin. The shouting and chaos traveled around the square. Howbert recalled being ordered to immediately fall into line to repel an Indian attack. "We rushed out," he said, "but in our sleepy condition had difficulty forming a line, as we hardly knew what we were doing." In Coffin's estimation, "There is no telling the result of a sudden and determined attack of even one hundred Indians at such a time."

The officers had every fourth man form a skirmish line several rods in front around the camp perimeter. The dying fires of the burning tipis still glowed, and occasional shots echoed across the plains. In the orange glow of the fires, men

2 Chubbuck, "Sand Creek," 2; Howbert, *Indians of Pike's Peak*, 108.

3 Shaw, *Pioneers of Colorado*, 84–85.

thought they spotted approaching Indians. Howbert saw "what looked to be hundreds of Indian ponies running hither and thither." The horses all appeared to be riderless, but in the soldiers' imaginations they were certain to be ridden by warriors clinging to the far sides. Howbert was convinced he and his fellow soldiers "should surely be overwhelmed." While nervously awaiting the attack, the volunteers finally discovered they were being charged by hundreds of dogs that had lost their masters and were simply running wildly about in every direction.[4]

Much more was moving about beyond the glow of the burning lodges than just dogs or phantoms. The Coloradans may have spent a trying night, but for the surviving Indians, it was much worse. George Bent recalled how most of them lay in their pits until dark, suspecting that the soldiers might return. They eventually crawled out, "stiff and sore, with the blood frozen on our wounded and half-naked bodies." Many slowly retreated up Sand Creek. Occasional wails from women and children broke the stillness, but everyone did their best to muffle their cries. Many women and children met up with warriors who had left the camp before the fighting to gather up the horses. The warriors had driven the ponies out of the battle area and waited until dark to return. One of Bent's cousins gave him a pony, but his hip hurt so badly that he had to be lifted onto its back. The survivors moved slowly north, some mounted and many on foot, until they were too exhausted to continue and stopped on the open plains for the night. The ground was frozen, there was no shelter, and no wood to build a fire. Some gathered grass to ignite small intermittent blazes, close to which the wounded and children were placed. Bent would never forget those tortuous hours, which he described as "the worst night I ever went through."[5]

Some Indians who had lost relatives crept back to the battlefield to search for them, but only a very few wounded were found and carried out alive. Black Kettle searched in the darkness for the body of his wife, Medicine Woman, and almost miraculously found her alive. Her clothes were frozen to the clotted blood from nine wounds. Black Kettle carried her away on his back until someone gave him a pony, and they started for the Smoky Hill camps. Old Yellow Fingernails had been scalped alive, but somehow managed to crawl away and find his family. The botched scalping left his forehead skin hanging loose over his eyes. He wanted to say goodbye to his grandchildren, but they

---

4   Coffin, *Sand Creek*, 32; Howbert, *Indians of Pike's Peak*, 109.

5   Hyde, *George Bent*, 156-57.

were afraid to look at him. He grabbed his loose skin in his hand and held it back, bade them farewell, and died. Tallow Woman, the 14-year-old who told of hearing whistling sounds the previous night, disappeared completely. The Cheyenne Strong Bow managed to get his family out before the soldiers reached them, but they fled with little except the clothes on their back. The child Black Bear was lifeless when they stopped late in the day to rest. Strong Bow thought he had frozen to death. They were burying him in the sand when the sun broke through the clouds. Perhaps it was the combination of light and warmth, but it was enough to revive him.

When Bent's group could stand the cold no longer, they picked up and began walking east toward the camps on the Smoky Hill some 50 miles away. Luckily for them, a number of Indians who had escaped on horseback early in the fighting had ridden directly to Smoky Hill, which they reached about nightfall. When they spread the news of the attack, many rescuers set out with ponies loaded with blankets, robes, and food. The column met the fugitives after daybreak and no doubt saved some of their lives.

The Sand Creek attack was one of the worst blows to ever hit the Cheyenne. Black Kettle's people lost more than any other band. White Antelope and Lone Bear (One Eye) were killed, and their bands suffered heavy losses. The oldest of the chiefs, Yellow Wolf, and his brother Big Man were dead. Bear Man was killed, and War Bonnet and half of his band were wiped out. Stand in the Water, chief of the Southern Elkhorn Scrapers, was killed, as were Two Thighs of the Kit Foxes and Yellow Shield of the Bowstrings. Spotted Crow, Bear Robe, and Little Robe also were killed, as were most of the Arapaho. Sand Hill, who had camped farther away, suffered the lightest losses.[6]

Unfortunately, the killing was not yet at an end.

---

6 Hyde, *George Bent*, 158; Powell, *Sacred Mountain* I, 308; *Sand Creek Massacre Project*, 190, 203, 233.

Chapter 12

The Death of Jack Smith

After the fighting ended, Colonel Chivington scribbled a hurried if short after-action report to General Samuel Curtis.

According to the colonel, he and his men had ridden 300 miles in 10 days, 100 miles of it through snow a couple feet deep. After a 40-mile night march, at daylight he attacked a Cheyenne village of 130 lodges with more than 900 warriors. He thought his men had killed Chiefs Black Kettle, White Antelope, Notanee, Little Raven and 400 to 500 other Indians, and captured hundreds of horses and mules. His own loss, he added, was but nine killed and 38 wounded. "All did nobly," Chivington concluded. He went on to note that he thought he could catch more Indians on Smoky Hill. "Found white man's scalp, not more than three days' old, in one of the lodges," he added. The colonel also dashed off a similar report to William Byers in Denver, adding, "I could mention many more things to show how these Indians that have been drawing Government rations at Fort Lyon are and have been acting."[1]

On November 30, Lieutenant Colonel Bowen, with John Smith and a small escort including Lt. Frank DeLamar of Company M, Third Colorado, Theodore Chubbuck, Billy Breakenridge, and Sergeant Decatur, rode the field to identify bodies. Decatur, who was now acting as Bowen's battalion adjutant, counted the slain and recorded the names of the Indians they recognized. Smith

---

1 Chivington to Curtis, December 16, 1864, *OR* 41, pt. 1, 948-51.

did find the bodies of several chiefs, "lying there in the water and sand; most of them in the bed of the creek, dead and dying, making many struggles." One of those found was One Eye, "who was employed by our government at $125 a month and rations to remain in the village as a spy." War Bonnet, Stand in the Water, and a chief he thought was Black Kettle, were also found. He was unsure of Black Kettle's identity because his corpse had been mutilated.[2]

Breakenridge did not like what he saw. "I had no conscientious scruples in regard to killing an Indian," he explained, "but I did draw the line at scalping them or mutilating them after they were dead." Lieutenant Colonel Bowen felt differently. When he came across White Antelope's body, which had already been scalped, Breakenridge claimed that Bowen "cut off his ears for pocket pieces. A long time afterward, he was treated to free drinks if he would show the ears." Breakenridge refused to scalp anyone, but he did want one for himself. He traded a buffalo robe for two scalps, although they might not have been whole ones. "There were a lot of scalps of white men and women, some very fresh, found in the tepees," explained Breakenridge, "but so far as scalps went, our boys had the best of it, for every dead Indian was scalped once, and some of them two or three times."

"Most of the Indians yielded four or five scalps," claimed Joe Cramer in a letter to Ned Wynkoop. According to Silas Soule, "They were all scalped, and as high as half a dozen taken from one head." Simeon Whiteley agreed: When the regiment returned to Denver, he noted, the soldiers carried with them many scalps "or parts of scalps." They were exhibited at a theatrical performance. Whiteley believed there were as many as 100.[3]

If, as Whiteley thought, there were about 100 scalps, and if, as others claimed, many Indians were scalped more than once, the total number of scalps could have come from 50 or fewer Indians. We know several soldiers took more than one, and it was said that Lt. Harry Richmond took eight.[4] There were about 600 soldiers at Sand Creek, so percentage-wise, very few of the Colorado volunteers engaged in the scalping. The practice was as atrocious to many contemporaries as it is to us today, and although some men participated, it is inaccurate to portray the soldiers as an army of ghoulish mutilators.

2   "Sand Creek Massacre," 135; "Massacre of Cheyenne Indians," 8-9.

3   "Chivington Massacre," 71; "Sand Creek Massacre," 195; Breakenridge, *Helldorado*, 49, 55-56; Roberts and Halaas, "Written in Blood," 26-27.

4   "Chivington Massacre," 61.

* * *

During the morning of the 30th, after the night phantoms had faded away, the sleep-deprived soldiers made their fires, boiled their coffee, and waited for orders. They soon learned the Indians were still nearby.

While he was working picket duty, Francisco Medino of Company C, Third Colorado, left his post to go after some ponies he saw running loose. Riding nearby were Jesse Greenley, William Hopkins, Hank Farrar, Hi Lockhart, and Frank Smith, all of Company D. Several miles from camp they spotted about six Indians on the top of a ridge. The men dismounted and got ready for a fight, but the Indians noticed Medino riding alone and went after him. They caught up to him before the boys of Company D could do the same. Medino fired several shots and turned to run, but the Indians overtook him. One shot an arrow into his neck, and another knocked him from his horse with a hatchet. The pursuing soldiers arrived in time to prevent his scalping, but not in time to save his life. One managed to shoot a fleeing Indian, who was picked up and carried off by his companions.

In the afternoon, three soldiers of Company G, Third Colorado, including Marion (John) Wells and William Davenport, rode off together. Somehow, Wells separated from the others and was not seen or heard from again. No effort was made to look for him.

Morse Coffin, Melanthon Williams, and a man Coffin called "Mory" received permission to look over the battleground. On their way out, they crossed paths with Bowen, Breakenridge, Smith and others, just returning from their body count and identification trip. Coffin and his comrades came across White Antelope's body in the creek bed near the village. Coffin guided his horse upstream, where in one sand pit, in a space not more than 30 feet across, he counted 23 dead warriors, "not a woman or child among or near them." Only a few bodies were found along the east bank of the creek where the first fighting took place, but there were more along the west bank in the makeshift rifle pits. All told, Coffin's party counted about 125 dead Indians. Coffin added in another 50 he heard about, but did not see, to reach an estimate of 175.[5]

That morning, as David Louderback cooked breakfast for the Indians and mixed bloods being held in War Bonnet's lodge, soldiers arrived claiming they had been ordered to take all the robes, blankets, and provisions for the

5   Coffin, *Sand Creek*, 33-34, 37; Roberts, "Sand Creek," 439.

wounded. John Smith complained to Chivington about "his" goods being taken, and Colonel Shoup placed a temporary guard around the tipi. Meanwhile, there was some talk in the camp that Jack Smith had himself participated in raids with the Cheyenne and that he ought to have been killed with the rest. As word spread that Jack Smith was going to be killed, some officers decided to check with Chivington. "I heard Lieutenant Dunn ask Colonel Chivington if he had any objections to having Jack Smith killed," testified Captain Soule. "Colonel Chivington said that he need not ask him about it; he knew how he (Chivington) felt about it, or words to that effect."

The problem with Soule's story is that he wasn't there. Soule, it will be recalled, had left the battlefield with Major Anthony by 3:00 p.m. on the 29th to ride to Fort Lyon. Nor was Soule there the next day when Jack Smith was killed. His story is often cited as proof that Chivington approved of the killing of young Smith, but Soule testified to so many questions that he sometimes forgot what he had said and contradicted himself. Later, he would testify that he had only heard all these things. "All I know is from hearsay," he finally admitted, "except seeing the dead body."

Neither would Major Anthony have known about any plan to kill Smith, for he was with Soule. Back in the village on December 1, Anthony wrote to his brother, "We, of course, took no prisoners, except John Smith's son, and he was taken suddenly ill in the night and died before morning." From this candid letter it is clear Anthony knew absolutely nothing about how many prisoners were taken, and nothing at all about a conversation between officers and Chivington regarding the fate of Jack Smith. By the time of his December 15 report to district headquarters at Fort Riley, however, Anthony was more informed. "One prisoner (half breed), son of John S. Smith, Indian interpreter, was taken and afterward killed in camp," he wrote. "One other prisoner, Charles Bent (son of Col. William Bent), was taken, and sent to this post, where he is now confined."

By the time the Sand Creek investigations were going full-tilt, Anthony realized something had definitely gone wrong. What the soldiers believed had been a hard-fought battle was now being portrayed as a massacre, and this time it was the authorities who were out for scalps. Like Silas Soule, Major Anthony changed his tune. On March 14, he testified that he had gone directly to Chivington and told him that Jack Smith would be killed by the next morning unless the colonel ordered the men not to harm him. He claimed he had told Chivington that Smith could be useful, but that the colonel interjected, "I do not want any prisoners taken, and I have no further instructions to give." By the

Colonel George L. Shoup. It was Shoup, not Chivington, who commanded the Third Colorado at Sand Creek.

History Colorado, Denver, CO

late winter of 1865, it was very clear that being in sympathy with Chivington and the manner in which he had handled the affair was not a particularly smart career move. Anthony was trying his best to distance himself from a man he had once admired, and a battle that he had once wanted to fight. Memories were changing.[6]

Colonel Shoup, who was with Chivington when the matter of Jack Smith was broached, Shoup testified that Smith was killed on November 30 between ten in the morning and two in the afternoon. He reported Chivington's comments as "we must not allow John Smith and family, father of Jack Smith, to be harmed," even though he did not intend to take any Indian prisoners. Shoup also claimed the colonel said "he would allow the half-breed Bent to return to his father." This is just what Chivington had promised Anthony before the battle.[7] Of all those who claimed firsthand knowledge, only Shoup could have been there during this time, yet his testimony is seldom cited and rarely believed. Shoup is perceived as a biased witness, yet he was no more or less biased than Soule, Cramer, or Anthony. All had something to gain or lose by the positions they assumed.

Back in War Bonnet's lodge, the situation went downhill for Jack Smith. When the battle began the day before, his father knew "he had little hope of being spared," so he broke out and ran for about one mile before realizing that he might be killed hiding with the Indians. He walked back to the village, found Major Sayr, gave himself up, and was placed back in the lodge where he

6 Michno, *Battle at Sand Creek*, 249-50.

7 "Chivington Massacre," 74; "Sand Creek Massacre," 51, 177.

remained through the night. The soldiers believed Smith had fought with the Indians during their summer attacks. Louderback heard one soldier call his son Jack "a son of a bitch" and that Jack "ought to have been shot long ago." Jack supposedly replied that he "did not give a damn; that if he wanted to kill him, shoot him."

Late in the afternoon of the 29th, about one dozen soldiers entered the lodge, and Louderback figured it was time for him to get out, "as men had threatened to hang and shoot me as well as uncle John Smith and the teamster that was with us." As Louderback left, one of the soldiers called to John Smith to accompany him to Chivington's mess, which was 60 yards away. After walking a distance, the soldier told Smith, "I am sorry to tell you but they are going to kill your son Jack."

The elder Smith figured this was coming and replied that "there was no use to make any resistance." He supposedly told the soldier, "I can't help it," and walked toward Chivington's campfire—an incomprehensible reaction for a father just informed that his son was going to be murdered. A number of men figured they had good reason to kill the younger Smith. Private Shaw was more than ready to do the job and had been hanging around the tipi, waiting for a chance when no one was around. He was lingering there when he was surprised by another soldier.

"What are you doing here, Shaw?" asked the man.

"Oh, just wandering around because I couldn't sleep," Shaw replied.

"Now see here," the other soldier said. "I know why you are just wandering around; it is for a chance to kill Smith, and I wanted that job myself."

"Well," Shaw shot back, "if you are sure you will do the job up right, I will leave it to you." Shaw left the man, whom he dubbed a "First Regiment boy."

In the lodge, James Beckwourth and Pvt. George Roan witnessed what took place. While some soldiers confronted Jack, telling him that he would not leave the camp alive, someone outside poked a pistol through a hole in the lodge skin. The shot thundered inside the tipi and the bullet hit Jack below the right breast. According to Beckwourth, "He sprung forward and fell dead, and the lodge scattered, soldiers, squaws, and everything else." Shaw recalled hearing Smith give "a war whoop,"and Beckwourth rushed out and saw a man with the pistol in his hand.

"I am afraid the damn son of a bitch is not dead. I will finish him," said the man.

"Let him go to rest;" Beckwourth replied. "He is dead."

As Shaw quickly walked away from the scene, he met Colonel Shoup, who inquired about what had just happened.

"I guess some of the boys' guns have gone off accidentally," was how Shaw framed his reply.

Louderback and Smith were both near Chivington's campfire when they heard the fatal gunshot. According to Louderback, Chivington said, "Halloo; I wonder what that is?" Louderback claimed he told the colonel that Jack Smith had been shot, and that "it was a damned shame" the way he been killed. No matter what a man had done," he added, "they ought to give him a show for his life." An officer, claimed Louderback, told him he had better be careful about how "I shot my mouth off." Louderback snapped back that his tongue was his own, and it didn't belong to the government.

Sergeant Lucien Palmer of Louderback's Company G, First Colorado, was standing nearby when the supposed exchange took place, calmed the private down, and told Louderback to stay with the company or he'd be shot before he left the village.[8]

---

8 "Massacre of Cheyenne Indians," 10, 32; Shaw, *Pioneers of Colorado*, 95-96; "Sand Creek Massacre," 71, 136, 141.

Chapter 13

Aftermath

The night of the 30th was nearly a repetition of the previous night. Soldiers slept on their arms, peering into the darkness looking for ghosts. Sporadic firing broke out. Those who could fall asleep were shaken awaken by the 7:00 p.m. arrival of Lt. Andrew J. Pennock, Company D, Third Colorado, who had been left behind at Fort Lyon and now was bringing in about 40 wagons of provisions, forage, and ammunition.

About 9:00 a.m. on Thursday, December 1, the command finally packed up and headed out—but not toward the Smoky Hill. Coffin was aware they were going to pursue Little Raven's band, but Irving Howbert didn't know why they went south. He assumed it was because of "our regiment's inferior horses, arms, and equipment."

In truth, Chivington did not know exactly where the Indians were or in what numbers, and he had lost the equivalent of three companies to casualties, wagon escorting, wounded, prisoners, and captured horses. Chivington, however, did have new intelligence about a closer Indian camp. Sam Colley was "desirous so that I should find and also attack the Arapahoes," explained Chivington, "that he sent a messenger after the fight at Sand Creek, nearly forty miles, to inform me where I could find the Arapahoes and Kiowas." These Indians had been camped near the junction of Rush Creek and Sand Creek, about 15 miles below the battle site, and that was Chivington's destination.

About one mile south of the battleground, the column came across a few women and children huddled in the grass by the trail. Coffin felt sorry for them. They begged to be taken on the wagons, but were left behind so they could be picked up by other Indians. According to Jim Dubois, "they were left by the road side with some considerable rations." However, he also thought they might have been killed by soldiers bringing up the rear. The command stopped for the day near the mouth of Rush Creek, but the Arapaho were already gone.

Anthony and Soule had left Fort Lyon at 11:00 p.m. the night before and met up with Chivington at Rush Creek. On December 2, Chivington continued riding down Sand Creek to its junction with the Arkansas River. Anthony was given charge of the dead and wounded to take back to Fort Lyon. Once there, Anthony wrote to headquarters: "This has certainly been the most bloody and hard-fought Indian battle that has ever occurred on these plains." He also observed there were too many wounded for the current surgeon to handle, and that he would ride to catch up to Chivington, after which he hoped to continue on to the Smoky Hill and end up near Fort Larned in a couple of weeks.[1]

On the night of December 2, Chivington broke camp and moved down the Arkansas, riding 42 miles through the night and into the next day. He reached the reported site of the last Arapaho camp, but no Indians were found. The morning of the 4th, the column came across a westbound stage whose passengers announced another Indian camp 15 miles to the east. Colonel Shoup took 30 men from each company of the Third Colorado and made for the reported camp. They arrived there at dusk, but there were no Indians in sight. Scouts reported Indians another 15 miles below, and on December 5, they moved east once more, with the same result. The Indians, it seemed, were always about one day ahead of the pursuing soldiers. On the 6th, another scout was sent 20 miles downriver, but returned without spotting anything of interest.

That night, recorded Major Sayr, was the "coldest night we have had during the campaign." Billy Breakenridge also commented on the cold, as did Irving Howbert, who observed that from the day they left the original battleground, "it had been very cold and disagreeable. Sharp, piercing winds blew from the north almost incessantly, making us extremely uncomfortable . . . . The thin, shoddy government blankets afforded only the slightest possible protection against the bitter winds."[2]

---

1   Coffin, *Sand Creek*, 37-38; Howbert, *Indians of Pike's Peak*, 111-12; "Massacre of Cheyenne Indians," 108; Anthony to Chivington, December 1, 1864, OR 41, pt. 1, 952.

2   Perrigo, "Sayr's Diary," 56; Breakenridge, *Helldorado*, 58-59; Howbert, *Indians of Pike's Peak*, 113. These statements contrast with what Major Anthony wrote to his brother on December 23, when he was trying to emphasize that they could have attacked all the Indians, not just those

The extreme cold, the inability to catch the fleeing Indians, the exhaustion of the horses, and the near-expirations of the enlistments of the Third Colorado convinced Chivington it as time to turn back. On December 7, he headed back upstream and reaching Fort Lyon on the 10th. It was there Chivington learned what had happened to much of the stock captured at Sand Creek.

Lieutenant Chauncy M. Cossitt, the quartermaster at Fort Lyon, was always short on horseflesh. Before the battle, Lt. D. Perry Elliot, the quartermaster of the Third Colorado, jokingly told Cossitt they had "to have a fight in order to get even on their stores." When the captured San Creek ponies were brought in, it was like manna from heaven. Cossitt counted 450 head. Before they were officially turned over to the post quartermaster, however, some of Lieutenant Autobees's men drove a portion of the herd up the Arkansas River. Thus, only 327 were turned over to Cossitt at Fort Lyon. Lieutenant Henry H. Hewitt of Company I, Third Colorado, was sent to retrieve the horses that had been cut from the captured herd. He found them at Autobees's ranch and surrounded the corral, but soldiers there told Hewitt they had driven off the stock during the battle under Autobees' orders, and both Chivington and Shoup knew it.

Hewitt had little choice but to arrest the men and took them back to Fort Lyon in an effort to sort through the mess. When Hewitt reached the post about December 9, he learned that more stock had been driven off to the Cimarron River. When Chivington arrived the next day, Hewitt reported to him to clarify the situation.

"You have done perfectly right," Chivington told him. "I am glad you did it; the men had no authority from myself or Colonel Shoup to drive the stock off when they did." Autobees, he explained, was only authorized to drive the horses back to Fort Lyon. Chivington added that "it was a scandal, that while the troops were fighting the Indians, some scoundrels should shrink to plunder." Later, at the military tribunal, these missing horses were used as a vehicle to further discredit Chivington, although his attempted disposition of the stock was quite legitimate.[3]

*   *   *

on Sand Creek. According to Anthony, the weather was "delightful," and "I did not wear my overcoat two days during the whole trip, and all my bedding stolen besides." Scott J. Anthony Papers **[what is this a reference to?]**

3   "Sand Creek Massacre," 153-54, 200-01.

Word of Sand Creek fight broke in the *Rocky Mountain News* on December 8. The "whipping" of the Indians was the "chief subject of comment and glorification" in the town. The *Rocky Mountain News* gloated that the local Colorado boys had "collectively 'cleaned out' the confederated savages of Sand Creek, have won for themselves and their commanders, from Colonel down to corporal, the eternal gratitude of dwellers on these plains." As the troops marched back to Denver, the papers daily spilled forth with additional bits of news about the fight, all couched in grandiloquent terms. "Among the brilliant feats of arms in Indian warfare," editorialized the *Rocky Mountain News* on December 17, "harkened, the recent campaign of our Colorado volunteers will stand in history with few rivals and none to exceed it in final results." Ironically, the statement would prove to be both very right wrong, and very wrong.

On December 22, the Third Colorado rode victoriously into Denver. According to the *Rocky Mountain News*, Chivington, Shoup, Bowen, Sayr, and "the rank and file of the 'bloody Thirdsters' made a most imposing procession," with all observers "expressing their admiration for the gallant boys." The stories were pouring in, continued the paper, and "there's no exaggeration in stating that no two men give the same version of the big battle, and, of the stories of a score of them, there ain't three alike, respecting the minutiae of the great glorious victory." On Christmas Day, Major Sayr recorded in his diary: "In camp—None of our Regiment mustered out yet—Some of the boys trying to have a Merry Christmas by getting drunk."

It was a fine old time for all, at least until the 29th of that month, when the *Rocky Mountain News* ran a short and disturbing snippet: "Washington, Dec. 28—The affair at Fort Lyon, Colorado, in which Colonel Chivington destroyed a large Indian village and all its inhabitants, is to be made the subject of a Congressional investigation. Letters received from high officials in Colorado say that the Indians were killed after surrendering, and that a large proportion of them were women and children."

The news exploded on the scene like a bombshell. Who were the "high officials" who claimed that friendly Indians had surrendered before being killed? These officials may believe the Indians were friendly, the paper editorialized, "but the mass of our people 'can't see it.'" Possibly those white scalps found in the lodges "were taken in a friendly, playful manner," continued the sarcastic editorial, but they certainly weren't taken from the heads of the wives or daughters of those "high officials."

Many citizens welcomed an investigation to prove that the actions undertaken by the volunteers were justified. The *Rocky Mountain News* begged the Congressional Committee to come forth, but the paper also warned the committee members that they had better "get their scalps insured before they pass Plum Creek on their way out." On the last day of 1864, the *News* speculated again about the "contemptibly mean" people who would drag Colorado down to further their own political ambitions or line their own pockets with money. These men did not care for peace, or for Colorado's security, or for the lives of defenseless citizens, carped the paper. Instead, they spread malicious lies "Solely and simply to vent their spite upon two or three men against whom they have personal animosities, or whose power and popularity they envy and fear."

The editorial ended with these words: "Let the investigations go on."[4]

---

4   Perrigo, "Sayr's Diary," 56-57; Williams, *Through the News*, 269, 280, 291, 299, 300, 304-05, 317-20, 323-24.

Part II:

IN COURT

Chapter 14

Opening Rounds

When the troops returned to Fort Lyon, the consciences of some of the officers were rightly bothering them, and they began arguing amongst themselves. The pro- and anti-Chivington factions were already developing.

Major Scott Anthony wanted to kill Indians, but he wasn't so sure they had gone after the right ones. Captain Silas Soule and Lt. Joseph Cramer agreed to fight with the understanding that some of the "friendlies" would be saved, but it is difficult to understand how they could have believed they'd fight a battle without killing anyone. Both would affirm they had moral objections. Waiting at the fort was Lieutenant Colonel Samuel F. Tappan, a willing conduit for the complaints.

Captain Theodore G. Cree and Lieutenant Cramer had a confrontation the day after the command returned to Fort Lyon. Cramer was angry about what he considered Colonel Chivington's disregard of his wishes not to fight the Indians at Sand Creek. Cramer told Cree that Chivington "was working for a brigadier general's commission, and that he did not care how many lives he lost in getting it so that he got it." According to Cree, Cramer also told him, "We (meaning he and I don't know who else) were going to crush him if we could. He said he thought they could make a massacre out of the Sand Creek affair and crush him." When Cree asked Cramer what Chivington had done to him to make Cramer hate him so much, the lieutenant replied "that he did not know that he had done anything." He went on to tell Cree that he'd like to see the Indians killed just as much as anyone else, but "they had got their play in on Chivington and they were going to play it." Perturbed by this irrational attitude, Cree broke off the conversation. "I told him that there was no use of our discussing that question, as we would only make enemies of ourselves, and I thought it was best for us not to say anything more about it."[1]

Something else was brewing. The wounded Captain Presley Talbot was given a room next to Agent Colley's office in which to recuperate. There, John Smith showed him papers that Smith and Colley had drawn up against the government, papers claiming they were owed "for 105 buffalo robes, two white ponies, and a wagon-load of goods." "This account," claimed Talbot, "was made out in favor of Smith and Colley for $6,000." The two told Talbot that they had other demands against the government, and, Smith added, "they would realize $25,000 out of it, and damn Colonel Chivington." The government bill they had, Talbot explained, was "sworn and subscribed to by one David Louderback, stating that he would go to Washington City and present the same, and that he had friends who would help him get it." Talbot noted that Louderback "was detailed as a nurse to me, but he did the writing for Smith and Colley."

While Talbot was recuperating, he heard John Smith and Colley in an adjoining room reading a letter written to the superintendent of Indian affairs denouncing Chivington. Smith later boasted to Talbot that the eastern papers would soon be filled with letters blaming Chivington for the death of his son and "that he would be avenged by using every effort with the department possible." Tears filled Smith's eyes when he told Talbot that Jack "was a bad boy and deserved punishment, but it was hard for a father to endure it." Perhaps money would soften the sorrow.

Private Asbury Bird of Company D heard about part of the deal while talking to Dexter Colley, who told him that they had sent Indian goods worth $2,000 to sell in Denver, and they expected the money to arrive any day. Bird heard John Smith explain that the goods did not cost them anything—the implication being that they were government annuities meant for the Indians— but that he would just trade them to the Indians, "and if he lost them he would not be out anything."[2]

---

1   "Sand Creek Massacre," 190-91.

2   "The Chivington Massacre," 68, 72; "Sand Creek Massacre," 25, 51; Craig, *Fighting Parson*, 274.

It quickly became clear that some who had fought at Sand Creek hated Chivington, some felt betrayed, and others saw it all as a way to make money. The colonel's gruff manner and bullying tactics may have cowed people when he was riding high, but he was more likely to be attacked when vulnerable, as he clearly was now. Letters were soon on their way to "high officials" (unnamed in *Rocky Mountain News* stories), a plethora of tales filled with details of recrimination and obfuscation that would make finding the truth of what had taken place nearly impossible.

As early as December 7, word from an unidentified member of the First Colorado was carried to Judge Stephen S. Harding in Denver, a political foe of Governor John Evans and Chivington, about a horrible massacre along Sand Creek. Harding wrote to John Wright, Evans's former adversary in Washington, but a friend of both Colley and Secretary of the Interior John P. Usher. Harding's sensationalist letter contained phrases such as "the attack on the defenseless savages was one of the most monstrous in history," the Indians were "quiet and at peace," the "victims were women and papooses," and "none were spared." "These Indians, I am assured," he added, "molested no travelers who passed among them. The most of them had given up their firearms before the attack was made."[3]

The public condemnations of Sand Creek soon appeared in the eastern newspapers. Harding's letter was reprinted on December 26 in the *New York Herald*. The *Auburn* (New York) *Advertiser & Union* printed the words of former Colorado Judge Benjamin F. Hall, in which he "authorizes us to state that those Indians are entirely pacific." Soon after, similar stories appeared in other prominent eastern papers. According to the *Washington Star*, Sand Creek was "a massacre of helpless savages." The next day, the *Auburn Advertiser & Union* wrote that Chivington "murdered two hundred families of Cheyennes . . . without provocation." In another article, the same paper claimed Chivington "is low and brutal enough to believe that an Indian has no right to live and ought to be exterminated."

All of this negative publicity, of course, served to help bring about an inquiry into the fighting. On January 4, 1865, the *National Intelligencer* published a story about the Committee on the Conduct of the War, which had not even heard the evidence yet, but noted that it would be investigating "a wholesale

3 Roberts, "Sand Creek," 445, 457.

massacre of Indians in Colorado for no just cause, so far as is known at the Indian Bureau."[4]

Samuel Tappan was quick to enter the fray. He knew several eastern politicians including Secretary of War Stanton and Orville Babcock, General Grant's adjutant, and his letters of condemnation were quickly disseminated through the hierarchy. Letters went to John Slough, the first commander of the First Colorado who knew Stanton, and Senator Benjamin F. Wade. Cramer wrote to Major Wynkoop, who went wild with anger and passed on a copy of the letter with his own denunciation to other politicians. Agent Colley wrote to his cousin, the Commissioner of Indian Affairs William Dole, to Secretary of the Interior Usher, and to Senator James R. Doolittle, chairman of the Senate Indian Affairs Committee. Colley, who had been complaining about "hostile" Indians for months, wrote to Senator Doolittle that the Indians were "under his protection." "All the chiefs were in camp and doing all they could to protect the whites and keep the peace," he wrote, "when Colonel Chivington marched from Denver, surprised the village, killed one half of them, all the women and children, and then returned to Denver."[5]

Comanche and Kiowa Agent Jesse Leavenworth conveyed a passel of hearsay and incorrect information to Commissioner Dole. He said that almost every peaceful chief of the Arapaho and Cheyenne tribes "who had remained true to the whites, and were determined not to fight the whites, were cruelly murdered when resting in all the confidences and assurances from Major Wyncoop." Peace was already restored to the frontier, Leavenworth claimed, when Sand Creek destroyed it all. Leavenworth went on to fabricate and attribute words to the Indians at the Camp Weld Council that they did not say, and repeated the false story that the Indians "had purchased from their captors white prisoners and set them free." Leavenworth also claimed the Cheyenne had "two more white women and one child they had sold horses to purchase, and who would have been restored to their friends in forty-eight hours more had not Colonel Chivington committed this homicide." It is impossible to know where Leavenworth obtained such erroneous information. Even Major Anthony jumped into the act of trying to distance himself from Chivington,

---

4 Roberts, "Sand Creek," 464-66; John M. Coward, *The Newspaper Indian: Native American Identity in the Press, 1820-90* (Urbana, IL, 1986), 117-18.

5 Roberts, "Sand Creek," 457-59.

writing to his brother that the colonel "whipped the only peaceable Indians in the country."

Senator Doolittle soon proposed that the matter be referred to the Indian Affairs Committee for study, and another proposal was made that the Joint Committee on the Conduct of the War also investigate. James Harlan of Iowa called for pay to be withheld from the men of the Third Colorado Regiment; his position was the result of letters from an Indian agent, a judge, and a few "private gentlemen" who said that the affair at Sand Creek was a massacre "unprovoked, premeditated, and cold-blooded," and "probably perpetrated for plunder." A few cooler heads decried the rush to judgment, claiming that it was punishment without proof of guilt. Radicals such as Senator Charles Sumner, however, won out. "Exceptional crimes," intoned the senator, "require exceptional remedies." Before the inquiries began, legislators were already certain Sand Creek was a crime, and "one of the most atrocious in the history of our country."[6]

Sand Creek was indeed an atrocious affair, but the rush to judgment in official circles almost guaranteed that an accurate account of what had transpired there was never going to be discovered. However, whether a more methodic, reasoned, and judicious approach would have uncovered different facts is also unknown.

One set of circumstances that negatively impacted the process of finding the truth developed after Major Wynkoop's trip to Fort Leavenworth once he was relieved of command at Fort Lyon. There, the major explained to General Curtis why he had been feeding the Indians, providing them with government stores, and trying as best as he could to make peace with them. Wynkoop produced letters from Lieutenant Cramer and some Arkansas Valley settlers who had approved of his conduct. Wynkoop's story cooled some of Curtis's anger. The general explained to the major that his main problem was that the major had left his district without orders and gone to Governor Evans instead of riding to him.

Major Wynkoop left Leavenworth with his hide intact and made his way to Fort Riley, where he learned of the Sand Creek controversy. By this time, General Blunt had been replaced as commander of the District of the Upper

---

6   U.S. Department of the Interior, Bureau of Indian Affairs, *Report of the Commissioner of Indian Affairs, 1865* (Washington, DC, 1865), 387-88; Scott J. Anthony Papers [Folder? Letter?]; Roberts, "Sand Creek," 465-67.

Arkansas by James Ford of the Second Colorado Cavalry. Ford, perhaps not fully realizing the depth of Wynkoop's involvement in the matter, ordered his former acquaintance of Glorieta Pass days to return to Fort Lyon to take command and investigate the Sand Creek affair. Major Wynkoop, a man whose good intentions had backfired into a series of unfortunate events that led to the disaster, slipped free from the scapegoat hook that had been wrapping itself around his own neck and was allowed to help determine who would be the next fall guy. A great tragedy requires a great villain.[7]

Amidst the uproar, General Curtis summarized the issues, as he believed them to be, to Governor Evans. The army had been known to treat the Indians roughly before, he explained, since that was the nature of its job. Chivington's attack, however, may have been perceived as "a kind of betrayal, accidental or otherwise, of a confidence which had improperly been given to the Indians." He also believed that the traders were part of the problem because Chivington had disturbed their operations, and certain officials were anxious to stir things up for their own benefit. Curtis let it be known that he was a general at war, and he would fight bandits, Rebels, and Indians with equal determination. "Our troops everywhere," Curtis explained, "now consider it right to kill bushwhackers, even after they surrender." The implication was clear: Indians could expect the same treatment. Curtis hoped that Evans would explain to the commission that the fuss about Sand Creek had a lot to do with personalities and politics, especially Chivington's, "which are no doubt likely to interfere with other men's hopes in this regard."[8]

Governor Evans had likely overplayed the threat of an Indian war, and made some poor decisions that exacerbated a potentially dangerous situation. With the similarly minded Chivington as military commander of the district, they formed a self-reinforcing loop of paranoia that proved itself every time the Indians made a raid. Reactions provoked justifiable retribution, which resulted in more revenge as a remedy, all of which became part of a spiral of increasing savagery. Evans and Chivington tried to fix the situation in their own way, but a violent solution rarely leads to reduced violence. In any event, these two men became caught in a crossfire between those who believed Indians should be

---

7   Roberts, "Sand Creek," 463; "Sand Creek Massacre," 92.

8   Curtis to Evans, January 12, 1865, *OR* 48, pt. 1, 504; S. E. Browne to Curtis, October 3, 1864, Curtis to S. E. Browne, October 15, 1864, *OR* 41, pt. 3, 596, 899-900; Lonnie J. White, *Hostiles and Horse Soldiers: Indian Battles and Campaigns in the West* (Boulder, CO, 1972), 36.

treated humanely and fairly, those who believed extermination was the only solution, those who cared only about their own enrichment, and others who sought to use the episode as a smokescreen to cover their own mistakes.

These motivations would become more clear during the Sand Creek investigations.

Chapter 15

The Denver Military Commission

She first investigation was performed by a military commission. In all practical aspects it was a court of inquiry initiated by Colonel Thomas Moonlight, Chivington's successor as district commander, at the order of General Curtis. Its impartiality depends upon the eye of the beholder.

Chivington was unhappy from the outset by this turn of events, for the officers appointed to run the proceedings were all First Colorado men: Captain Edward A. Jacobs, Captain George H. Stilwell, and Samuel F. Tappan, who was tasked as president of the commission. Before it began, Chivington objected six times, requested that the hearings be conducted in public, and asked for the dismissal of Tappan since the lieutenant colonel "for a long time past was my open and avowed enemy." Chivington also complained that Tappan said the Sand Creek affair "was a disgrace to every officer connected with it, and that he [Tappan] would make it appear so in the end." Tappan overruled each of Chivington's preliminary objections and refused to remove himself. It was an indication of things to come.[1]

One seemingly minor detail that appeared to pass unnoticed would prove to be of enormous importance for its impact on witnesses and their perceptions and recollections of all things related to Sand Creek: From the outset, the affair

---

1 "Sand Creek Massacre," 1-7.

Lt. Col. Samuel F. Tappan,
First Colorado

Tappen had considered Colonel
Chivington an enemy since 1862,
when Chivington was promoted
over him to colonel.

The Denver Public Library, Western History Collection

was consistently reffered to as a "massacre." The record of the proceedings was printed in *The Report of the Secretary of War for 1867, Executive Document 26, 39th Congress,* as "Sand Creek Massacre." It may indeed have been a massacre, but that was what the commission was trying to find out. Describing it so beforehand was almost guaranteed to prejudice participant recollections.

* * *

The commission, called into session in Denver on February 9, was consumed with preliminary matters for a few days before it called its first witness. Silas Soule took the stand on February 15. Tappan was determined to unlimber the big guns from the outset. Soule's testimony was important, but demonstrated how confusing the events in question were to those who experienced them.

According to Soule, Governor Evans at the Camp Weld Council told the Indians "that he could not make peace with them," but he also testified that when they returned to Fort Lyon, Major Wynkoop told the chiefs to bring in all in their tribe who were anxious for peace and they could camp near the post.

The next day, Soule talked about the fight itself and that Major Anthony ordered his company to move up Sand Creek "for the purpose of killing Indians." Soule obeyed, but because there were troops firing on both sides of him he felt "it was unsafe" and moved across the creek, taking himself out of the action. Soule offered no testimony that it was lofty principles that kept him from shooting Indians, as he had earlier claimed. He was not heavily engaged, and about 3:00 p.m. received orders to accompany Major Anthony and the supply wagons back to Fort Lyon. Soule explained that he returned to the field later in December and counted 69 dead Indians. He also testified that he saw soldiers scalping and mutilating Indian women and children.

Soule continued his testimony on February 20, but this time when he was asked if he had seen soldiers scalping and mutilating Indians he answered, "I think not." At Fort Lyon, Soule claimed to have heard Major Anthony, Lieutenants Baldwin, Cramer, Cannon, and Minton, and Lieutenant Colonel Tappan argue that Chivington ought to be prosecuted. On February 21, his last day of testimony, however, Soule said he saw Jack Smith's body, but didn't know anything about how, where, or when he was killed.[2]

Lieutenant Cramer was the next officer to take the stand. Cramer also talked about the confusing results of the Camp Weld meeting. He claimed that Major Wynkoop thought a preliminary peace accord had been reached, and that he believed he could thereafter use the Cheyenne to fight other tribes. Evans' and Chivington's impressions, he continued, were "mixed." Evans made no direct peace proposition, arguing that was in the hands of the military. Chivington, he continued, wanted to delay any resolution "until such time as we could get troops here to fight them." Chivington, claimed Cramer, said they had been "bad" Indians and should be punished. Cramer added that he also believed Chivington had endorsed the actions of Wynkoop, which would have been mutually contradictory. In addition, Cramer testified that back at Fort Lyon, Major Anthony had a council with Black Kettle and other chiefs and he told them he could not feed them at the post, and that they must move away, but "they would be perfectly safe." Like Captain Soule, Cramer, Wynkoop, Evans, Chivington, and the chiefs each had different understanding of whether there would be peace or war.

At Sand Creek, Cramer also received orders from Anthony to move up the creek and engage the enemy. Cramer's men were firing, but at times troops got in line of each other's fire and, he said, "several times during the fight I ordered my men to cease firing." He also said that his men were firing at the Indians, including White Antelope, as he "came running towards the troops with both hands raised." This contradicts what he had previously written to Major Wynkoop after the fight, i.e., "I swore I would not burn powder, and I did not."

In keeping with the rest of the testimony, Cramer probably made the most honest statement of anyone when wrote, "Major, I am ashamed of this. I have it gloriously mixed up."[3]

The commission moved from Denver to to Fort Lyon and reopened questioning there on March 20. The first witness was Major Wynkoop. That officer wasn't at Sand Creek, so all he could contribute was hearsay testimony. According to Wynkoop, Major Anthony issued goods and food to the Indians in "greater quantity than ever I had issued," when in truth, Anthony had only given food to the Arapaho for about ten days, between the token surrender of their weapons and when the they were told to leave the area (with their weapons). Anthony only fed them while they were considered prisoners of war. Wynkoop also repeated the nonsense that there were no Indian depredations for more than two months between the time he had his Smoky Hill talk and the Sand Creek incident. What is notable in this face-to-face hearing is its contrast with his written affidavit: the lack of venomous accusations against the colonel. Chivington and his attorney, Jacob Downing, were in the room during Wynkoop's testimony. All of Wynkoop's epithets about Chivington and his behavior ceased. Wynkoop even admitted that at the Camp Weld Council, Chivington told the Indians that he was the war chief "and his business was to kill Indians, and not to make peace with them." Wynkoop could bluster and accuse and blame others, but when in the presence of men who could easily call his bluff, he folded up like a losing poker hand.[4]

Tappan's court had just returned from Fort Lyon to Denver on April 20 when Silas Soule was shot and killed while acting as provost marshal in Denver. The usual accusations followed, with two camps developing: one certain that Soule had been assassinated through the influence of Chivington, and the other just as certain his death was the result of shots fired by drunken soldiers. The commission met the day after the killing and agreed to adjourn for one day "in respect to the memory of the deceased," who they explained, had been "assassinated." The use of the word "assassinated" implies Tappan suspected Chivington had a hand in Soule's death.

The inference is borne out in Tappan's diary. On April 27, Tappan recorded, "'The barbarism of slavery' culminated in the assassination of Mr. Lincoln, the barbarism of Sand Creek has culminated in the assassination of

---

3 "Sand Creek Massacre," 45-46, 48-49; Roberts and Halaas, "Written in Blood," 27, 29.

4 "Sand Creek Massacre," 86-88.

Capt. Soule." On May 2, he wrote, "The authors of this horrible crime may escape punishment by the hand of man, but the real authors, those who have calculated to excite by their speeches and writing this spurt of assassination in our midst, the real and responsible parties, may still remain in the community. The origins of this dreadful deed may yet be found in the editorial columns of the press and the public speeches of Col. Chivington." Tappan poured out his feelings about Chivington and the battle in the pages of his diary over the following weeks. No one should be allowed to defend Sand Creek, he wrote, no one should "palm off on posterity a bloody massacre as a battle, the blackest perfidy as military strategy, assassination as (illegible), and the disgusting mutilation of the dead as victory."[5]

With the commission's president harboring such deep feelings against the accused, it was highly unlikely that the proceedings would or could be impartial. Chivington was correct to lodge his initial protest. Under Special Orders No. 23 the court was charged, not to put anyone on trial, "but simply to investigate and accumulate facts called for by the government, to fix the responsibility, if any, and to insure justice to all parties."

Chivington and his attorney tried several times to limit the illegal testimony and depositions. In their view, most of the testimony was "ex parte " (that is, brought by one person in the absence, and without representation or notification, of other parties) and irregular, because it was not "evidence that could be introduced before any properly constituted court," or they were in violation of the rule of law "that the accused shall be allowed to face his accuser face to face." Chivington's objections were overruled.

President Tappan's tribunal called 19 witnesses, every one of them hostile to Chivington. If the court was charged to accumulate facts and insure justice, one might reason it would call both friendly and hostile witnesses. Since it did not, Chivington called 16 witnesses of his own to testify on his behalf. Those in Tappan's camp included Wynkoop, Soule, Cramer, Cannon, Minton, Cossitt, Beckwourth, Smith, Combs, Prowers, and Louderback. These men generally viewed the Indians as peaceful, and believed the attack was unjustified. Some of the most damning testimony came from Major Wynkoop, who had no firsthand knowledge of the affair.

---

5   Diary and Notebook of Samuel F. Tappan, 1865, MSS #617, Colorado Historical Society, 246-59, 280.

Chivington's witnesses included Cree, Talbot, Richmond, Dunn, Shoup, Decatur, Gill, Burdsal, Safely, and Valentine. These men viewed the Indians as hostile and deserving of punishment. Most of the anti-Sand Creek witnesses were men of the First Colorado, while the majority of Chivington's defenders were from the Third Colorado. Throughout the course of the inquiry, most of Chivington's objections were overruled while most of Tappan's objections were sustained.

Given its charge, did the court follow its orders or fail miserably?[6]

6   "Sand Creek Massacre," 164; Craig, *Fighting Parson*, 255-56; White, *Hostiles & Horse Soldiers*, 36-37.

Chapter 16

The Joint Committee in Washington

While the military commission in Denver was in session, a second investigatory committee, the Joint Committee on the Conduct of the War, met in Washington, DC in March 1865. Its purpose was "to inquire into and report all the facts connected with the late attack." It was quickly evident that the issue of "massacre" would be the principal theme.

The committee heard live witnesses and took depositions, plus received documents, reports, and correspondence that had little bearing on the subject. Some of the depositions were written in January at Fort Lyon under the direction of Major Wynkoop.

Some of those testifying—including Jesse Leavenworth, Sam Robbins, Dexter Colley, and A. C. Hunt—were not at the battle. Sam Colley gave a deposition and testified and, in doing so, made several false statements including one that Wynkoop also made: that the Indians were peaceful after Wynkoop's September talk on the Smoky Hill. Colley also falsely claimed that the Cheyenne purchased the white captives.

John Smith testified and made a deposition that the Indians were peaceful, but indicated that many of the principal chiefs who died at Sand Creek died fighting in the creek bed and not peacefully in front of their tipis.

Major Anthony claimed that he never made any peace offers to the Indians, nor did he tell them where to camp other than between Sand Creek and the Smoky Hill. He also testified that the Arapaho might have surrendered at one time, but not the Cheyenne; the Arapaho, he added, besides the few who had joined the Cheyenne, were not attacked.

James Cannon, who was at the battle, remonstrated that he did not want to go to Sand Creek to fight. He was a hostile witness toward Chivington, yet he never once claimed to have seen any atrocities committed. Instead, on four different occasions he testified that he had only "heard" about them.

Leading questions proffered to the witnesses contained words or phrases like "massacre," "mutilation," or "unsuspecting friendly Indians," as if they were established facts and not the very points to be determined by the investigation. Chivington sent an affidavit from Denver claiming that the Indians were indeed at war, and if there were a few friendly Indians in the village when he arrived, there was no way to distinguish that fact. He also claimed that both Colley and Anthony had told him that the Indians were hostile. Not a single man from the Third Colorado was called to testify.

The most damaging indictment came from Major Wynkoop's unsworn affidavit written after his assumption of duty at Fort Lyon—a vituperative diatribe with few facts based upon his own knowledge. Wynkoop gave incorrect information about the letter written by Bent and Guerrier, about the Indians' desire for peace, about their non-hostility, and about his ability to have annihilated the Indians at any time. He passed on secondhand stories regarding mutilations of the dead as if he had personally witnessed them, and accused Chivington of "all the time inciting his troops to these diabolical outrages." Wynkoop also claimed Chivington knew the Indians were friendly, and yet "this inhuman monster committed this unprecedented atrocity." According to Wynkoop, the Indians had not been plundering and killing, and the settlers were "resting in perfect security." He also wrote that all the officers at Fort Lyon were in unanimous agreement with him, and that since "the horrible murder by Colonel Chivington," the country was desolated and all but ruined.

Wynkoop's statements were a travesty, but the true damage and insult occurred when they were accepted as gospel. The committee favored the testimony its members wanted to hear as truth, and rejected as false all testimony that did not fit its members' perspective of Sand Creek. The summary of the proceedings contained constant mention of friendly Indians and brutal massacre. The soldiers were barbarians, and the Indians "in every way conducted themselves properly and peaceably." Chivington and Anthony were on a "mission of murder and barbarity," concluded the committee, and the colonel "deliberately planned and executed a foul and dastardly massacre which would have disgraced the veriest savage." It was John Evans and Major

Anthony who tried to foster a false image of the Indians as hostile through their own "prevarication."

The final report noted that all those who disgraced the government should be removed from command and punished "as their crimes deserve." The report was released over the signature of Ben Wade, who, a year later on the Senate floor admitted that he had never even attended the hearings, nor did he understand the full import of the committee report.[1]

John Evans was very upset about the committee's portrayal of him as a liar. He complained that this conclusion was "unfair," "partial," "erroneous," and slanderous enough to do him "great injustice." He soberly reviewed the events, cited the numerous errors the committee made, and insisted that the committee itself was "culpably negligent" for not examining the actual facts that would have exonerated him. It was wrong to conclude "that I had prevaricated," stressed Evans, "because my statement did not agree with the falsehoods they [the committee members] had embraced." Evans had demonstrated that the whites were captured, not purchased, that the Indians were not friendly, that he did not grant them safety, that he had tried to stop the war on numerous occasions, and that he did not lie. Evans' complaints hit the proverbial nail on the head: Sometimes facts do not matter, and one's prior prejudices can determine who will be seen as honest and who will be considered mendacious.[2]

The season of investigation was not yet over.

1   "Massacre of Cheyenne Indians," 81-84; Michno, *Battle at Sand Creek*, 261-63.

2   Carroll, *A Documentary History*, xix-xxi.

Chapter 17

Doolittle's Committee

Concurrent with the Joint Committee investigation, a Joint Special Committee under Senator James R. Doolittle assessed the Indian tribes's situation and reviewed their treatment by civil and military authorities. The committee wanted to determine, among other things, "the reasons for the latest round of warfare."

The assessment was divided into three geographical areas, each investigated by a separate investigative group. One group addressed Kansas, Colorado, New Mexico, Utah, and Indian Territory, another covered Minnesota, Nebraska, the Dakotas, and part of Montana, while the third covered California, Oregon, Nevada, Washington, Idaho, and the remaining part of Montana. Senator Doolittle's committee interviewed or took depositions from 30 people, many of whom were interviewed by the other commissions. More than half of these men were not at the battle of Sand Creek. The committee members heard testimony in Washington, then moved west and took affidavits at Forts Riley, Larned, and Lyon, as well as in Denver and Santa Fe, New Mexico.

The fresh round of testimony did not always match that gathered by the other investigations. In Washington, Colley began changing his story by stating that the Indians at Sand Creek were friendly and had not been plundering. He told about the chiefs being shot down in front of their tipis, the American flag flying, and the horrible scalping and mutilation—although he had obviously not seen any of it. He also made a statement that apologists seem so prone to make, inadvertently exposing the reality of the situation faced by both sides. The villagers, he explained, "were butchered in a brutal manner, and scalped and mutilated *as bad as an Indian ever did to a white man* [emphasis added]."

Several affidavits were collected from civilians and soldiers who had only secondhand information to provide. Most of the eyewitness statements were from men of the First Colorado, but not all were hostile to Chivington. Lieutenant Luther Wilson reported that he had not seen any flags in the village, but he did recall see several white scalps, some old and some fresh, plus white women's clothing. The men of Wilson's three-company battalion at Sand Creek did not appear to have issues with Chivington or the conduct of the fight. It was in Major Anthony's battalion, with officers once under Major Wynkoop, where the discontent was centered.

Discontent with Chivington was alive elsewhere and not always based on fact. "I have heard . . . that the authorities of Colorado, expecting that their troops would be sent to the Potomac," explained Kit Carson, "determined to get up an Indian war, so that the troops would be compelled to remain." In fact, Chivington had once tried very hard to get his First Colorado sent east to fight Rebels. How such obviously false statements could be accepted without challenge and admitted into the record is a mystery. Also, the same Wynkoop hearsay document loaded with falsehoods that had made it into the Wade Committee hearing also founds its way into Doolittle's committee.[1]

Doolittle's conclusions were printed in 1867 as the *Report of the Joint Special Committee on the Condition of the Indian Tribes, Senate Report 156, 39th Congress, 2nd Session.* The report, portions of which had different authors, included a sub-report entitled "The Chivington Massacre." As it was in the other two investigations, the word "massacre" was found throughout to document. Given the nature of much of the testimony, it is no surprise that Chivington was directly named as the perpetrator of the massacre.

Doolittle offered several observations in the preface to his report. He noted that, with the exception of Indian Territory, the numbers of Indians were rapidly decreasing due to disease, intemperance, white emigration, railroads, loss of hunting grounds, and war. Another reason was because of the "Almighty" himself. It was His will, concluded the senator, that "one race of men—as in races of lower animals—shall disappear off the face of the earth and

---

1 "Chivington Massacre," 29, 67, 96, passim; Craig, *Fighting Parson*, 250. Doolittle interviewed a number of men who were not at Sand Creek.

give place to another race." Doolittle and his cohorts could readily give a nod and a wink to that one because they all "knew" which race God favored. But being enlightened and educated men, they knew it was not Christian-like to add guns and bullets to God's divine plan. God, it seemed, would eventually see to it that the Indians vanished without further assistance.

According to Doolittle, almost all of the Indian wars "are to be traced to the aggressions of lawless white men" who lived on the boundary "between savage and civilized life." Frontier warfare is often a war of extermination, and it is difficult to restrain white frontiersmen "from adopting the same mode of warfare against the Indians." Doolittle observed that slaughter was frequent in Indian warfare. "But the fact which gives such terrible force to the condemnation of the wholesale massacre of Arapahoes and Cheyennes, by the Colorado troops under Colonel Chivington, near Fort Lyon," he added, "was, that those Indians were then encamped under the direction of our own officers, and believed themselves under the protection of our flag." As far as Doolittle was concerned, Sand Creek was a black and white issue—a massacre of peaceful Indians who were under Army protection.

According to the senator, at least some of the problem stemmed from conflicts and jealousies between men of the Interior and War departments. He recommended that the Indian Bureau continue to operate within the Department of the Interior because having the War Department care for and fight Indians simultaneously made little sense. He also wanted to de-politicize the situation by turning over the administration of Indian affairs to churchmen.[2]

Because Doolittle was the committee chairman, his portion of the report is the one most often cited. On the other hand, Oregon Senator James W. Nesmith, the former superintendent of Indian affairs for Oregon Territory, took a very different stance. His sub-report, however, did not receive the same level of publicity that Doolittle's had garnered. After making his study in the Pacific Northwest, Nesmith concluded that the Indians were very much to blame for the constant warfare in his region of investigation, particularly the Snakes. Nesmith called them "natural thieves and murderers [who] have taken many valuable lives and destroyed hundreds of thousands of dollars' worth of

---

2 Condition of the Indian Tribes. Report of the Joint Special Committee, Appointed Under Joint Resolution of March 3, 1865, Senate Report 156, 39th Congress, 2nd Session (Washington, 1867), 3-7.

property." Nesmith wasn't finished. The Indians, he continued,"infest all the routes of inland travel east of the Cascade mountains and south of the Columbia River, and pay their respects alike and simultaneously to the stage stations, the ranch men, the farmers, and the miners. They respect neither age, sex, nor condition, and seem to live solely for blood and plunder." Nesmith hoped the Indians would live up to past treaties, and that the government would negotiate new ones with the still-hostile bands, yet he had little hope any treaty would bring about real peace. The "Snakes," according to the senator, would never submit because of "their constitutional and ingrained tendency to rob and murder."

Senator Nesmith's view was just as biased as Doolittle's—the former's villains were the Indians, and the latter's villains were the whites. Doolittle of Wisconsin, and Nesmith of Oregon—men from very different parts of the country—saw the facts through very different lenses.[3] Was one right and one wrong? Were they both right, or both wrong? Did each viewpoint contain some parcels of truth? Perhaps the evidence heard by the committees was completely irrelevant because each man was already predisposed to reach certain conclusions. Did confirmation bias force them to reinforce one set of "truths" and discount others?

One man's fact is often another man's falsehood.

---

3 Condition of the Indian Tribes, Appendix, Sub-Report of Hon. J. W. Nesmith, 4-5; Gregory Michno, *The Deadliest Indian War in the West The Snake Conflict, 1864-1868* (Caldwell, ID, 2007), 204.

Chapter 18

Conflicting Testimony

When dealing with the Sand Creek testimony, it becomes readily apparent that it is easy to select testimony and build a case for a massacre, and just as easy to select other pieces of testimony and assemble a case supporting a battle. There is plenty of evidence to blame the Indians for what happened, and other evidence to blame the whites. There is proof that the Indians were shot down where they stood, and other proof that they put up a staunch fight. In other words, the contradictions are numerous and often seemingly irreconcilable.

When examined in detail as a whole, how one comes to view the evidence depends upon one's own preconceptions and biases. The following eyewitness accounts from the Sand Creek affair demonstrate the contradictory nature of the evidence.

Was Peace Made Before Sand Creek?
Were the Indians Under Army Protection?

"The time when you can make war best, is in the summer time; when I can make war best, is in the winter. You, so far, have had the advantage; my time is just coming." (Governor Evans to Cheyenne chiefs, Carroll, *Documentary History*, v.)

"The governor declined to make any peace with them." (Sam Colley testimony, "Massacre of Cheyenne Indians," 31.)

"The governor told them that he could not make peace with them." (Silas Soule testimony, "Sand Creek Massacre," 9.)

The Cheyenne knew "things looked dark," and "that we were at war with them." (Scott Anthony testimony, "Massacre of Cheyenne Indians," 20.)

Black Kettle and the chiefs had been to Denver and Evans and Chivington told them "that they could not make any treaty of peace with them." (John Prowers testimony, "Sand Creek Massacre," 104.)

"The Indians had sent him (Anthony) word that if he wanted to fight he could get as big a one as he wanted by coming out there to Sand Creek." (Alexander F. Safely testimony, "Sand Creek Massacre," 220.)

Anthony was asked if peace was made. "I do not think they thought so. I think they were afraid I was going to attack them. I judge so from words that came to me like this: 'That they did not like that red-eyed chief; that they believed he wanted to fight them.'" (Scott Anthony testimony, "Massacre of Cheyenne Indians," 28.)

"Major Anthony told them that they would be perfectly safe." (Joseph Cramer testimony, "Sand Creek Massacre," 46.)

Major Anthony "urged an immediate attack upon the Indians . . . they were hostile." (Jacob Downing statement, "Chivington Massacre," 69-70.)

The Indians talked with Major Anthony, "received assurances of safety," and "had no fears of their families being disturbed." (John Smith testimony, "Massacre of Cheyenne Indians," 87.)

Major Anthony "told me that those Indians that were encamped on Sand Creek were hostile, and not under the protection of the troops at the post." (Clark Dunn testimony, "Sand Creek Massacre," 182.)

"I heard Wynkoop tell some of the chiefs… in case he got word from Curtis not to make peace with them, that he would let them know, so that they could remove out of the way and get to their tribe." (Silas Soule testimony, "Sand Creek Massacre," 28.)

The Indians were "under assurances of perfect safety and protection from the government, given to them by myself. . . . They were perfectly satisfied with the assurances that I had given them." Major Anthony said "he would insure them the same protection as I had." (Edward Wynkoop testimony, "Sand Creek Massacre," 87.)

"I told them I had no authority... to make peace with them." "I never made any offer to the Indians." Scott Anthony testimony. ("Massacre of Cheyenne Indians," 18.)

William P. Minton said he understood that "there should be no hostile parties sent against them..." but "I did not understand that they were to be protected by the troops if attacked; there was nothing of that kind thought of." (William Minton testimony, "Sand Creek Massacre," 148.)

"The day before the attack Major Scott J. Anthony . . . told me that these Indians were hostile." (John Chivington testimony, "Massacre of Cheyenne Indians," 104.)

Sam Colley told Chivington "that he had done everything in his power to make them behave themselves, and that for the last six months he could do nothing with them. That nothing but a severe whipping would bring a lasting peace with them." (John Chivington testimony, "Massacre of Cheyenne Indians," 105.)

How did Sam Colley regard the Indians? "I regarded them as at that time friendly." (Sam Colley testimony, "Chivington Massacre," 28.)

"The chiefs present there had been laboring over a year to keep the peace between the Indians and whites." (Sam Colley testimony, "Massacre of Cheyenne Indians," 15.)

"I now think a little powder and lead is the best food for them." (Sam Colley letter, "Chivington Massacre," 80.)

Sam Colley to George Shoup: "These Indians had violated their treaty," and some should not be punished, but those "affiliated with the hostile Indians we could not discriminate; that no treaty could be made that would be lasting till they were all severely chastised; he also told me where the Indians were camped." (George Shoup testimony, "Sand Creek Massacre," 178.)

The Indians were told "to move in near Fort Lyon, where they could be protected and taken care of," and "they went there with all the assurances in the world of peace promised by the commanding officer." (John Smith testimony, "The Chivington Massacre," 42.)

"The Indians were encamped at the place where they were attacked in full faith and assurance that they would be protected as friendly Indians." (Edmund Guerrier testimony, "Chivington Massacre," 66.)

"I did not understand from any source that the Indians had been placed there at Sand Creek under the protection of the government." (Presley Talbot statement, "Chivington Massacre," 68.)

According to the above statements, the Indians were definitely at peace, definitely at war, unquestionably under US Army protection, and unquestionably not under US Army protection. Which are correct?

There is often a discrepancy in testimony concerning what someone else said, versus what that person actually *said* that he said. For instance, several people claimed Major Anthony gave the Indians promises of peace, while others testified that he did no such thing. Anthony himself swore he did not do anything of the kind. Is it safer to believe someone's perception of what Anthony said, or is it more trustworthy to rely upon what Anthony claims he said?

It is doubtful that all of the memories of those who offered testimony were faulty, but it is possible many or all offered evidence that best served each individual's personal and professional interests.

How Many Indians Were in the Village?
How Many Soldiers Were Present?

The Indians numbered "from 900 to 1,000." (John Chivington report, "Massacre of Cheyenne Indians," 49.)

There were in the camp "about eleven or twelve hundred Indians." "[S]even hundred were warriors." (John Chivington testimony, "Massacre of Cheyenne Indians," 102-03.)

The Indians were "numbering nine hundred or one thousand." (Clark Dunn report, "Massacre of Cheyenne Indians," 55.)

The Indians numbered "from nine hundred to one thousand." (J. J. Kennedy report, "Massacre of Cheyenne Indians," 55.)

The Indians "numbered about 1,100 persons." (Scott Anthony report, "Massacre of Cheyenne Indians," 54.)

The number of Indians were "in the neighborhood of 700 men, women, and children." (Scott Anthony testimony, "Massacre of Cheyenne Indians," 22.)

Doolittle question to Sam Colley: How many Indians were in the camp? "About 500." ("Chivington Massacre," 31.)

Doolittle question to John Smith: How many warriors in the camp? "About 200." ("Chivington Massacre," 41.)

"There were, I think, about eighty lodges." Edmund Guerrier testimony. ("Chivington Massacre," 65.)

"There were from 600 to 800 Indians in all." (Luther Wilson statement, "Chivington Massacre," 67.)

"I think there were six hundred Indians in all." (Robert Bent statement, "Chivington Massacre," 96.)

The Indians numbered "from five hundred to six hundred souls." (James Cannon testimony, "Massacre of Cheyenne Indians," 88.)

In the village there were "not more than 500 souls, two-thirds of which were women and children. " (R. W. Clarke and D. Louderback testimony, "Massacre of Cheyenne Indians," 93.)

"There were not any more women and children in the village at Sand Creek than are usually in Indian villages." (David Louderback testimony, "Sand Creek Massacre," 139.)

Totals for the soldiers were 750 men. (John Chivington report, "Massacre of Cheyenne Indians," 49.)

Chivington had "a command of about 1,000 men." (R. W. Clarke and D. Louderback testimony, "Massacre of Cheyenne Indians," 93.)

Chivington had "about one thousand men." (James Cannon testimony, "Massacre of Cheyenne Indians," 88.)

Chivington had "between 800 and 1,000 men in this command." (John Smith testimony, "Massacre of Cheyenne Indians," 6.)

"The command consisted of from nine hundred to one thousand men." (Robert Bent statement, "The Chivington Massacre," 96.)

Watson Beach counted them as they left Fort Lyon; there were "640 men in the ranks." (Coffin, *Sand Creek*, 17.)

"Our regiment had about five hundred men, as, when we got orders to move, a lot of soldiers were home on leave of absence and were not notified in time to join us." (Breakenridge, *Helldorado*, 47.)

Regarding the matters of how many Indians were in the Sand Creek village, and how many soldiers attacked them there, there is a definite division between the pro-Chivington personnel (who overestimated the numbers of Indians), and the anti-Chivington crowd (who overestimated the number of soldiers).

Were There Flags in the Indian Camp?

"Black Kettle ran this American flag up to the top of his lodge, with a small white flag tied right under it." (John Smith testimony, "Massacre of Cheyenne Indians," 5.)

"I saw no flag of any kind among the Indians." (Luther Wilson statement, "Chivington Massacre," 67.)

"I did not see any flags displayed by the Indians." (Presley Talbot statement, "Chivington Massacre," 68.)

"I did not see any flag over the village, but afterwards saw a man with a small flag, who said he got it out of a lodge. I saw no person advancing with a white flag, but I think I should have seen it had it happened." (Jacob Downing statement, "Chivington Massacre," 70.)

"I did not see any kind of a flag in the Indian camp Caleb." (Caleb Burdsal statement, "Chivington Massacre," 72.)

"[A great deal had been said about a white flag—about the Indians sending out a white flag, a flag of truce. I saw none." (Stephen Decatur testimony, "Sand Creek Massacre," 200.)

"I saw someone with a white flag approaching our lines, and the troops fired upon it." "After the fight I saw the United States flag in the Indian camp." (Joseph Cramer statement, "Chivington Massacre," 74.)

"I looked towards Black Kettle's Lodge and he had [a] Flag on [a] Lodge pole in front of his Lodge. Just than the Soldiers opened fire from all sides of the Village." (George Bent letter, "Letters of George Bent to George Hyde," March 15, 1905.)

Little Bear hurried through the village and "as I ran by Black Kettle's Lodge he had Flag tied to [the] Lodge Pole and was holding it." (Little Bear statement to George Bent, "Letters of George Bent to George Hyde," April 14, 1906.)

"I saw the American flag waving and heard Black Kettle tell the Indians to stand round the flag." (Robert Bent statement, "Chivington Massacre," 96.)

"I saw none during the fight; I saw one in camp after the fight." (Joseph Cramer testimony, "Sand Creek Massacre," 50.)

Did you see an American flag? "Yes, at the lower end of the village." (Naman Snyder testimony, "Sand Creek Massacre," 77.)

Did you see any white flag? "I did not." (Alexander Safely testimony, "Sand Creek Massacre," 221.)

"I saw a camp of Indians, and the stars and stripes waving over the camp." (George Roan testimony, "Sand Creek Massacre," 142.)

"Permit me to say that these statements (about flags) are unqualifiedly false." (Milo Slater statement, "Indian Troubles," Bancroft Library.)

Was an American flag or a white flag seen in Black Kettle's village? Slightly more witnesses indicated they had not seen any flags before or during the event than those who claimed otherwise. If someone testified to seeing a white flag, it would be reasonable to conclude that there was one. Not seeing one, however, does not mean there was no white flag, but only that that individual did not see a white flag. Of course, each account could be a function of self-interest as much as the simple truth.

Were the Indians Scalped and Mutilated?

"I never saw anything of that; and I never heard it until I saw" the affidavits. (Scott Anthony testimony, "Massacre of Cheyenne Indians," 26.)

"I did not see a body of a man, woman, or child but was scalped; and in many instances their bodies were mutilated." (James Cannon testimony, "Massacre of Cheyenne Indians," 88-89.)

"I saw some of the first Colorado regiment committing some very bad acts there on the persons of Indians, and I likewise saw some of the one-hundred-day men in the same kind of business." (John Smith testimony, "Chivington Massacre," 42.)

"I heard men say they had cut out the privates, but did not see it myself. It was the 3rd Colorado men who did these things." (Amos Miksch statement, "Chivington Massacre," 75.)

"I saw no soldier scalping anybody." "I saw no scalps or other parts of the person among the command on our return." (Jacob Downing statement, "Chivington Massacre," 70.)

"I saw in the hands of a good many of the privates a great many scalps, or parts of scalps . . . as many as a hundred scalps." (Simeon Whiteley statement, "Chivington Massacre," 71.)

"Everyone I saw dead was scalped." (Robert Bent statement, "Chivington Massacre," 96.)

Question on February 17, 1865: Did you [Silas Soule] witness any scalping and mutilating of Indians? Reply: "I did." (Silas Soule testimony, "Sand Creek Massacre," 14.)

Question on February 20, 1865: Did you [Silas Soule] witness any scalping and mutilating of Indians? Reply: "I think not." (Silas Soule testimony, "Sand Creek Massacre," 23.)

"White Antelope was the only one I saw that was otherwise mutilated." "I saw several men scalping." (James Beckwourth testimony, "Sand Creek Massacre," 70-71.)

Question: Was there scalping and mutilating? "It was very near a general thing." (James Cannon testimony, "Sand Creek Massacre," 112.)

"I heard one man say that he had cut a woman's private parts out, and had them for exhibition on a stick." (James Cannon statement January 16, 1865, "Sand Creek Massacre," 129.)

"I heard one man say he had cut a squaw's heart out, and he had it stuck up on a stick." (James Cannon testimony, March 28, 1865, "Sand Creek Massacre," 113.)

"I saw one or two men who were in the act of scalping, but I am not positive." (George Shoup testimony, "Sand Creek Massacre," 177.)

"I do not think I saw any but what was scalped; saw fingers cut off, saw several bodies with privates cut off, women as well as men." (Lucien Palmer statement, "Chivington Massacre," 74.)

The propensity to recall either extensive scalping or very little scalping largely depended upon whether the witness one was a pro- or anti-Chivington man. Also, as has been previously noted, testimony on this issue changed with time and circumstances.

Were There White Scalps in the Village?

"I never heard a word about a white woman's scalp being found in the camp until afterwards." (Scott Anthony testimony, "Massacre of Cheyenne Indians," 26.)

"I saw them take therefrom [the tipis] a number of white person's scalps—men's women's, and children's." (Stephen Decatur testimony, "Sand Creek Massacre," 195.)

"I saw a good many of white scalps there. Some were not very old. The fresh scalp was from a red haired man." (Thaddeus P. Bell testimony, "Sand Creek Massacre," 223.)

"I was shown, by my chief surgeon, the scalp of a white man taken from the lodge of one of the chiefs, which could not have been more than two or three days taken." (John Chivington report, "Massacre of Cheyenne Indians," 48.)

"We found in the camp the scalps of nineteen white persons." (John Chivington testimony, "Massacre of Cheyenne Indians," 104.)

"In the Indian camp I saw one new scalp, a white man's, and two old ones." Luther Wilson testimony. ("Chivington Massacre," 67.)

I saw "five or six scalps he had in his hand. I should judge, from a casual look, that they were the scalps of white persons." The hair was white and sandy brown. "My impression is that one or two of them were not more than ten days off the head." (Caleb Burdsal testimony, "Sand Creek Massacre," 203-04.)

"In these same tents we found a dozen or more scalps of white people." (Howbert, *Indians of Pike's Peak*, 110.)

"It is a mistake that there were any white scalps found in the village." (Joseph Cramer statement, "Chivington Massacre," 74.)

Were white scalps found in the village? As with the case of the flags, it is reasonable to conclude that if several people saw them, the scalps existed, and that those who did not see them simply missed seeing them. Then again, some witnesses may have had something to gain or lose buy affirming or denying the presence of flags or scalps. What is important is to avoid choosing the testimony that confirms our biases and dismiss the non-confirmatory evidence.

How Many Indians Were Killed?

"Between five and six hundred Indians were left dead upon the field." (John Chivington report, "Massacre of Cheyenne Indians," 49.)

The number of Indians killed was "about 175 to 200." (Hal Sayr testimony, "Massacre of Cheyenne Indians," 52.)

"I think about seventy or eighty, including men, women, and children, were killed." (John Smith testimony, "Chivington Massacre," 42.)

"There were one hundred and forty-eight killed and missing [and] about sixty were men—the balance women and children." (Edmund Guerrier testimony, "Chivington Massacre," 66.)

"There were some five hundred or six hundred Indians killed." (Jacob Downing statement, "Chivington Massacre," 70.)

"I should judge there were between 400 and 500 Indians killed." "I think about half the killed were women and children." (Asbury Bird statement, "Chivington Massacre," 72.)

Downing counted two hundred Indians killed, but only "about twelve or fifteen women, and a few children." (Jacob Downing statement, "Chivington Massacre," 70.)

"I counted 130 bodies, all dead." (Lucien Palmer statement, "Chivington Massacre," 74.)

The loss of Indians was "from one hundred and twenty-five to one hundred and seventy-five killed." (Joseph Cramer statement, "Chivington Massacre," 73.)

"Saw sixty-nine dead Indians." (Silas Soule testimony, "Sand Creek Massacre," p. 11.)

Question: How many dead Indians did you see? Reply: "Two hundred." (Naman Snyder testimony, "Sand Creek Massacre," 77.)

Question: How many Indians were killed? Reply: "About two hundred, all told." (James Cannon testimony, "Sand Creek Massacre," 111.)

"I counted four hundred and fifty dead Indian warriors." (Stephen Decatur testimony, "Sand Creek Massacre," 195.)

Question: How many Indians were killed? Reply: "I should say about three hundred." (George Shoup testimony, "Sand Creek Massacre," 176.)

"One-half were men, and, the balance were women and children. I do not think that I saw more than 70 lying dead." (John Smith testimony, "Massacre of Cheyenne Indians," 9.)

"The loss to the Indians was about three hundred killed." (Scott Anthony report, "Massacre of Cheyenne Indians," 54.)

"[T]here were not over 125 killed." (Scott Anthony testimony, "Massacre of Cheyenne Indians," 22).

"I counted 123 dead bodies; I think not over twenty-five were full-grown men." (Amos Miksch statement, "Chivington Massacre," 75.)

Once again, testimony varied depending upon the witness's assessment of Chivington, or how the witness wanted to be perceived. Officers generally inflated Indian causalities, perhaps to improve their reputations as Indian fighters. Anti-Chivington men, however, offered lower numbers, perhaps to support the idea that the soldiers were not efficient killers. By doing so, they also eroded the idea that a massacre had taken place. One officer, Major Scott Anthony, once testified that 300 Indians had been killed, but later decreased that number to 125.

How Did the Soldiers Attack?

"They came on a charge." (John Smith testimony, "Chivington Massacre," 41.)

John Smith was trading "in One Eye's Lodge at the time when Chivington's men charge[d] through the Village." (George Bent letter to Hyde, January 20, 1915.)

"[W]e proceeded through the village on a walk. I think the town at this time was entirely deserted by the Indians, as not one was to be seen thereabouts, though plenty were not far away." (Coffin, *Sand Creek*, 19.)

"I went to Major Anthony, who had his battalion in line, and, under the supposition that he was going to charge the village with his cavalry, advised him not to do it, believing that the horses were liable to become entangled among the ropes and fall." "Most of the command were dismounted, and fought in that way." (Jacob Downing statement, "Chivington Massacre," 70.)

According to the testimony of two non-soldiers, the cavalry charged into the village; two soldiers, however, claimed they had simply walked in.

The Death of White Antelope

"White Antelope was the first Indian killed, within a hundred yards of where I was in camp at the time." (John Smith testimony, "Chivington Massacre," 41.)

"Left Hand (White Antelope?) stood with his hands folded across his breast, until he was shot saying: 'Soldiers no hurt me—soldiers my friends.'" (Joseph Cramer letter to Edward Wynkoop, Roberts and Halaas, *Written in Blood*, 27)

"White Antelope . . . never left his Lodge and was Killed in front of his Lodge. Black Kettle ask[ed] him to come on with him but [he] said he would not leave and sung [his] death song." (George Bent letter to Hyde, April 25, 1906.)

White Antelope "came running out to meet the command at the time the battle commenced, holding up his hands and saying 'Stop! Stop!' He spoke it in as plain English as I can. He stopped and folded his arms until shot down." (James Beckwourth testimony, "Sand Creek Massacre," 70.)

"White Antelope and Stand-in-the-Water started to their lodges, got their guns, came back, and commenced firing at the troops. Both of them were killed within fifty yards of each other; White Antelope was killed in the bed of the creek and Stand-in-the-Water was killed right opposite to him." (David Louderback testimony, "Sand Creek Massacre," 137-38.)

"About the first Indian killed was the head chief, White Antelope. Duncan Kerr, the scout, killed him." (Breakenridge, *Helldorado*, 55.)

"He (White Antelope) came running directly towards Company H; he had a pistol in his left hand, and a bow with some arrows in his right. He got within about fifty yards of the company; he commenced shooting his pistol, still in his left hand." "I got off and fired at the Indian, the ball taking effect in the groin. . . . Billy Henderson . . . shot the Indian through the head." (Alexander F. Safely testimony, "Sand Creek Massacre," 221.)

According to this testimony, White Antelope did not move from the front of his tipi, and he made an armed attack on the approaching soldiers. The stories of course are irreconcilable. Which one we choose as the "truth" could depend upon our predilections. Can we somehow split the extremes and pick something in between? That solution, of course, does not necessarily discover the truth.

Did Men of the First Colorado Fire Their Weapons?

"Officers of the first regiment told me they did not fire a gun, and would not or could not." (Sam Colley testimony, "Chivington Massacre," 30.)

"I swore I would not burn powder, and I did not." (Joseph Cramer letter to Edward Wynkoop, Roberts and Halaas, "Written in Blood," 27.)

"[S]everal times during the fight I ordered my men to cease firing." (Joseph Cramer testimony, "Sand Creek Massacre," 49.)

"I refused to fire, and swore that none but a coward would." (Silas Soule letter to Edward Wynkoop, Roberts and Halaas, "Written in Blood," 25.)

Major Anthony moved us "within about one hundred yards of the lodges, and ordered us to open fire; some firing done." (Silas Soule testimony, "Sand Creek Massacre," 11.)

"I don't ask you to shoot, but follow me and we will mix in this fuss and go through it." (Soule's words according to Jesse Haire.)

The testimony offered by Soule and Cramer is contradictory. How should we reconcile this?

What Did Chivington Say About Killing Prisoners?

"Don't ask me; you know my orders; I want no prisoners." (Joseph Cramer statement, "Chivington Massacre," 74.)

"I heard him say we must not allow John Smith and family, father of Jack Smith, to be harmed." (George Shoup testimony, "Sand Creek Massacre," 177.)

"I have given my instructions; have told my men not to take any prisoners." (Scott Anthony testimony, "Massacre of Cheyenne Indians," 22.)

In this instance, two officers heard they were not to take prisoners, while one claimed they were instructed not to harm at least some of the prisoners.

* * *

Reading the testimony, which runs about 400 printed pages, is an exercise in futility and frustration. It seems at this late date impossible to determine the truth of the matter because there is so much firsthand evidence that conflicts.

Several years ago, the author was involved in an exchange of e-mails with another man regarding which witnesses were telling the truth, and which witnesses were lying. The specific subjects of the testimony were whether there was an American flag flying over the village, and whether or not white scalps had been found there. The author contended that if one accepts a witnesses's claim that he saw a flag, one must also accept the testimony of those who claimed they saw scalps. It would be inconsistent to accept or deny a witness's testimony based upon any personal feelings about them. The other e-mailer, however, adamantly insisted that the witnesses who claimed they saw scalps were "thugs, lowlifes, criminals," all animated by self-interest, while those who denied there were scalps and claimed they saw an American flag were somehow honest, upright, pillars of the community.

This disagreement encapsulates the entire Sand Creek controversy. Many or most of us who have studied or read about Sand Creek have already picked out our heroes and villains, and no amount of "fact" or "logic" will change our mindset. This is a rather disturbing conclusion, and one supported by many studies conducted over the last half-century.

The fact is that humans generally make poor witnesses. We are all biased, have poor or shifting memory, and we are often illogical, irrational, and ill-equipped to do much about it depending upon the circumstances. Our truths are individual and relative. The same was true with our ancestors.

Chapter 19

Battle or Massacre?
The Fallacy of the False Dichotomy

the time of this writing, the most recent book to examine Sand Creek is a collection of essays entitled *Battles and Massacres on the Southwest Frontier*. This book undeniably places the engagement in the massacre category. One of the contributors, Ari Kelman, examines the historical angle and makes a reasonably good case that it was indeed a massacre. Still, it is not difficult to notice that he had a proclivity to use the testimony to prove a point.[1]

For instance, in his use of Silas Soule's court testimony, Kelman references Soule's statement that he saw soldiers with scalps, but omits Soule's later statement that he did not see any soldiers scalping Indians. Kelman quotes Sam Tappan's statement that the barbarism of Sand Creek culminated in Soule's assassination. However, he does not identify Tappan or note that he was the president of the military inquiry. Instead, he describes that important player only as "one federal official looking into Sand Creek." Tappan's attitude and his position are germane to the investigation. Kelman also went on to note that after Soule's death, he was "unavailable to provide further testimony." This is obviously true. What was left unsaid was that his death did not impact the

---

1 Richard K. Wetherington and Frances Levine, eds., *Battles and Massacres on the Southwestern Frontier: Historical and Archaeological Perspectives* (Norman, OK, 2014).

information he could have shared because Soule completed his testimony a month before he was killed.[2]

This use of select pieces of testimony could be a conscious attempt to steer readers toward the conclusion favored by Kelman. Or, it could be just a matter of space limitation that would not allow for a complete discussion of relevant matters. More likely, however, this is the work of the subconscious mind, implicit memory, confirmation bias, and other psychological factors going about their stealthy business—all of which will be examined in more detail in Section Three.

In addition to Kelman's historical assessment of Sand Creek, there is an archaeological perspective on Sand Creek by Doug Scott, a superb historian and archeologist. Scott has investigated and written on many different events in attempts to discover, among other things, the accuracy of the relationships of the historical record to the physical record. His work on the Little Big Horn, for example, is ground-breaking. As far as he his concerned, Sand Creek "unequivocally qualifies as a massacre."[3]

Scott makes many good arguments, but there are other points to also consider. He discovered that there was a striking absence of firearm calibers likely to have been used by the Cheyenne or Arapaho. "Few bullets in trade gun calibers or firearm types known to have been issued as annuity items are present," he observed, "thus supporting earlier conclusions that the Indians offered little resistance to the soldiers' attack."[4]

On its face, this sounds reasonable. But what if the absence of firearm evidence in the village and on the retreat route has another explanation—like many of the Indians used bows and arrows instead of other weapons? By examining the soldier casualties in the appendix, we can see that of the 76 casualties, 29 were attributed to a specific weapon. Of those 29, 16 were from arrows and 13 were from bullets. Perhaps a valid explanation for the dearth of firearm evidence was not entirely that the Indians put up little resistance, but that in more than half the cases, they inflicted damage with arrows, and not firearms. This also demolishes the contention some have made that most of the

2   Ari Kelman, "What's in a Name? The Fight to Call Sand Creek a Battle or a Massacre," in Wetherington and Levine, ed., *Battles and Massacres on the Southwestern Frontier*, 123.

3   Douglas D. Scott, "Reassessing the Meaning of Artifact Patterning," in Wetherington and Levine, eds., *Battles and Massacres on the Southwestern Frontier*, 147.

4   Scott, "Artifact Patterning," 144.

soldier casualties were self-inflicted via "friendly fire." It is also important to note that both sides are susceptible to "friendly fire." It is therefore reasonable to conclude that if some of the soldiers shot themselves, so did some of the Indians.

Scott also observed that, "Among the contemporary and survivor accounts of the fight, from both sides, there is little disagreement that the affair was very one-sided," and that among the accounts "there is general agreement that the Colorado soldiers attacked a protected camp." The Sand Creek affair may well have been very one-sided and the camp "protected," but the eyewitness accounts in no way agreed on these points. If anything, one is struck after a careful reading of the records sampled above by the great disagreement over these very assertions.[5]

Scott also observes that one can discern the difference between a battle and a massacre by the numbers engaged, and by the wounded-to-killed ratios. It makes sense that in a massacre, the number of killed would exceed the number of wounded. So how many Indians were killed and wounded at Sand Creek? As already demonstrated, the estimates in the number of Indians killed ranges from about 70 to as many as 600, with most estimates falling in the 150 range. How many Indians were wounded? It appears as though estimates on that issue do not exist, or at least they have never been found and published. We can estimate the number of Indians killed, but we have no idea of the number of Indians wounded. How, then, can we draw conclusions about the ratios of wounded to killed and whether that indicates a battle or a massacre?

We will have more success in using the soldiers as an example. Studies of conventional warfare demonstrate that the wounded-to-killed ratio can be from two-to-one (two wounded for every man killed) to as many as five-to-one (five wounded to every man killed). In recent conflicts, the number has been estimated as high as 13-to-one, with the high modern ratios mostly the result of expeditious battlefield evacuation, expert medical treatment, and body armor. More wounded survive today than they did in the nineteenth century.[6] Scott suggests that in conventional warfare, the wounded-to-killed ratio should be

5   Scott, "Artifact Patterning," 147-48.

6   "Statistical Summary of America's Major Wars," www.civilwarhome.com/warstats.htm (accessed July 13, 2014); "Costs of War," http://costsofwar.org/article/us-and-allied-wounded accessed July 13, 2014; "Mortality associated with use of weapons in armed conflicts, wartime atrocities, and civilian mass shootings: literature review," www.bmi.com/contents/319/7207/407, accessed July 13, 2014.

about five-to-one. We don't know the Indian warfare wounded and killed rates, but we can be certain they were not be anything near that ratio. For example, Billy Breakenridge and Morse Coffin estimated the numbers of soldiers marching out of Fort Lyon to be from 500 to 650. Let's reasonably assume the number was 600. We must then subtract Soule's and Cramer's companies from the mix because we know they did not actively take part in any hard fighting. That knocks out roughly another 100 men, leaving about 500 soldiers who were actively engaged in fighting at Sand Creek.

Historians have had a penchant for undercounting the soldier casualties at Sand Creek. According to Scott, 10 soldiers were killed and 38 wounded.[7] Based on a thorough assessment of the official reports, newspapers, letters, and other documents, the number appears to be 24 killed and 52 wounded. This is a big difference. Scott claims, for example, that "The percentages of soldier dead (1.4 percent) and wounded (6 percent) are far more typical of conventional war, even in a one-sided battle, thus reinforcing by scientific methods the interpretation of the Sand Creek event as a war crime and massacre."[8]

However, it appears as though there were about 500 soldiers engaged in the fighting and not 700, and 76 total casualties instead of 48. If so, then five percent of the soldiers engaged were killed and ten percent were wounded. That's about a two-to-one ratio. If a five-to-one (wounded-to-killed) ratio is the norm, then it appears that the soldiers were the ones who were massacred at Sand Creek.

It might also be better to use Civil War-era statistics than comparing Sand Creek fighting with battle in Afghanistan in the twenty-first century. Trevor Depuy, who devoted years to military studies about numbers and war, stated that during the Civil War, which for the most part was a conventional fight, the North lost 2.1 men killed for every 100 engaged.[9] The Civil War-era troopers at Sand Creek lost five killed for every 100 engaged. Does this mean they were massacred?

What all of this illustrates is that a historian can reach just about any conclusion and support it with statistics. How you use them is important. As historians, we can't fire hundreds of bullets into the side of a barn and then draw

---

7   Scott, "Artifact Patterning," 135.

8   Ibid., 149.

9   Colonel Trevor N. Depuy, *The Evolution of Weapons and Warfare* (New York, 1980), 171.

a bull's eye around the spot with the most bullet holes to show the accuracy of the men pulling the trigger. For a valid test, the bull's eye would have be painted onto the side of the barn before pulling a trigger.[10]

If someone believes a massacre took place at Sand Creek, it is not difficult to set parameters accordingly, sift through the evidence, and find proof of a massacre. The same is true if you believe a battle was fought there. The task of trying to determine the truth from the preponderance of the evidence, scrupulously collected and studied with the best of intentions, cannot be divorced from one's predilections. Historians and archaeologists are trapped to some degree by forces we cannot control, and often we do not realize these forces are influencing our research and writing.

In the end, it seems as though no matter how hard we try, we cannot extricate ourselves from the battle vs. massacre quagmire. And therein lies the ultimate conundrum, because the question itself is fallacious to begin with. Asking whether Sand Creek was a battle or massacre is a false dichotomous question. As historian David Hackett Fischer notes, the dichotomous question is divided into two parts—mutually exclusive with no overlap, no opening in the middle, and nothing possible beyond either end. According to Fischer, it is rare that any two historical terms can be so related unless one is specifically defined as the negation of the other. The law of the excluded middle, he continues, might demand obedience in formal logic, but in history it just doesn't cut it. The dichotomous historical question is false because it is "constructed so that it demands a choice between two answers which are in fact not exclusive or not exhaustive."[11]

Fischer makes his point by listing a number of book titles, including *Napoleon III: Enlightened Statesman or Proto-Fascist?*; *The Abolitionists: Reformers or Fanatics?*; *Plato: Totalitarian or Democrat?*; *The Robber Barons: Pirates or Pioneers?*; *The Medieval Mind: Faith or Reason?*; *Martin Luther: Reformer or Revolutionary?*; *The Dred Scott Decision: Law or Politics?*; *What is History—Fact or Fancy?*

These, and more like them, drive Fischer to distraction. According to Fischer, they are unsatisfactory, grossly anachronistic, very shallow, imprecise, and ambiguous. They are evidence of a "faulty pedagogical practice" that encourages "simple-minded moralizing." He sympathizes with the poor

10 Gary Smith, "How to Lie with Statistics," *Skeptic*, Vol. 19, no. 4 (2014), 47.

11 David Hackett Fischer, *Historians' Fallacies: Toward a Logic of Historical Thought* (New York, 1970), 9-10.

students faced with such false dichotomies. Does the student try to demonstrate that dichotomous terms can coexist, demonstrate that there is a third possibility, or repudiate one or the other or both propositions? Fischer believes the questions serve only to shackle the student to false options, and the best response is to try to indicate the serious problem of structural deficiencies in the question as it is framed.[12]

So Sand Creek could have been a conventional battle, a massacre, both, or something in between. As we have seen, even those who were there did not agree. It is important to be mindful of the challenges facing historians who are trying to explain complicated events.

[12] Ibid., 11-12.

PART III:
THE END OF HISTORY

Chapter 20

Eyewitness Testimony

Eyewitness testimony provided the foundation of the three hearings about Sand Creek. Although a significant portion of the testimony was not from actual eyewitnesses, but from so-called experts or other interested parties, the fact finders were supposed to build the base on a rigorous examination of those who had seen the events with their own eyes. After all, the American jurisprudence system, including military courts, is built upon eyewitness testimony.

There is little that is more convincing to a jury than a witness who is confident, consistent, and certain that he saw what he saw and that he heard what he heard. According to the U.S. Supreme Court, the "level of certainty of the witness" was usually the most important factor in gaining a conviction. Psychologists who testify about the memories of witnesses, however, claim that "an eyewitness's confidence is not a good predictor of his or her identification accuracy." In fact, mistaken eyewitness identifications confidently presented to the jury are the main cause of more than 75 percent of wrongful convictions.[1]

A large body of research demonstrates that eyewitness testimony is not as reliable as we think. According to Professor Richard Wiseman, "the truth of the

---

1 Christopher Chabris and Daniel Simons, *The Invisible Gorilla: How Other Ways Our Intuitions Deceive Us* (New York, NY, 2009), 111-12.

matter is that, without realizing it, we tend to misremember what has happened right in front of our eyes and frequently omit the most important details."[2]

A classic example of this phenomenon is the "invisible gorilla" experiment. One version of this at Cornell University had students watch a one-minute film with two basketball teams, one wearing white uniforms, and one wearing black. The teams passed a basketball back and forth and the students were asked to count the passes. In the middle of the short movie, a student in a full-body gorilla suit walks into the middle of the players, faces the camera, thumps her chest, and walks off after spending about nine seconds on camera. The actual number of basketball passes was irrelevant because the real test was to see how many people saw the gorilla. One might think such an interruption in the middle of the scene would be like a pie hitting the viewer in the face. In fact, fully one-half of the witnesses saw nothing but teams passing a basketball. When asked if they saw the gorilla, many answered, "A what?"[3]

A related phenomenon is referred to as "weapon focus." It would be like a witness in the gorilla experiment seeing only the gorilla and none of the basketball players. For example, one test involved a staged fight by two students. The test ended with a gun held by one of the students going off and the other student falling to the floor. The teacher, a German criminologist, halted the proceedings, explained the test, and quizzed the students about what they had seen. Most of the students could not recall who had been involved in the "fight," what the students looked like, what they wore, or what they had argued about only a few minutes after watching the test. What they did remember, however, was the gun. Their minds had focused on what they believed to be the most important issue—and forgot much of the rest.[4]

Research psychologists have been intensively studying the reliability of eyewitness testimony since the early 1980s. The studies have included staging mock crimes and asking the witnesses to identify the perpetrators from photos, testing interviewing techniques, and trying to learn if eyewitnesses could be misled by questions after the event. One test conducted on television staged a purse-snatching event and asked viewers to identify the thief from a six-person lineup. Some 1,800 of the 2,000 respondents identified the wrong man. The

2   Richard Wiseman, *Paranormality: Why We See What Isn't There* (Lexington, KY, 2010), 72.

3   Chabris and Simons, *Invisible Gorilla*, 6-7.

4   Wiseman, *Paranormality*, 71.

studies demonstrate that eyewitness testimony can run the gamut from reasonably accurate to completely worthless.[5]

So what does all this say about memories? If every memory can be called into question, how does that affect the memories of the Sand Creek participants of their own actions and of the actions they witnessed?

We have already read how some of Edward Wynkoop's recollections changed over time. Let us consider George Bent, who provided about the only surviving testimony (with the exception of short statements from Edmund Guerrier) we have from the Indian side of events. Bent corresponded voluminously with George Bird Grinnell and George E. Hyde during the first two decades of the 20th century. His letters are a treasure of information about Indian life on the frontier during the mid-1800s. However, they were written four and five decades after the events.

Bent wrote twice to Hyde about the number of Arapaho who were in the Sand Creek camp. In March 1905, he claimed there were 15 lodges of Arapaho and only four individuals managed to escape. Eight years later in April 1913, he wrote that there were only seven Arapaho lodges in the camp and that three individuals escaped. As to the number of Indians captured, Bent wrote Hyde in March 1905 that Colonel Chivington took nine prisoners (six women and three children). In October 1916, Bent wrote to Grinnell that the soldiers captured three women and three children—two Cheyenne women and two children from the lodges, and one Arapaho woman and one child from the sand pits.

In the winter of 1865, many Indians were raiding along the South Platte River. There, they attacked and killed a band of soldiers, or ex-soldiers, heading east. According to Bent, among the soldiers' possessions were scalps of Indians who had been killed at Sand Creek. In March 1905, he told Hyde they found two scalps. A year later, he wrote and added information that the two scalps belonged to White Leave and Little Wolf. Seven years later in December 1913, Bent wrote to Grinnell that only one scalp had been found, and it belonged to an Indian named Coyote.

Bent offered differing numbers for prisoners and scalps. Which should we accept as correct, and why? It does not appear that Bent had anything to gain or lose by relating these recollections. Instead, his letters demonstrate a malleable

---

5   Ibid., 72; Kathryn Foxhall, "Suddenly, a Big Impact on Criminal Justice," *American Psychological Association* (January 2000), no. 1, accessed January 29, 2014, www.apa.org/monitor/jan00/pi4.aspx.

George Bent, the mixed blood son of William Bent and the Cheyenne, Owl Woman, offered the most complete description of the Sand Creek incident from the Indian perspective. *History Colorado, Denver, Colorado*

memory that subconsciously changed with each retelling. Different motivations may have influenced Bent's 1913 letter to Hyde that 53 men and 110 women were killed at Sand Creek. Contrast those numbers with Colonel Chivington's 500, or John Smith's significantly lower 80. Bent did not remain in the area to do any counting. Instead, he garnered the numbers from the reports of others who may or may not have had their own incentives to inflate or deflate the casualty figures.[6]

We like to believe that our memories are exact accounts of what we witnessed, but that is not the case. According to psychology professors Christopher Chabris and Daniel Simons, "What we retrieve often is filled in based on gist, inference, and other influences," more like a vague melody than a digital recording. "We mistakenly believe that our memories are accurate and precise, and we cannot readily separate those aspects of our memory that accurately happened and those that were introduced later."[7]

6   Bent, "Letters of George Bent to George E. Hyde"; George Bent, "The Letters of George Bent to George Bird Grinnell, 1901-1918." Southwest Museum, Los Angeles, CA.

7   Chabris, *Invisible Gorilla*, 62–63.

Chapter 21

False Memories

Even eyewitnesses have a tough time accurately recalling things they see, but what may be worse for historians is when eyewitnesses recall things they never saw in the first place, which may be the case with some of what have come down to us as Sand Creek "facts."

Most people have had what are called "flashbulb" memories— recollections of where they were, who they were with, and what they were doing when something very important or memorable took place. For those of us alive during the past half-century or more, the assassination of President John F. Kennedy offered a powerful "flashbulb" moment, as did the catastrophic Challenger explosion or the Islamic terrorist attacks on 9-11 against the World Trade Centers in New York, the Pentagon in Washington, D.C., and the downing of Flight 93 in a Pennsylvania field. Memories of these sorts of events (which are typically disasters) are vividly recalled days, months, and years after they take place. Unfortunately, even these vivid memories may be wrong.

Karim Nader, a neuroscientist at McGill University in Montreal, was in New York when the World Trade Center was hit. He later said he "knew" he had seen a video of the first plane hitting the north tower as it happened, but was completely surprised when he later learned that no such footage aired that day. Two years later, a study of more than 500 college students found that 73 percent of them shared the same mistaken perception as Nader. According to Harvard psychology professor Daniel L. Schacter, "Memories are imaginative reconstructions of past events" shaped by the person's attitude, expectations, and general knowledge. People construct their own subjective realities.[1]

Nader's studies show that the very act of remembering can alter our memories. Memory is malleable, and whenever something is rethought, it can and often does change. People may have gotten the day wrong when they recalled the film of the plane striking the tower, but it can be much worse than that. Hundreds perhaps thousands of people remember seeing the footage of United Flight 93 crashing into the countryside in Pennsylvania. No such film exists. The memory is a fusion of various images implanted in our brains of a visual that never occurred.

The Flight 93 case is reflected in many experiments that have shown such fusion to be a natural occurrence. A test group read a list of words including candy, sugar, taste, honey, cake, sour, chocolate, and so on. Only minutes later, most people when asked believed that the word "sweet" was on the list. It was not. The experimenters wrote that the "people not only believe that sweet was on the list, but claim to remember it vividly."[2]

Profound events can even change an individual's perceptions. Consider how the assassination of President Kennedy changed people's views of him. He barely won the election of 1960 over Richard Nixon with only 49.7 percent of the vote. In the years after the assassination, however, two-thirds of all Americans insisted they had voted for him. Are they purposely lying or is their memory simply wrong?[3]

Even though "flashbulb" memories are lucidly recalled, and subjects will believe strongly in their accuracy, the accuracy as it pertains to the details of an event inevitably decays over time. False memories can be plainly recalled also, but they can become stronger over time. Perhaps it was your high school reunion. Your friends have told you so many times what a memorable evening it

1   Chabris and Simons, *The Invisible Gorilla*, 62-63; Daniel L. Schacter, *Searching for Memory: The Brain, the Mind, and the Past* (New York, NY, 1996), 40, 101, 200.

2   Greg Miller, "How Our Brains Make Memories: Surprising New Research about the Act of Remembering May Help People with Post-Traumatic Stress Disorder," *Smithsonian Magazine* (May 2010), accessed January 29, 2014, www.smithsonianmag.com/science-nature/how-our-brains-make-memories-14466850/; Tara Thean, "Remember That? No You Don't. Study Shows False Memories Afflict Us All," Time (November 19, 2013), accessed January 29, 2014, http://science.time.com/2013/11/19/remember-that-no- you-don't-study-shows-false-memories-afflict-us-all; Schacter, *Searching for Memory*, 103.

3   Linda Shopes, "Making Sense of Oral History," *Oral History in a Digital Age*, accessed February 10, 2014, http://ohda.matrix.msu.edu/2012/08/making-sense-of-oral-history/.

was, especially when the old prom queen dropped the cake on the floor. You laugh with them as you recall every detail. However, you forgot that you didn't go to that reunion because you were home with the flu. You've heard the stories so often that you've incorporated them as your own.

So the very act of remembering can change a person's memories. According to researcher Nader, "When you retell it, the memory becomes plastic, and whatever is present around you in the environment can interfere with the original content of the memory."[4]

Humans believe their memories contain exact accounts of what they saw and heard. According to psychology professors Christopher Chabris and Daniel Simons, however, "What we retrieve often is filled in based on gist, inference, and other influences," more like a vague melody than a digital recording. "We mistakenly believe that our memories are accurate and precise, and we cannot readily separate those aspects of our memory that accurately happened and those that were introduced later." In other words, vivid memories can lead us to forget their actual source, and we can assume memory details came from our own experience. This could account for some Sand Creek witnesses who testified about specific events that they could not have seen or heard themselves. Their emotions mixed with other peoples' memories, and by doing so made memories of their own.

Since so many of our memories never happened as was believe and we will often unknowingly concoct them, how susceptible are we when others deliberately try to manipulate our recollections?

---

4 James Gorman, "Scientists Trace Memories of Things That Never Happened," *New York Times* (July 25, 2013), accessed January 29, 2014, www.nytimes.com/2013/07/26/science/false-memory-planted-in-a-mouse-brain-study-shows.html?_r=0; Miller, "How Our Brains Make Memories," May 2010.

Chapter 22

Leading Questions and Lies

discussed in prior chapters, eyewitness testimony is less reliable than most people think, and its use raises many significant issues. This, of course, is also true for the events that unfolded at Sand Creek, so a firm understanding of the fallibility of eyewitness accounts is important.

Every attorney knows that in most cases, leading questions are not allowed on direct examination of a witness because the manner in which a question is asked will prompt or imply the desired answer. For example, "Where were you when the defendant murdered the victim?" implies the defendant is guilty of murder, when that may be the underlying purpose of the trial itself.

Recounting events to police can also be problematic. How did the police question the witness? What techniques were utilized? Did the authorities lead the witness to a preordained conclusion? Many people have been convicted of crimes based upon memory and eyewitness accounts, only to be exonerated years later by DNA evidence. The manner in which interrogations are conducted is crucial in finding the truth of a matter. Investigators and trial attorneys are not unlike historians, asking questions and investigating something in an effort to get at the truth.[1]

In 1974, Elizabeth F. Loftus and J. C. Palmer demonstrated that memory is not a factual recording of an event, and that leading questions can and do distort

---

1 Foxhall, "Suddenly, a Big Impact on Criminal Justice," *American Psychological Association.*

a person's memory. For example, in an experiment at the University of Washington, students were shown short driver education films showing traffic accidents. After each clip, each group of students answered questions about the incident, such as, "About how fast were the cars going when they contacted each other?" The questions were altered a bit for the next group, with the verb "contacted" changed to "hit," "bumped," "collided," or "smashed." The answers confirmed what the researchers suspected: Students recollected faster speeds each time the verb increased in severity.

When "contacted" was used, students thought the cars were traveling at an average of 32 mph. When the verb "hit" was used, the speed increased to 34 mph. "Bumped" upped it to 38, "collided" to 39, and "smashed" to 41 mph. The researchers concluded that either the memories of how fast the cars were traveling were distorted by the verbal cues the students received, or the memories were "response-bias factors," meaning the students were not sure of the speed and simply adjusted their estimates to fit the expectations of the questioner.

In a second experiment, 100 students viewed a short film involving an accident with multiple cars. Half of the participants were asked the speed of the cars when using the verb "hit," and the other half were asked about the speed of the cars using the verb "smashed." One week later, without seeing the film again, the same students were all asked, "Did you see any broken glass?" Even though there was no broken glass shown in the film, those students who heard the verb "smashed" were more than twice as likely to recall seeing non-existent broken glass.

From these experiments, the researchers concluded that two types of information go into a person's memory of a complex event. The first is information a person obtains from perceiving the event, and second is the information supplied to the person after the event. Over time, input from the two sources (seeing an event and information garnered later) can be integrated to the extent that a person is unable to tell from which source his or her memory originated. The study is especially instructive for how police and lawyers use leading questions, and has led judges to warn juries that it is not safe to convict a person on a single eyewitness testimony without corroborating evidence.[2]

2   E. F. Loftus & J. C. Palmer. "Reconstruction of auto-mobile destruction: An example of the interaction between language and memory," *Journal of Verbal Learning and Verbal Behavior*, 13, 1974: 585–589; www.holah.co.uk/study/loftus/, accessed January 29, 2014.

False memories, suggestibility, and how leading questions can affect replies directly relates to the study of Sand Creek. For instance, during Senator Ben Wade's committee hearing on Sand Creek, D. W. Gooch asked John Evans if there was "any justification for the attack made by Colonel Chivington on these *friendly* [emphasis added] Indians?" William Windom asked if there was "any palliation or excuse for that *massacre* [emphasis added]." James Doolittle asked Sam Colley, "Was it the First Colorado Regiment that joined in this *massacre* [emphasis added], or was it the one-hundred-day men that were raised?"[3]

These questions are only a few of many such examples. Whether the Indians were friendly or whether they were massacred were the very issues the inquiries were organized to determine. The use of these (and other) suggestive words exposed the investigators' prejudices and may have profoundly influenced the answers they received.

A phenomenon related to leading questions is the matter of "anchoring." Witnesses often attach (i.e., anchor) a response to the most implausible suggestion. For instance, in one study subjects were asked to write down the first three digits of their phone number and then estimate the date of Genghis Khan's death, the length of the Nile River, or any other variation of question that most people would not know anything about. The study subjects used their phone number as an "anchor" upon which to base their guess. For example, if a phone number was 707, people would guess Khan's death as being in the 7th or 8th century (when it was in 1227 CE).[4] Was it is possible that many estimations of the number of Indians present or killed at Sand Creek, or the number of scalps present, were influenced by, or "anchored" to, someone else's suggestion?

Once a witness states facts in a particular way or identifies a particular person as having done something, he or she is usually unable, or even unwilling, to reconsider their position. Memory changes in the retelling, and we rarely tell a story without inserting our own biases, preconceptions, prejudices, and/or third-party considerations that affect us. Confidence and accuracy are sometimes correlated, but "when misleading information is given, witness confidence is often higher for the incorrect information than for the correct

---

3 Lt. Col. William R. Dunn, *I Stand by Sand Creek A Defense of Colonel John M. Chivington and the Third Colorado Cavalry* (Fort Collins, CO, 1985), 147; "Massacre of Cheyenne Indians," 42; "Chivington Massacre," 30, 48.

4 Joseph T. Hallinan, *Why We Make Mistakes* (New York, 2009), 102–05.

information." Laura Engelhardt, writing for the *Stanford Journal of Legal Studies*, concluded that "since the very act of forming a memory creates distortion, how can anyone uncover the 'truth' behind a person's statements?"

The chief problem with testimony is the unreliability of personal observation. Witnesses can and do distort their own memories without any outside influence. "Rarely do we tell a story or recount events without a purpose," explained Engelhardt. "Every act of telling and retelling is tailored to a particular listener." Every time we tell a story, we add "another layer of distortion, which in turn affects the underlying memory of the event. This is why a fish story, which grows with each retelling, can eventually lead the teller to believe it."[5]

Very few of us consider ourselves to be liars. Our brains work overtime to make us feel we are competent, truthful, and moral people. Almost certainly, most of the witnesses relating what they saw and experienced at Sand Creek believed they were telling the truth, and were not engaged in purposeful deception. But some were. Some people deliberately lie, and do so often.[6]

How truthful is the average person? According to one researcher, "Lying is pervasive. At some level, most of us lie most days of the week. We lie about almost anything." A 2002 study at the University of Massachusetts found that, on average, people tell two to three lies during every 10-minute conversation. Over the course of a day, a person can be lied to as many as 200 times, and most people can only detect a lie about 50 percent of the time.[7]

---

5   Laura Engelhardt, "The Problem with Eyewitness Testimony Commentary on a talk by George Fisher and Barbara Tversky," *Stanford Journal of Legal Studies*, Vol. 1:1, April 5, 1999, 25–29. http://agora.stanford.edu/sjls/Issue%20One/fisher&tversky.htm, accessed January 30, 2014.

6   Martha Stout, Ph.D., *The Sociopath Next Door The Ruthless Versus the Rest of Us* (New York, 2005), 136; Adriane Raine, *The Anatomy of Violence The Biological Roots of Crime* (New York, 2014), 122, 169. According to the FBI, one percent of Americans are psychopaths. Harvard Medical School Psychologist Martha Stout estimates that four percent of people in the Western world are sociopaths, which translates to one in 25. Adriane Raine, a professor of Criminology and Psychology at the University of Pennsylvania, believes that about three percent of Americans today meet the definition of a psychopath. A key trait of the psychopath or sociopath "is pathological lying and deception. They lie left, right, and center. Sometimes for good reason, and sometimes, perplexingly, for no reason."

7   Raine, *Anatomy of Violence*, 169; "10 Research Findings About Deception That Will Blow Your Mind," http://liespotting.com/2010/06/10-research-findings-about-deception-that-will-blow-your-mind/, accessed June 19, 2014.

People living in the 19th century were no different. According to what we know today, if about 700 soldiers were at Sand Creek, and about 500 participated in the fighting, then about 28 were inveterate liars. Fifty-nine men were interrogated. Of those, research concludes about three would have been sociopaths or inveterate liars. What if one or all of them offered testimony that was critical to the proceedings, like Chivington, Wynkoop, Cramer, or Soule? What if George Bent fit that category and poured out pages of deception to his correspondents Hyde and Grinnell? When you add the unreliability of memory, and the use of leading questions by interrogators, the difficulty of finding out exactly what happened at Sand Creek (or at any historical event) becomes readily obvious.

The courts and commissions at the time of Sand Creek knew all about leading questions, hearsay, and what could or could not be entered into evidence. John Chivington, for example, made 86 objections, and 32 of them were sustained (granted). Samuel Tappan made 15 objections, 14 of which were sustained (although it should be noted that as head of the tribunal, Tappan sustained or overruled his own motions).

One of the three commissions was organized to find out about Sand Creek and "the condition of the Indian tribes," while the other two were organized solely to investigate the nature of the fighting there. As we know, however, of the nearly 700 soldiers who participated in the Sand Creek campaign, only 59 were ever formally questioned and only one-half of those, only 28 were eyewitnesses of the actual events.

Chapter 23

Stress and Memories

Although Colonel Chivington's memories shifted in certain respects, he was more consistent regarding the number of Indians he believed were killed at Sand Creek.

In his initial report he prepared after the fight, written on November 29, 1864, Chivington claimed that his attack killed 500 Indians. Chivington added some information in a letter to Governor Evans a little more than one week later (December 7) when he noted that 500 Indians had been killed and his own losses were nine killed and 38 wounded. In a report written a little more than one week after that letter (December 16), Chivington upped the number of Indians killed from 500 to between 500 and 600, and added that he had not taken any prisoners. He also reported his own losses as eight killed instead of nine, and 40 wounded (with two having since died) instead of 38. In this report he also claimed to have seen the scalp of one white man in the camp, and that it was not more than two or three days old.

His account changed in several respects by the time he prepared his written testimony for the inquiry. On April 26, 1865, Colonel Chivington reported that his losses were seven soldiers killed, 47 wounded, and one missing. He still claimed between 500 and 600 Indians had been killed, and explained that officers had informed him that only a few women and children were among the dead at Sand Creek. Previously, he had written that no prisoners had been taken, and that he had seen but one white scalp, but his latest testimony claimed that eight Indians had been captured, and had found 19 white scalps in the Indian camp.[1]

Why did Chivington hold to the outrageously high number of Indian dead? He may have believed it enhanced his image as an Indian fighter and thus he was worthy of promotion. Perhaps for the same reasons, he undercounted his own casualties. Once again our own biases come into play. Some historians will rightly dismiss Chivington's estimate of Indians killed as nonsense, but readily accept as accurate the low estimate of his own casualties. Chivington shift in memory that increased the count of white scalps discovered in the village made the Indians look more like savage murderers, which in turn served his own personal interests. Did he purposely lie? We don't know, but we do know that he stuck to his position better than some other participants.

* * *

Stress profoundly influences memory. It is hard enough to accurately remember the mundane details of day-to-day events, but what if the memories are of traumatic events like a crime, accident, or war? Stress can impair or enhance memory, but there is a high correlation between increased stress and false memories. People perform worse at most tasks that involve memory when under stress, such as in battle or testifying as a witness. Trauma can and often does enhance initial memory consolidation, but impairs later memory retrieval.[2]

"Eyewitness testimony," explained an article in the *Journal of Neuroscience*, "often proves untrustworthy" with more false positives while under stress. Stress can enhance generalized processing, "such as extracting the central thematic information (gist) at the cost of specificity." In other words, the stressful event is remembered longer, but at the expense of accuracy.[3]

How true is this concerning the participants at Sand Creek? Each soldier knew something happened there, and something terrible, but what, exactly?

1   "Massacre of Cheyenne Indians," 48–49, 102–04.

2   Jessica D. Payne, et al., "Stress administered prior to encoding impairs neutral but enhances emotional long-term episodic memories," *Learning & Memory*, 14 (12), December, 2007: 861–868. http://www.ncbi.nlm.nih.gov/pmc/articles/PMC2151024/, accessed February 6, 2014.

3   Shaozheng Qin, et al., "Understanding Low Reliability of Memories for Neural Information Encoded Under Stress: Alterations in Memory-Related Activation in the Hippocampus and Midbrain," *Journal of Neuroscience*, 32 (12), March 21, 2012: 4032–4041. Http://www.jneurosci.org/content/32/12/4032.full, accessed January 20, 2014.

The chaos and stress of battle took a toll on their perceptions and memories, and the leading questions and suggestions during the investigations dragged at least some of them down a preset path. Yet, most of the witnesses were certain their memories were accurate. As noted, in everyday situations, people have different conceptions of distance, depth, direction, and numbers. Traumatic events like battle distort perception. Many men in combat, for example, consistently underestimate distances and believe danger to be much closer than it was in fact.[4]

Believing something is a threat further increases stress and impacts accurate assessment. Most men are not killers and avoid personal confrontations. In war, this might be considered cowardice, but most men in combat will show signs of neuroses—the "shell-shock" of the Great War, the "combat fatigue" of World War II, or the "thousand-yard stare" of soldiers from all eras who have been in battle too long. Stress and fear are constant companions in war, but the psychiatric, emotional, and memory-altering dynamics that accompany battle stress have not been understood until relatively recently. Stages of mental stress may include difficulty of concentration and response, apprehensiveness, confusion, and impaired judgment. All five senses can be impacted, ranging from hyper-sensitivities to insensitivities. Soldiers might hallucinate, receiving sensory perceptions without environmental input, or they might become delusional and misinterpret incoming sensory data. Environmental, temporal, and spatial dimensions may become distorted.[5]

Fear-induced stress can alter perceptions and those altered states can remain long after the fighting ends. Many of the men who fought in campaigns during the Indian Wars of the 19th century may have experienced symptoms, undiagnosed or incorrectly diagnosed at the time, that have been given a name in the 20th century: post-traumatic stress disorder (PTSD). Many survivors with PTSD suffer from "survivor guilt," or suffer because of what they had to do in order to survive, or about killing another human being, or even because they enjoying the killing. There may be a "psychogenic amnesia" of the trauma,

4 John Keegan, *The Face of Battle* (Middlesex, UK, 1976), 166.

5 Richard A. Gabriel, *The Painful Field The Psychiatric Dimension of Modern War* (Westport, CT, 1988), 9, 22; George L. Engel, *Psychological Development in Health and Disease* (Philadelphia, PA, 1962), 284, 327; Gregory Michno, *The Mystery of E Troop Custer's Gray Horse Company at the Little Bighorn* (Missoula, MT, 1994), 287–89.

selective perceptions, and constriction or inflexibility of thought. Memories can be altered or even invented as coping mechanisms.[6]

Behavioral research of combat veterans found that regardless of their "duty" to kill the enemy, many men simply cannot pull the trigger. After the Battle of Gettysburg, for example, many thousands of weapons were found loaded with three to 10 rounds, and one weapon had 23 rounds still in the barrel. One World War II study calculated that 75 percent or more infantrymen would not fire their guns in combat. A high percentage of men simply did not want to kill the enemy, but acted as if they were doing so by going through the motions. Since human nature has not changed, it is very likely that only a comparatively small percentage of the 500 men actively engaged at Sand Creek took part in the killing.

Research also found that soldiers unable to kill rationalized their inability to do so, or become fixated and traumatized by it. Some men who passed through the "killing barrier" and actually took another life reached the exhilaration stage; killing became easier the more it was done, and the act itself provided an intense satisfaction. For some of these men, the war experience was described as "fun." Others felt intense remorse at having taken another life—a realization that brought on waves of revulsion and disgust. Regardless, the last stage was always the rationalization and acceptance process, an often life-long struggle that usually involved changing the conception of the enemy from a human being to an evil demon, an animal-like "other" who could be killed with as little regret as stepping on an ant. In addition to morphing the enemy into a savage beast, soldiers could rationalize that they weren't really killing, but were only following orders. Or, perhaps they had no choice, since it was either "him or me."[7]

Before Sand Creek, most of the troopers had expressed a desire to kill Indians. Later, when the affair began to be called a massacre and public opinion turned against them, many began distancing themselves from it and claimed

6 American Psychiatric Association, *Diagnostic and Statistical Manual for Mental Disorders DSM III-R* (Washington, D. C., 1987), 236–37, 248–50; Eva Kahana et al., "Coping with Extreme Trauma," in *Human Adaptation to Extreme Stress from the Holocaust to Vietnam*, John P. Wilson, Zev Harel, and Boaz Kahana, eds. (New York, 1988), 62–67, 70.

7 Lt. Col. Dave Grossman, *On Killing The Psychological Cost of Learning to Kill in War and Society* (Boston MS, 1995), 21–22, 119, 231–232, 233-240; S. L. A. Marshall, *Men Against Fire The Problem of Battle Command in Future War* (Gloucester, MA, 1978), 50. Some of Marshall's methodologies and statistics have been questioned.

they had not fired their weapons at all, had never approved of attacking the Indians, and/or were disgusted by the atrocities *others* had committed there.

The whites and the Indians who battled each other during the wars of the 19th century were compelled by the same psychological pressures, and reacted to them in all the various ways noted above. Most and perhaps all of them had one thing in common: They all justified their actions by reshaping and altering their memories, whether consciously or not.

Chapter 24

Memory Alteration and Cognitive Dissonance at Sand Creek

ationalizations and justifications are aspects of psychological processes that shape our memories. What is surprising is how little we have to say in the matter.

These same processes were impacting the participants on both side before, during, and after the encounter at Sand Creek. They include cognitive dissonance or motivated reasoning, as well as self-perception or self-affirmation. Understanding these processes helps us better understand past events, including Sand Creek.

The theory of "cognitive dissonance" was formulated in 1954 by social psychologist Leon Festinger. Cognitions (or thoughts) are bits of knowledge we possess, and dissonance (or conflict) occurs when we hold contradictory thoughts. According to Festinger, a person relies on a positive self-image to feel good about himself and therefore cherishes that self-image. Therefore, he will work hard to keep that positive self-image intact if he is challenged by any inconsistent attitudes or actions, i.e., he will experience "cognitive dissonance."

Most people believe they are morally conscientious and responsible, but when their behavior violates their self-expectations, an internal conflict arises. The more disparate the thoughts and actions, the greater the need is to correct them. Since we cannot change the reality of any past behavior, it is easier to change attitudes by incorporating harmonious thoughts. In other words, we either align our current ideas with our past behavior, which is often very difficult, or we live in psychological turmoil.[1]

Self-perception can be thought of as a flip side to cognitive dissonance. In the latter, the hypothesis is that attitudes cause behavior, while the hypothesis of the former is that behaviors cause attitude. Take, for example, a test that divided people into two groups, one strongly pro-environment and the second with weak or inconsistent views on the same issue. Leading questions about their behaviors were introduced into the test like the "frequent" versus "occasional" use of carpooling. When the word "occasional" was used, the subjects tended to answer "yes" (they did engage in that activity) and in later sessions were more likely to identify themselves as "pro-environment." When the word "frequent" was used, subjects were more likely to answer "no" (they did not engage in that activity frequently) and later saw themselves as "anti-environment." The correlation was strongest with those whose attitudes were tentative. Those people "are much more likely to infer their attitudes by observing their own behavior. Those who possess well-defined attitudes on a particular topic, however, are much less vulnerable to outside influences."[2]

There is little or no doubt that attitudes can affect behavior, and behaviors can also affect attitudes. But whatever theory one prefers, the brain has a mind all its own. Most people want to feel good about themselves. When their actions or words are challenged, many alter their attitudes, behaviors, and memories in order to maintain their positive self-image. Cynics are often critical of those who change their attitudes to justify their behavior and see them as hypocrites. Tests show, however, that "what looks like disingenuous rationalization from without may feel genuine from within."[3]

One important facet of cognitive dissonance addresses testimony, which can be related to some of our eyewitnesses at Sand Creek. Was what they swore

---

1 Leon Festinger, Henry W. Riecken, and Stanley Schacter, *When Prophesy Fails* (London, 2005), viii, 3; Joel Cooper, *Cognitive Dissonance Fifty Years of a Classic Theory* (London, 2007), 2, 6–8, 96–97; Herbert R. Ginsburg and Silvia Opper, *Piaget's Theory of Intellectual Development* (Englewood Cliffs, NJ, 1988), 23.

2 "Cognitive Dissonance and Self-Perception Theory." *e LearnPortal.* http://www.elearn portal.com/courses/psychology/social-and-community-psychology/social-and-community-psychology-cognitive-dissonance-and-self-perception-th, accessed February 4, 2014.

3 Matthew D. Lieberman, et al., "Do Amnesics Exhibit Cognitive Dissonance Reduction? The Role of Explicit Memory and Attention in Attitude Change." *Psychological Science*, 12, no. 2, March 2001: 135-140. http://pss.sagepub.com/content/12/2/135.full.pdf, accessed February 9, 2014.

under oath to have seen and heard going to be accurate months later, assuming it was even accurate when it was first experienced? A set of experiments that involved potential buyers of an inexpensive, fuel-efficient car and a flashy sports car helps us better understand this issue. Some of those who initially believed that economy was the most important selling point still ended up buying the fuel-guzzling sports car. Their original dispassionate analysis and validation had succumbed to an impulse, and the dissonant cognitions had to be eliminated. Ill at ease with the change of heart, the subconscious mind adjusted itself to accommodate the decision. Most people are adamant they have made the right choice after they have made it, especially when the choice was economically or socially costly. The more important a decision is, the greater the need to reduce the resultant dissonance by overemphasizing the correctness of the choice—subconsciously, of course.[4]

It is possible to see the workings of cognitive dissonance reduction by examining the testimonies of Silas Soule, who was nearly universally depicted as a hero for speaking out against the Sand Creek attack. Captain Soule was once a Colonel Chivington supporter, but he experienced a radical change of mind. In an outraged letter to Major Wynkoop penned on December 14, 1864, Soule insisted that he had not taken part in the massacre. "I refused to fire and swore that none but a coward would," he wrote. "My Company was the only one that kept their formation, and we did not fire a shot." Soule went on to tell Wynkoop that the others killed "about 140 women and children and 60 bucks."[5]

Four days later on December 18, Soule wrote a letter to his mother in Kansas. After having recently experienced an event that so outraged him (Sand Creek), he noted that he was lazy, "and have so little that would interest you." Eventually he got around to writing, "I was present at a massacre of three hundred Indians mostly women and children it was a horrable scene and I would not let my Company fire." He blamed the slaughter on the "100 day men who accomplished the noble deed." He also told her that he had a horse shot from under him, apparently a wild long shot, since he claimed he was not in the fight. The soldiers, he added, lost twelve killed and forty wounded.

---

4 Cooper, *Cognitive Dissonance*, 11–12; Carol Tavris and Elliot Aronson, *Mistakes Were Made (But Not by Me) Why we Justify Foolish Beliefs, Bad Decisions, and Hurtful Acts* (Orlando, FL, 2007), 22–23.

5 Roberts and Halaas, "Written in Blood," 25–26.

A month later on January 18, 1865, Soule again wrote to his mother that he had spent New Year's Day "on the battleground counting dead Indians there were not as many killed as was reported there was not more than one hundred and thirty killed." He once more noted, "I would not fire on the Indians."[6]

Captain Soule appeared in Denver as a witness at the military commission inquiring into the Sand Creek affair. On February 16, 1865, he testified that Major Anthony moved his battalion to within 100 yards of the Indian lodges "and ordered us to open fire; some firing done," but when the battery moved behind them and prepared to open fire, Anthony had ordered Soule's company "to move up the creek and for the purpose of killing Indians which were under the banks." Soule testified that he complied, but the hot firing "was unsafe" and so he moved across the creek and then upstream. He also testified that he saw only 69 dead Indians on the battlefield.

The next day on February 17, Soule was asked if he saw soldiers doing any scalping and mutilating. "I did," he answered. He also replied that by noon, Major Anthony had pulled him out of the battle and that he was guarding wounded and some captured property. On February 20, when asked again if he saw any soldiers scalping or mutilating Indians, Soule answered, "I think not."[7]

As is readily apparent, Soule's correspondence and his testimony is often at odds. Perhaps he was embarrassed by his behavior of firing on Indians he claimed were friendly, so he insisted to his mother and to Wynkoop that he had not allowed his company to participate in the battle. Despite his attempt to ease his conscience, when he had to testify at the inquiry, he confirmed under oath that he had complied with Major Anthony's orders to fire and take part in the fight—assertions possibly influenced by a concern that other potential witnesses could counter testimony to the contrary. Had Soule admitted to disobeying orders in battle, he would also have been liable to court martial. On the stand, the now-humble captain made no such indignant claims that lofty principles had kept him from shooting Indians.

Was Soule trying to reduce his dissonance by denying his participation, or did he really not participate, but told the court that he had in order to save his own hide? His reconstituted memories served his best personal interest—which was no different than those offered by Wynkoop and Chivington.

---

6   Silas S. Soule Papers, *Kansas State Historical Society*, WH1690, Box 1.

7   "Sand Creek Massacre," 11, 14, 21, 23.

One problem for someone who rationalizes his conduct is that he may not remember what he said from one day to the next. For example, one day Soule testified seeing soldiers scalping Indians. Just three days later he claimed he didn't see any such thing. The number of Indians Soule remembered being killed also changed. When he wanted to emphasize the *massacre*, for example, he told Wynkoop that 200 had been killed, and he increased that number to 300 when writing to his mother. The next month in another letter to his mother, however, he reduced the number to 130. In court, Soule dropped the number all the way down to 69—while Chivington inflated it to more than 500.

Here we come across the rather odd situation of a commander trying to increase the enemy body count to make himself appear to be a great warrior, but by doing so, he counter-intuitively pushed the incident into the category of a massacre—the very charge against which he was defending himself. We also have subordinate officers trying to prove perfidy on part of their commander and make the massacre charges stick, but who paradoxically lowered the number of Indian dead to keep Chivington from being seen as a hero. As Lieutenant Cramer put it to Captain Cree: They "thought they could make a massacre out of the Sand Creek affair and crush him." And to Major Wynkoop, Cramer wrote: "for God's sake, Major, keep Chivington from being a Bri'g Genl."[8]

Every soldier noted above had reasons to enhance his own image or to malign others deemed an enemy. This clearly shows how testimony and memory can be nothing more than fables constructed to enhance one's self-esteem and self-interest, or to hurt another. Bent, Chivington, Soule, Wynkoop and everyone else involved told so many contradictory stories that the actual "facts" concerning some details of what happened at Sand Creek will likely never be known. The congressmen and officers conducting the hearings were charged with finding the "truth," but they were subject to the same social, political, and psychological forces as those on the witness stand. They had their own self-image and self-interest to sustain. Their truths may already have been established before they began, and possibly reinforced by any number of factors as the hearings progressed.

As is now quite clear, eyewitness testimony can be very inaccurate for many reasons: leading questions and suggestibility, false implanted memories, trauma distortion, and altered attitude and behavior to make us feel good. Once we

8 "Sand Creek Massacre," 190; Roberts and Halaas, "Written in Blood," 28.

have packed our brains with all these thoughts, some of them indubitably false, we sometimes try our best to convince others (and ourselves) that they are accurate.

How, then, do we ever get at the truth? When people are presented with incontrovertible facts, will they adjust their attitudes and behaviors?

Chapter 25

Don't Confuse Me with the Facts

Would any of us consciously hold an irrationally obstinate opinion? Unfortunately, the answer is a resounding "yes."

Facts don't matter for many people who already have made up their minds. "A man with a conviction is a hard man to change," explained social psychologist Leon Festinger. "Tell him you disagree and he turns away. Show him facts or figures and he questions your sources. Appeal to logic and he fails to see your point." We love to protect our beliefs, and the stronger they are, the more we will fight to keep them intact. Suppose one is strongly committed to a belief and has taken irrevocable actions because of it. Now suppose one is presented with unequivocal and undeniable evidence that the belief is wrong. What happens? "The individual will frequently emerge, not only unshaken, but even more convinced of the truth of his beliefs than ever before. Indeed, he may even show a new fervor about convincing and converting other people to his view."[1]

Dr. Festinger posited this argument in 1956, and numerous studies have borne it out. When someone questions your deeply held beliefs in which personal values are at play, they are implicitly questioning your sense of self. Questioning value beliefs increases one's stress and leads to highly charged responses. It is nearly impossible to find common ground when disparate

---

1 Festinger, *When Prophesy Fails*, 3.

deeply held beliefs are involved, no matter what the "facts" might be. Threatened people can and do resist.[2]

Economist John Maynard Keynes once famously asked, "When my information changes, I alter my conclusions. What do you do, sir?" Unlike Keynes, most people will disregard incongruent new information on matters of import. They will not allow facts to interfere with their belief system. We do not like to be proven wrong because belief is tied to a sense of self, so it is much easier to deceive ourselves than to change belief. When under stress, we don't process information calmly and logically, so we seek comforting input based on our preconceptions—we strain our input through a sieve, admitting only the facts that nourish and sustain our beliefs.[3]

Confirmation bias, or the "I know I'm right" syndrome, is a formidable problem, and may have implications for some students of the Sand Creek affair. When we realize that facts do not always get us anywhere, and that they are just raw data with no particular meaning until processed through the software of our feelings, we hit a wall. How can this be?

Philosophers since the early Enlightenment have insisted that man is a rational, reasoning creature. The archetype of the reasonable, enlightened man was Marie-Jean-Antoine-Nicolas Caritat, the Marquis de Condorcet, known as Nicolas de Condorcet. To him, reason was God, and every man armed with reason could defeat any error and prejudice. "The time will therefore come," he wrote while imprisoned, "when the sun will shine only on free men who know no other master but their reason." Armed with sense, logic, and reason, men would conquer falsehood and be "emancipated from its shackles, released from the empire of fate and from that of the enemies of its progress, advancing with a firm and sure step along the path of truth, virtue, and happiness!" One writer has wittily named this hope the "Condorcet handicap"—trying to use factual, sound, well-researched, well-reasoned arguments and then being amazed each time when the arguments are discarded and attacked.[4]

---

2   Matt Huston, "Now It's Personal Arguments are Harder to Resolve when Values are on the Line," *Psychology Today*, 47, no. 3 (May/June 2014), 23.

3   Tavris and Aronson, *Mistakes Were Made*, 2, 18; Stuart A. Vyse, *Believing in Magic The Psychology of Superstition* (New York, 1997), 119–20, 200.

4   Marquis de Condorcet, "The Future Progress of the Human Mind," in Isaac Kramnick, ed., *The Portable Enlightenment Reader* (New York, 1995), 30, 38. Condorcet died in prison. Chris Mooney, *The Republican Brain The Science of Why they Deny Science—and Reality* (Hoboken, NJ, 2012), 83. Condorcet may have been completely wrong about reason being the savior of man.

Persuasion is therefore more essential than reason, because fact and reason interfere with beliefs and objectives. The philosophers were wrong too, in claiming man is an individualist, for tests show that we often exhibit sheep-like behavior, which surely infected the Sand Creek affair.

This inclination is demonstrated with an experiment in which the participants were secretly coached beforehand to provide the wrong answers to questions. When a significant number of the group consistently gave the wrong answers, a portion of the test subjects—even though they knew the answers were incorrect—nevertheless followed the group and also gave the wrong answers.

Humans are in many respects herd animals. We seldom try to disconfirm, but will very often follow whatever stance the group has adopted. Individuals in a group will often reinforce one another. Some psychologists call this group polarization: the idea that we shape our opinions to conform to the view of the group with which we identify. This creates group solidarity and increases the chances that our group's views will prevail in society. The more threatened we feel by non-confirming group members—the press, opposing political parties, or courts of inquiry in the Sand Creek case—the more we circle the wagons and go into a defensive shell. It is tough to change an individual mind; it is nearly impossible to change the mind of a group.[5]

So how do we discern the real from the fake as we sift through the disparate accounts at Sand Creek?

Philosopher Hugo Mercier and cognitive scientist Dan Sperber have proposed that our cherished estimation of the merits of reason is fundamentally incorrect. They argue that we have never understood what reason was for. They suggest that reason did not evolve as a device for discovering the objective truth. Instead, its purpose was to facilitate selective arguing in defense of one's position in a social context. When our ancestors developed into hunter-gatherer communities, there was survival value in getting others in the group to listen to and follow the leader. Persuasion, not reason, was a priority. We needed to be good rhetoricians, cobbling together evidence to support our own position. If we could persuade others to follow, we all had a better chance to survive (and presumably refute the counter-claims of any challenge to the leader). Mooney, *Republican Brain*, 52–53.

5   Daniel Gardner, *The Science of Fear How the Culture of Fear Manipulates Your Brain* (New York, 2009), 103, 110–11, 113; David Ropeik, "Why Changing Somebody's Mind, or Yours, is Hard to Do," *Psychology Today*, July 13, 2010; www.psychologytoday.com/blog/how-risky- is-it-really /201007/why-changing-somebody-s-mind-or-yours-is-hard-do, accessed February 13, 2014.

Chapter 26

Oral History

*W*e have a tough time accurately remembering what happened to us, and a worse time remembering something when misinformation is inserted into the narrative. Experiments have shown that misinformation has the most impact on test subjects when they read it (43%). The second most impactful way to receive misinformation is when test subjects recall something but cannot give a specific source (17%). The third is when we see something (15%). These results highlight the role that the written word plays in spreading misinformation. If inaccurate information is spread in large part by reading it, will telling something, such as in verbal testimony, be more accurate?[1]

Oral history, based upon eyewitnesses and participants, remains as storytelling. Some cultures place a premium on recording those experiences in books, while others, in what an anthropologist might label as "preliterate," transmit their cultural knowledge and lore orally from one generation to another. Messages or stories or testimony are verbally transmitted in speech or song in the form of folk tales, sayings, ballads, or chants. It is tough enough to achieve accuracy in writing, but it is even harder to attain and then maintain it through storytelling.

---

1 Elizabeth Loftus, "The Reality of Illusory Memories," in Daniel L. Schacter, ed., *Memory Distortion How Minds, Brains, and Societies Reconstruct the Past* (Cambridge, MS, 1995), 58–60.

Take, for example, the 1950 film Rashomon, a classic story of four eyewitnesses to the rape of a woman and the murder of her samurai husband. The witnesses tell mutually contradictory stories of what they saw, all of them heavily influenced by their biases and egos, and all of them convinced in the validity of their version of events. The film highlights what recent memory studies have proven: There are multiple realities, memory output differs substantially from input, and "truth" can subjectively relative. If these Japanese witnesses had lives in a preliterate society, which tale would have eventually displaced the others to be then passed down to later generations as "truth"?[2]

In 1932, Sir Frederic Bartlett wrote a book entitled *Remembering*. In it, he explained how he conducted his now-classic test of exposing his subjects to an old Indian legend called "The War of the Ghosts" in an effort to see how accurately they repeated the story in later sessions. Not surprisingly, the study participants rarely recalled all of the events accurately. In some cases the story was dramatically shortened, and many times the participants recalled a generalized tale of events that fit their expectations of what should have happened, even when these events were not part of the original story.

Bartlett also discovered that recollections changed dramatically across several retellings. He concluded that memories are imaginative reconstructions, heavily influenced by preexisting knowledge, and that remembering is fundamentally a social activity distorted by one's attitudes and needs. How one remembers reflects the nature of the person doing the remembering.[3]

There is an obvious danger in relying on word of mouth to pass on traditions. Eyewitnesses are challenged to accurately reconstruct what they recently experienced, and it gets harder when they try to write it on paper or try to remember it later. Numerous studies reveal what most of us would acknowledge as *a priori* truth: The incidence of false memories increases dramatically with the passage of time. It is therefore important to use caution in accepting as accurate letters, diaries, or memoirs written months or years after the fact, and even more caution should be exercised with oral traditions passed down one generation to the next.[4]

2 Daniel L. Schacter, "Memory Distortion: History and Current Status," in Schacter, ed., *Memory Distortion*, 1.

3 Schacter, "Memory Distortion: History and Current Status," 8–9; Hallinan, *Why We Make Mistakes*, 125–27.

4 Schacter, "Memory Distortion: History and Current Status," 26.

There are additional caveats when using Indian testimony about Sand Creek. The language barrier led to inevitable errors as the story was told by an Indian participant to an interpreter, and then passed along again in another language to the person who recorded it. It is a more complicated process than most people imagine. The Indian witness may not have told the truth, or may have misremembered the event under discussion. The translator may not have been fully proficient in the native language, or may not have been objective, or may have replaced or reordered words to match patterns familiar with his world view. All of this is also true for the recorder, who preserved the testimony for later use.

Some historians of the Indian wars do not use Indian testimony because they believe it is irreconcilable with what they deem "facts," and so rely solely on white accounts. For example, Fred Dustin (1866-1957) cherished white officers' recollections about the Battle of the Little Bighorn because of "the traditional truthfulness of their class." General George Crook, on the other hand, believed that "if you make it to the Indian's interest to tell the truth, you get correct information; a white man will lie intentionally, and mislead you unintentionally."[5]

An additional caution to consider when relying upon Indian testimony was the possibility that participants in a recent battle may have felt intimidated when facing white interrogators. As Indian wars historian Jerome Greene explained it, "Fearing retribution, they either subordinated their personal roles or told what they believed their questioners wanted to hear." Therefore, a later recollection, "by its distance from an event, was often more bias-free for both giver and receiver than testimony delivered soon afterwards."[6]

This conclusion seems to be an attempt to make problematic eyewitness testimony more palatable for the consumer/reader, as well as for the historian. When studies definitely show that recollections only gets worse with the passage of time, how can we lend credence to eyewitness remembrances given years later, especially when much of memory is distorted by subsequent input? And how much worse will it be when the storyteller has been purposely lying for many years, but now decides he wants to tell you the "truth"?

5 Richard G. Hardorff, ed., *Lakota Recollections of the Custer Fight New Sources of Indian-Military History* (Spokane, WA, 1991), 17; Michno, *Mystery of E Troop*, 63.

6 Jerome Greene, ed., *Lakota and Cheyenne Indian Views of the Great Sioux War, 1876–1877* (Norman, OK, 1994), xxiii.

A recent assessment of oral history suggests even more cautions are in order. Linda Shopes, a historian at the Pennsylvania Historical and Museum Commission, has been studying oral history for 25 years. She explains it as a self-conscious dialogue between two or more people in which the interviewer and responder have possibly contesting frames of reference. The questions and answers play off each other as both sides try to cater to the others' sensibilities in an effort to establish rapport. The narrators are a self-selected group, usually more articulate and self-assured than those who chose not to participate. They are predisposed to want to interview, creating an implicit bias.

According to Shopes, oral history, by its immediacy and emotional resonance, "seduces us into taking it literally, an approach . . . criticized as 'Anti-History.'" Oral history takes on the glow of something beyond historicity, interpretation, and accountability and it must be used with prudence. "Just because someone says something is true, however colorfully or convincingly they say it, doesn't mean it is true. Just because someone 'was there' doesn't mean they fully understand 'what happened.'"

According to Shopes, we must consider the reliability of the narrator and the verifiability of the account. What is the narrator's relationship to the events, his or her personal stake or physical and mental states? It may help if we check the story with related documentary evidence, but we have to remember that documentary evidence can be as tainted with memory imperfections as the verbal tale. Oral history is not just another source to be evaluated as simply more raw data, but an interpretation, an expression of identity, consciousness, and culture.[7]

This does not mean that oral history should be ignored or has no value. In Henry Wadsworth Longfellow's poem "There was a Little Girl," we learn: "When she was good, she was very, very good, and when she was bad she was horrid." Or, put another way we can apply to history in general, and Sand Creek in particular, "When she was bad she was extremely effective."

Oral history can be inspiring when told with verve, but it is always more impactful and "better" when the tale is a heartrending story filled with pathos. The "gut," explained author Daniel Gardner, "is a sucker for a good story." We have an instinct for storytelling stretching back from our earliest ancestors and we love the stories most when they are about conflict. Homer's *Iliad* leaps readily to mind. We have all heard the clichéd but true phrase "If it bleeds, it

---

7   Shopes, "Making Sense of Oral History."

leads" regarding news coverage. People in the media have even developed a "death-per-news-story" ratio that "measures the number of people who have to die from a given condition to merit a story in the news."[8]

Storytelling frequently beats statistics, and anecdotes frequently conquer evidence. People are much more easily convinced by personal stories than numbers, and that is why companies trying to sell us a product use testimonials instead of statistics. According to Joseph Hallinan, "the power of anecdotes to lead us astray is so strong that an influential CIA study advises intelligence analysts to avoid them. Analysts, it concluded, 'should give little weight to anecdotal and personal case histories,'" and it might be best to give them no weight at all if valid statistics can be found. "So ask for averages, not testimonials."[9]

How does all of this fit into our study of Sand Creek? It might be put like this: Seventy-six dead white soldiers is just a statistic, but the mutilated, pregnant Indian woman is the headline—our anecdote. That is human nature, or as Daniel Gardner might put it, "our gut talking."

The Cheyenne and Arapaho who passed down stories of what their ancestors experienced at Sand Creek were subject to all the foibles of relating oral history. They may have, as author Ari Kelman stated, "Unwritten rules about truthfulness in storytelling." But as we have seen, far more prevalent than purposeful lies are the unconscious distortions and false memories that are accepted as the truth by the speaker. The more invested in the outcomes of the memories, the more distorted they will be in favor of self-esteem.

This can be even more widespread when the storyteller sees himself as a victim, for instance, an Indian at Sand Creek who felt unjustly attacked, or a soldier who was later pilloried in the press for participating in a massacre. As Daniel Schacter has shown, traumatic memories can be partially accurate, false implants, or completely confabulated. Socio-cultural factors influence and distort recollections, and the culture of victimization enhances one's tendency to believe in repressed traumatic memories. Distorted memory passed down through oral history can be as prevalent for a culture as for an individual. Once

---

8   Gardner, *Science of Fear*, 44, 169.

9   Hallinan, *Why We Make Mistakes*, 215.

The historic site is now named the Sand Creek Massacre National Historic Site. Indian oral tradition has become official. *Author*

the myth becomes embedded in the cognitive fabric of the society, it is virtually impossible to determine its origin or to correct it.[10]

White Americans take pride in their history and, as Professor Patricia N. Limerick explained, now the Indians have put forth a counterclaim: They also want a history that belongs to them "in which the owners should take pride and which should make them feel better about their inherited identity." That idea might make some historians uncomfortable, possibly because they sense they are guilty of the same desires. Corporations, bureaucracies, religions, politicians, interest groups and many others have always written affirmative justifications as history.[11]

But is this history or heritage? History or cultural celebration? According to author Michael Kammen, the "heritage" trend in history is troubling because it

10 Ari Kelman, *A Misplaced Massacre: Struggling over the Memory of Sand Creek* (Cambridge, MS, 2013), 117; Schacter, "Memory Distortion: History and Current Status," 27, 29–30.

11 Patricia Nelson Limerick, *The Legacy of Conquest The Unbroken Past of the American West* (New York, 1987), 48, 219–20.

is selective in memory and anti-intellectual. In his view, it recalls the good, suppresses the unpleasant, and denigrates the written.[12]

Nevertheless, one might accede to the inevitable and admit what is good for the goose is good for the gander. The whites have dominated the stage for so long that it is time for the others to stand up. Unfortunately, it is unlikely that this will produce accurate history.

12 Michael Kammen, *Mystic Chords of Memory The Transformation of Tradition in American Culture* (New York, 1993), 625.

Chapter 27

Supernatural Insights

As demonstrated, our memories are altered by a multitude of conscious and subconscious factors that can lead to inaccurate history in a natural world made up of nuts and bolts reality. It should come as no surprise, then, that all of the processes influencing our brains also have an impact or influence on what some of us might consider the supernatural world.

One year after the Sand Creek fighting, a buffalo hunter named Kipling Brightwater claimed to have seen a band of Cheyenne camped on the site. He sent his partner out to talk to them, but no one was there when the man arrived. Although the man sent to investigate did not see anything, he "felt that something very wrong had gone on in the area." Brightwater reported his experience at Fort Lyon and soldiers investigated but found nothing. The next year, however, Brightwater and more hunters found themselves back in the Sand Creek area. This time around he claimed he saw Indians, tipis, animals, and fires. According to Brightwater, he rode closer to investigate and the entire assemblage simply disappeared into the mist. The perplexed hunter later explained that the only thing he heard was "the sound of a woman crying out in mourning."

In 1911, a local woman said she was traveling near the site when she said she heard crying, but a search turned up nothing. Similar stories were told for the next hundred years. In the 1990s, visitors to the area were said to feel pain, anguish, and grief. Even members of archaeological teams searching for the village site allegedly felt "overwhelming senses of grief and sadness." Recent visitors to the area have reported being overcome with such feelings. But do they have anything to do with the supernatural, or are they merely human emotions?[1]

Don Vasicek, who made a documentary film about Sand Creek, said in an interview with *Ghost Story Magazine* that he was overcome with emotions on his first visit to the field. Bill Dawson, the rancher who owned the land where the fighting was said to have taken place, gave Vasicek a tour and shared his interpretation of events. "At that moment," claimed Vasicek,

> I saw Colonel John M. Chivington, on a dark-colored horse, with his saber drawn, thrashing down this butte into Sand Creek leading a charge right into the heart of the Cheyenne and Arapaho village. I saw his flaming eyes, orbs of hatred and terror. It was at that point, I felt coldness penetrate my body. I shivered. I rubbed the back of my neck. It was rigid. I closed my eyes. I didn't want to look anymore. I could hear gunshots, the thud of rifle butts colliding with human heads, sabers slashing through the air, people screaming, and I could smell globs (sic) gun powder."[2]

As we know, however, soldiers testified that they had walked into the Indian camp without any sabers in play.

Even more than a place of personal emotional impact, the Dawson's Bend site has taken on spiritual connotations. A chief of the Cheyenne Council of 44 named Laird Cometsevah visited the site many times over the years and performing sacred rituals there. He claimed to have "heard the voices of children, of mothers, crying for help." Because he heard voices he "knew that's where Black Kettle's people got killed." Years earlier, Cometsevah had accompanied the a Cheyenne named Sacred Arrow Keeper to Sand Creek, where he consecrated soil to make it "Cheyenne earth." "Spiritually and religiously," Cometsevah explained, we "claimed that spot for the Cheyenne." "The Arrow Keeper wasn't wrong," he insisted. "I wasn't wrong. That's exactly where the massacre happened." Unfortunately, no physical evidence of the

---

1   "Mystery History the Paranormal and More," http://mysteryandhistory.blogspot.com/ 2011/05/ghosts of-sand-creek.html, accessed December 17, 2013; "The ghosts of Sand Creek," http://www.examiner.com/article/the-ghosts-of-sand-creek, accessed December 17, 2013.

2   "Donald L. Vasicek: The Zen of Writing," http://donvasicek.com/uncategorized/1516/, accessed December 18, 2013.

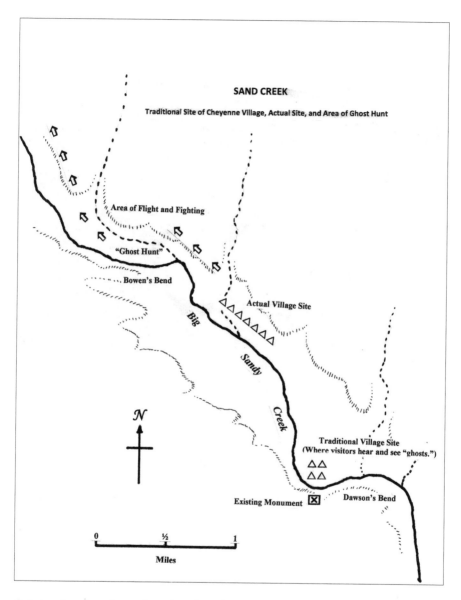

SAND CREEK

Traditional Site of Cheyenne Village, Actual Site, and Area of Ghost Hunt

Area of Flight and Fighting

"Ghost Hunt"

Bowen's Bend

Actual Village Site

Big Sandy Creek

Traditional Village Site
(Where visitors hear and see "ghosts.")

Existing Monument ☒   Dawson's Bend

N

0   ½   1

Miles

fighting has ever been found at that site. In what appears to be an exercise in circular logic, the village had to have once stood at Dawson's Bend on Sand Creek because a sacred ceremony was performed there. Why was it performed there? Because that's where the village was located.

Many Cheyenne, however, could not accept the fact that the traditional village site contained none of the artifacts that should have been associated with a village and a battle. In addition, archaeological surveys demonstrated that the

The old monument on the bluff overlooking the traditional village site.
Author

village and the fight took place at least one to three miles upstream. "They're calling our ancestors liars," was Cometsevah reply. Of course Cometsevah's ancestors were not being called liars, but not being a liar is not the same thing as being accurate.[3]

The reality is that the deficient memories of everyone involved wreaked more than enough havoc on the historical truth of what happened at Sand Creek, and where it happened. The simple fact is that Vasicek, Cometsevah, and hundreds of other visitors were mistaken about where the village was located and the fighting took place. Black Kettle's village was not on the spot where these people stood and envisioned all the horrors of warfare and heard weeping women and crying babies.

The lack of archeological evidence did not stop the National Park Service (NPS) from acting. While the NPS was negotiating the purchase of the land, a team of professional archaeologists inspected the area and found that actual site

3   Kelman, *Misplaced Massacre*, 126, 140–41.

of Black Kettle's village was a mile to a mile-and-a-half north of the area where the so-called spiritual encounters had occurred. Despite this information, the NPS constructed its visitor center near a stone monument that sits atop a bluff overlooking Sand Creek—but nowhere near the site where the actual Cheyenne village once stood. But the Park Service now owns the land, so it serves a purpose (and brings to mind the famous movie line "If you build it, they will come").

Chuck Bowen grew up on a ranch a few miles north of the NPS site. He spent many years searching the the area and discovered numerous village- and battle-related artifacts. He and his wife Sheri intensified their efforts to find the real site of the battle after 1993, when the Colorado Historical Society began inspecting the area. By 1997, they were hard at work with metal detectors, history books, and maps, and as a result assembled a remarkable collection of more than 3,000 relics—all found on Bowen property starting about two miles northwest of the traditional site at Dawson's Bend.

When the NPS entered the picture as a result of a 1998 public law, Chuck Bowen suggested to park representatives that the U.S. soldiers got their first view of the village from the bluffs near the monument above Dawson's Bend, but that the real village site was nearly two miles farther north. That area, he explained, was where they should begin looking for artifacts. The NPS located a concentration of artifacts a mile and more north of Dawson's Bend, which they soon determined was the actual site of Black Kettle's village. The artifact patterns also indicate that the village was not drawn up in a tight circle as is usually depicted, but was instead strung out along the course of the creek for at least a mile. The archaeologists noted that the "absence of definitive artifacts of resistance" was consistent with the Indian accounts that the attack came as a complete surprise.[4]

If the lack of weapon relics in the village suggest the Indians were surprised and did not put up much if any of a fight, it also supports what a number of soldiers claimed: The Indians had already vacated the camp before they reached it, they had simply walked in, and that there was no battle in the village proper.

Thus, the relativism— knowledge and truth existing in relation to historical context—and its parent, postmodernism, are reflected even in scientific study.

---

4   Jerome A. Greene and Douglas D. Scott, *Finding Sand Creek: History, Archaeology, and the 1864 Massacre Site* (Norman, OK, 2004), 96.

Chapter 28

The End of History?

The relativism involved in the study of history is encompassed within Postmodernism—a radical reappraisal of assumptions about culture, identity, history, and language that was in evidence since the mid-20th century. It was largely a reaction to the assumed certainty of scientific, objective efforts to explain reality, and stemmed from recognition that truth is not universal, but is constructed on an ad-hoc basis as the brain tries to understand its own personal reality.[1]

Postmodern interpretation essentially demolishes comprehensive narratives. According to this view, history isn't progressive and knowledge cannot liberate. Philosophy and history are metaphorical. Objectivity is a chimera and history is myth—no different from literature because all meaning is socially encoded, just like fiction.

It would be very dangerous if history is indeed myth, because whoever controls the official discourse can use it to marginalize subordinate groups. The lesson gleaned from postmodernism is that master narratives are not trustworthy. This, in turn, offers some irony, for while postmodernism contributed to the growth of diverse cultural histories, it simultaneously worked at the same time to dissolve the sense of history in culture. Exploding diverse

---

1 Bertrand Russell, *A History of Western Philosophy* (New York, 1945), 679; Joyce Appleby, Lynn Hunt, and Margaret Jacob, *Telling the Truth About History* (New York, 1994), 112–13.

cultural histories while imploding history out of culture, however, creates something akin to a relativistic, historical black hole.[2]

There are other internal contradictions. Scientific objective efforts to get at the truth supposedly cannot work because we invest the objects of our study with our own values and biases. That contention is not simply postmodernist rhetoric. Scientific studies have shown that even scientific studies have inherent biases we cannot overcome. Put another way, science impartially proves that it cannot prove impartially. A postmodernist contention is sustained by the very science postmodernism disdains. The entire process is akin to tumbling down the rabbit hole.

It is the historian's job to find order and pattern in history. While we search for connections and cycles, we sometimes forget that coincidence and contiguity are not causes, and eyewitness sources can be very inaccurate.

The demise of history has been written about for millennia. In the Plato's *Republic*, the philosopher wrote about the "dialectic," a type of logical process or method of argumentation that employs contrary cases to ultimately settle on a final solution, thus ending the controversy.

This idea was refined and expanded upon by German philosopher Georg Wilhelm Friedrich Hegel (1770–1831), who incorporated logic, metaphysics, and history into his famous Hegelian Dialectic. The dialectic (logical argument) posits that every attempt to formulate conceptions about the world (thesis) is contradicted by another formulation (antithesis), and the conflict between the two is eventually resolved (synthesis). With synthesis, the dialectic is ended— for a time—for internal inconsistencies will eventually serve as a thesis for a new dialectic.[3]

A postmodernist might deride Hegel as being a traditionalist because his argument implies a harmonious solution. But will the dialectic ever lead us to the truth? Its course seems to be progressive and linearly ascendant, because each new thesis represents an advance over the previous thesis, and in the final culmination results in the objectification of thought and mind. For Hegel, existence without a functioning dialectic is hollow: "Periods of happiness are empty pages in history." Man is left with activity without opposition. Given his nature, he may heat and stir the pot just to see something boil. If that is his

2 Christopher Butler, *Postmodernism A Very Short Introduction* (New York, 2002), 13, 16, 24, 32, 33–36, 50, 59, 105, 110, 116.

3 Peter Singer, *Hegel A Very Short Introduction* (New York, 1983), 100–02.

course, then the end goal of Reason can never be achieved, and the entire process of history collapses into what Hegel calls a "bad infinity." Reason and order in the universe are lost. History becomes meaningless. If Reason is the final goal and it cannot exist within meaninglessness, the entire scheme collapses.[4]

To avoid the fate of Sisyphus—who in Greek legend was punished in Hades by eternally rolling a heavy stone up a hill, only to have it slip from his grasp and roll back down again—there must be a final solution: The end of history. Hegel believed the final truth would come by learning the lessons of history. But if truth is revealed over time, and if it depends on historical circumstances, the road is open for historical relativism, and when the dialectic derails there is no progress. He unknowingly set the stage for an arbitrary universe—and postmodernism.

Hegel's most famous construction—history as thesis, antithesis, and synthesis—proved to be dead right. Hegel's Dialectic is nothing other than cognitive dissonance and its reduction. The thesis is man at status quo, the antithesis is the dissonant cognition (thought) that upsets his equilibrium, and the synthesis is the rationalization and justification that hopefully restores harmony.

Hegel's model posits a final point of realization that becomes the end of history. In a postmodernist world there will also be an end of history, but only because there will be no universal truth to discover; the continuous dissonance and its constant reduction is on a personal, individual, never-ending treadmill. Discovering the final truth would end history as much as spinning in a perpetual circle, trapped in a maze with no outlet, which is the actual case when we continuously battle our cognitive dissonance in search for an elusive equilibrium.

As we have witnessed with after-action testimony of the Sand Creek affair, events flowed from one crisis situation to the next as the participants did their best to buttress their own self-esteem and reduce dissonance. Changing memories of what took place eventually ran up against more dissonance—and the need to find new justifications to ease a troubled conscience. Even an honest man can lose his ideals gradually and unknowingly by offering

---

4   "A Historian Looks at Hegel Philosophically: Critical Examination of Hegelian Dialectic, Determinism, and Contingency," www.historicalinsights.com/dave/hegel.html, accessed February 13, 2014.

justifications for action or inaction. This stepladder of rationalization is dangerous because it only soothes the conscience and allows one to increase the lie.[5]

Constant debate swirls around what happened at Sand Creek, and no synthesis results because the thesis-antithesis is rarely discussed in terms of fact, but is instead molded while under the control of preconception, prejudice, false memory, confirmation bias, internal belief systems and more. There can therefore never be a valid synthesis, and no reduction of dissonance. If true, this represents the end of all practical history. All history stems from a nexus with memory, and we have witnessed how inadequate memory is at rooting out the truth. Thus, what happened at Sand Creek is never fully resolved and ends in a well of frustration between biased and eternally bickering minds.

For those of us still intrigued enough to pursue the matter, how can we find out what really happened at Sand Creek, in the other Indian war incidents, or in any other historical event? Which sources should we use? Is there a difference, or only a scale of poor options? Perhaps the best alternative is to provide a historiographical survey of the various sources and let the readers choose the one that most comfortably fits their own biases.

In the end, there are only our personal interpretations of events, filtered through individual lenses and bounced like a pinball through the synapses in different areas of our brains. The final understanding is true only for the one doing the filtering. After the "facts" have been either consciously or unconsciously transformed by the participants and the historians, the reader strains a book or article through the sieve of her own prejudices, experience, and judgment.

Today it appears we have even gone beyond Postmodernism. Not only have we likely reached the end of history, we may have entered unexplored territory: *extra mundum veri* (a world beyond truth). How will we ever determine what happened at Sand Creek?

1. APPLY LOGIC

2. REPLICATION = VERIFICATION

what do the majority of sources say?

5   Tavris, and Aronson, *Mistakes Were Made*, 4–5, 10, 37.

Appendix A

Ghosts Busted at Sand Creek

Believing is seeing, and when given a choice, most people with pre- conceived notions will usually hone in on things that best fit those preconceptions. Ghost hunters, as it turns out, are no different.

What happens when modern spirit-seekers hunt for the ghosts of the dead at the right place? Out of curiosity, Chuck Bowen, who owns much of the land upon which the actual fighting took place, allowed a ghost-hunting team to try its luck and invited the author to come along and observe. We assembled on a dirt road leading onto the Bowen property on a late afternoon in March of 2004. The Denver-based ghost hunters arrived just before twilight.

The group came equipped with all the must-haves for any reputable ghost hunter: infrared thermometers, electro-magnetic field detectors, audio recorders, full spectrum digital video cameras, night-vision cameras, laser lights, atmospheric meters, flashlights, and extra batteries. We drove to the south side of a cottonwood-lined bend where Chuck thought it would be a good place to start the hunt. Armed with their equipment, the hunters slowly walked toward the trees, adjusting meters and sweeping detectors left and right.[1]

We walked only a score of yards across the prairie when one of the women, apparently the "seer"—she did not carry any instruments but apparently picked up supernatural vibes with her own internal antenna—stopped and raised her arms out to her sides like a telephone pole. After a time she lowered her arms and I waited for what I believed was a respectable time for her to come out of her trance.

"What did you see or hear?" I finally asked.

---

1 When I jokingly asked if ghosts operated on infrared or electro-magnetically, my skepticism only served to make the hunters defensive. One of the rules on their website is that anyone asking for a ghost investigation or who wanted to be a member had to be a believer.

Bowen Bend northwest of the village, area of Indian flight and "ghost" hunt.
Author

"There were women," she answered, "Many were crying over their dead children, and one in particular was telling me about how awful it was for a mother to have her baby murdered."

I wondered whether these women were communicating to her in Cheyenne, or if they had learned English for their supernatural conversation. My offhanded remark about my dead grandmother sending me a message in Polish didn't impress her.

Near the creek bank, we walked to a place where Chuck had found a significant cache of relics, including bones. The hunters tramped right over the spot without a beep on their instruments or an inclination from the human antenna that they just stood on what presumably should have been one of the "hottest" spots on the field. The ghost hunters continued on, creeping among the trees and brush while slowly swinging their instruments left and right. Occasionally they stopped to take flash photographs. Speaking in whispers, they discussed their readings and appeared to be having success. I sidled up to one and tried to look at his meter. He smiled and showed me all the "activity" he was getting, but to me the gauge seemed fairly dead and unresponsive. I assumed the needle would be swinging like a pendulum.

When they finished sweeping the cottonwood grove, Chuck said there was another spot he wanted them to check, but we would have to walk back to the cars and drive there. By now it was quite dark. After following the lead vehicle's tail lights, we stopped at a new site nearly a mile upstream. The ghost hunters swept the area for a while before one halted to announce his battery was dead.

"Is this a common occurrence?" I asked.

"Oh yes," he said as he worked to replace the battery. "The spirits don't seem to like the interference and when their presence is strong they seem to take it out on us by killing our batteries."

"Wow," I replied. "How come our car batteries are working fine?"

That was another mistake. He turned away, walked up to another hunter, and whispered something. The pair shot me a glance and walked off in another direction.

When the investigation ended, we gathered back at the cars, which, miraculously, all started right up. Chuck led us out across the dry creek bed and over a few miles of prairie, jackrabbits scattering in front of us in the beams of our headlights. We all bid adieu when we reached the dirt road that would lead back to the paved highway.

The ghost hunters sent Chuck several "proofs" to show him the land was indeed haunted. "They took lots of pictures," Chuck explained. "It was well after dark and they used a flash on the camera. Some of the pictures had white and sometimes red dots." Chuck is an experienced photographer and well aware there were mundane explanations for these things, like reflections, lens flare from too much or uneven glass, an improperly opened aperture, dust, moisture, and in that location, floating cottonwood seeds. But the ghost hunters had an explanation of their own. "They said it was orbs," explained Chuck, "and the red dots were angry evil spirits." Overall, he concluded, "Taking the group out was a fun experience but for me I was underwhelmed." I agreed.

Later, I emailed the ghost hunters and asked about their findings. "We got some great stuff," the spokesperson wrote back. "EVPs (electronic voice phenomena) of screams and crying, cannons firing, soldiers yelling."

Those were some recordings. I never heard or saw any such things, but I guess my poor humanoid senses couldn't pick up all the activity that their instruments could. All I heard or saw were live humans talking, tramping through the undergrowth, or snapping an occasional twig underfoot. What I do know is that the areas we led them through where they had their "hits" were the very ones completely devoid of artifacts and conflict, while they walked over ground once laden with battle relics without generating so much as a beep or a buzz from their sophisticated instruments.[2]

The ghost hunters believed they would find a supernatural presence, were primed for it, and zeroed in on the places they felt should be haunted. They were little different from the visitors to the NPS-Dawson site who were told that the spot was where people were killed, and thus they imagined they could see or hear evidence of a massacre.

Believing is seeing. Like the ghost hunters, we historians and readers can search for and find exactly what we are looking to find.

---

2 The artifact concentrations can be found in Michno, *Battle at Sand Creek*, 288, and in Greene and Scott, *Finding Sand Creek*, 100. Much of the above story appeared in Gregory F. Michno, "Ghostbusters Busted at Sand Creek," *Skeptic*, Vol. 19, no. 1, 2014.

Appendix B

List of Killed and Wounded in the First and Third Colorado Cavalry at Sand Creek

The names below are from the Colorado State Archives (CSA), *Rocky Mountain News* (RMN), *Official Records War of the Rebellion* (OR), and eyewitness accounts (e.g., Coffin). Any uncertain casualties are denoted with an *.

FIRST COLORADO

Company C. Lt. Judson J. Kennedy

Ballou, Cornelius J., Pvt. (wounded, CSA, OR)

Batton, James (wounded, RMN)

Boyles, William, Pvt. (wounded, CSA, OR)

Calhoun, James Pvt. (wounded, arrow, right leg, RMN)

Calhoun, John B., Pvt. (wounded, gunshot in throat, CSA, OR, RMN)

Eaton, Joe Pvt. (wounded, arrow in back, RMN)

Linnell, Marshall H., Sgt. (wounded, CSA, OR)

Mattage, August, Pvt. (Mettge, Mettgo, Mattear) (wounded, CSA, OR, RMN)

Pierson, Oliver Pvt. (mortally wounded, right leg, arrow, CSA, OR, RMN)

Smith, Joseph (John) Pvt. (wounded, arrow in leg, RMN)

South, Elias Sadlr. (wounded, CSA, OR)

Tabor, Gus Pvt. (killed, RMN)

Weston, Pugh Pvt. (wounded, hip, RMN)

Wheatley, Augustus Pvt. (wounded, arrow in neck, RMN)

Company D. Capt. Silas S. Soule

Van Curen, John (wounded or sick, CSA, RMN)

Company E. Lt. Clark Dunn

Jackson, William C., Sgt. (wounded, broken leg, OR, RMN)

Mull, Henry Pvt. (wounded, gunshot leg, OR, CSA)

Company F. Capt. Samuel H. Cook.
(Men attached to Anthony's Battalion)

Aldrich, Joseph W., Pvt. (killed, CSA)

Pierce, George W., Pvt. (killed, RMN, CSA)

Company G. Lt. George H. Hardin (resigned 11-28).
Lt. Horace W. Baldwin.

Luckham, Thomas (wounded, CSA, RMN)

Company H. Lt. Luther Wilson, Lt. James Olney,
Lt. George H. Chase

Goodsell, Alvin H., Pvt. (wounded, right knee, CSA, RMN) (possibly in Co. A. Third CO)

Pingree, George W., Pvt.
(wounded, shot in face, CSA, RMN)

McGriffin, James D., Pvt. (wounded, Howbert,
CSA shows him unassigned in First CO)

Lt. Luther Wilson
(wounded, gunshot in arm, RMN)

Company K. Lt. Joseph A. Cramer

Nye, Alfred (wounded, CSA, RMN)

THIRD COLORADO

*Company A. Capt. Theodore G. Cree,
Lt. Charles L. Cass, Lt. Eldridge B. Sopris*

*Bennett, James A., Pvt.
(killed per CSA, in Third CO)

Connor, Joseph H., Pvt.
(killed, arrow in right breast, RMN, Shaw)

Gibbs, Lewis W., Pvt. (killed, CSA)

Metcalf, James A., Pvt.
(wounded, gunshot in neck and cheek, CSA, RMN)

Nesselton (Nettleton), George W., Pvt.
(wounded, neck and throat, CSA, RMN)

Parks, Ed Frank, Pvt.
(wounded, left leg, CSA, RMN, Shaw)

*Company B. Capt. Harper M. Orahood,
Lt. Charles H. Hawley, Lt. Harry Richmond*

Burghardt (Burckhart), Samuel H., Sgt.
(wounded, CSA, RMN)

Hawley, Charles H., Lt.
(wounded, shoulder, OR, CSA, RMN)

Manion, (Marrion) T.N., Pvt.
(wounded, gunshot in hip, CSA, OR, RMN)

Rowse, Zalmon Pvt. (killed, CSA)

*Company C. Capt. William H. Morgan,
Lt. Martin Wall, Lt. John F. Wymond*

*Baker, Thomas Pvt.
(wounded per CSA, Third CO)
Battenes (Battines), Bedal Pvt. (killed, CSA)
Field, Noah Pvt. (killed, CSA)

Field, Noah, Pvt. (killed, CSA)

Medino (Medina), Francisco Pvt.
(killed, CSA, RMN, Coffin)

*Company D. Capt. David H. Nichols, Lt. Andrew J.
Pennock, Lt. Lewis H. Dickson*

Carr, James O. (A.) (wounded, CSA, RMN)

Foster, Henry C., Pvt. (killed, CSA, RMN, Coffin)

Herrick, Amos Pvt. (killed, CSA, Coffin)

Maxwell, Andrew J. Cpl.
(wounded, bullet in chest, CSA, RMN, Coffin)

McFarland, Robert Pvt.
(killed, CSA, OR, RMN, Coffin)

Moore, Ewers Cpl. (killed, CSA, Coffin)

Phillips, Stephen Cpl. (wounded, Coffin)

*Company E. Capt. Jay J. Johnson,
Lt. Samuel H. Gibson*

McDermott, Patrick Pvt. (killed, CSA, RMN)

Wilson, Martin, blacksmith
(wounded, right breast, left shoulder, CSA, RMN)

*Company F. Capt. Edward Chase,
Lts. Joseph A. Foy, Charles Haines*

Bradley, John W., Pvt.
(wounded, gunshot left leg, RMN)

Dorsey, George W., Pvt.
(wounded, arrow in left side, CSA, RMN)

*Company G. Capt. Oliver H.P. Baxter,
Lts. Swain L. Graham, Andrew J. Templeton*

Wells, Marion John Pvt. (killed, CSA, Coffin)

*Company H. Capt. Thomas E. McDonald,
Lt. Mariano Autobees*

*Heath, Theodore T., Pvt. Wounded
(CSA says killed, Co. H. Third CO.)

*Holtz, David Pvt. Wounded
(CSA says killed, Co. H. Third CO)

*Company I. Capt. John McCannon, Lt. Thomas J. Davis,
Lt. Henry H. Hewitt (not at battle)*

Berkheimer (Buckhamer), Jesse Pvt.
(killed, CSA, RMN)

Douglass, James Sgt.
(wounded, arrow in left arm, CSA, RMN)

Duncan, John R., Pvt. (killed, CSA, RMN)

Hamilton, Richard Sgt.
(wounded, arrow in left arm, CSA, RMN)

Maxwell, Tom J. (wounded, CSA, RMN)

Parks (Parkes), John (James) Pvt.
(killed, gunshot in hip, CSA, RMN)

Richards, James Pvt. (killed, CSA)

Tisdale, James W. Cpl.
(wounded, in the back, CSA, RMN)

Zahan (Zahm), Horace B. (killed, CSA)

*Company K. Lt. William E. Grinnell,
Lt. Joseph T. Boyd, Lt. William R. Newkirk*

Bissell (Bisel), Benjamin F. Cpl. (wounded, gunshot
through right thigh, CSA, RMN)

Brown, Benjamin Pvt. (wounded, gunshot through
throat and left shoulder, RMN)

Stahl, Benjamin Ellis Pvt. (wounded, gunshot in
right breast, CSA, RMN)

Thomas, Jefferson Pvt. Saddler (wounded, gunshot
in right shoulder, CSA, RMN)

Woodworth, James H., Pvt. (wounded, arrow
through thigh, CSA, RMN)

*Company L. Capt. J. Freeman Phillips, Lts. Oliver M.
Albro, Maxwell D. Baslinger*

Parker, John Pvt. (killed, RMN)

Wilks (Wilkes), John W., Pvt. (killed, CSA)

*Company M. Capt. Presley Talbot,
Lt. Frank DeLamar, Lt. Thomas Peck*

Cree (Kaw), John Pvt. (wounded, arrow in bowels,
broken left thigh, RMN)

Cue, James (wounded, RMN)

Dolan, John Pvt. (killed, CSA)

Houston (Hueston), Thomas Pvt.
(wounded, arrow in elbow, RMN)

Mallory (Malroy), John H., Pvt.
(wounded, arrow in hip, RMN)

Millay, Thomas (John) Cpl. (wounded, CSA, RMN)

Morris, David (Daniel) Pvt.
(wounded, arrow in right side, RMN)

Orleans, Louis P., Sgt. (wounded, arrow in arm,
gunshot in side, CSA, OR, RMN)

Rice, Charles W., Pvt.
(wounded, right shoulder and elbow, CSA, RMN)

Sherman, Amos (Amas, Abel) Pvt.
(wounded, arrow in hip, CSA, RMN)

Talbot, Presley, Capt.
(wounded, gunshot in groin, CSA, OR, RMN)

*   *   *

Casualty Totals			
	Killed	Wounded	Total
1st Colorado	4	21	25
3rd Colorado	20	31	51
Totals	24	52	76

Bibliography

Archival Accounts and Papers

Anthony, Scott J., Papers, Colorado Historical Society.

Bent, George. "The Letters of George Bent to George Bird Grinnell, 1901–1918." Southwest Museum, Los Angeles, CA.

Bennett, Deborah J. "The Letters of George Bent to George E. Hyde, 1904–1918." Coe Collection, Beinecke Manuscript Library, Yale University, New Haven, CT.

Chubbuck, Theodore L. "Dictation. Battle of Sand Creek." P-L 135, Bancroft Library. University of California, Berkeley.

Slater, Milo H. "Indian Troubles in the Early Days of Colorado," P-L 169, Bancroft Library. University of California, Berkeley.

Soule, Silas, Letters. WH1690 Box 1. FF1 Denver Public Library.

Soule, Silas S., Papers. *Kansas State Historical Society*. WH1690, Box 1.

Tappan, Samuel. Diary and Notebook of Samuel F. Tappan, 1865. MSS#617. Colorado Historical Society.

Government Publications

U.S. Congress, Senate. "Sand Creek Massacre." Report of the Secretary of War Communicating, In compliance with a resolution of the Senate of February 4, 1867, a copy of the evidence taken at Denver and Fort Lyon, Colorado Territory, by a military commission, ordered to inquire into the Sand Creek Massacre, November, 1864. Senate Exec. Doc. 26. 39th Congress, 2nd Session. Washington: GPO, 1867.

U.S. Congress, Senate. "Massacre of Cheyenne Indians." *Report of the Joint Committee on the Conduct of the War at the Second Session Thirty-Eighth Congress*. 38th Congress, 2nd Session. Washington: GPO, 1865.

U.S. Congress, Senate. "The Chivington Massacre." Condition of the Indian Tribes. Report of the Joint Special Committee, Appointed Under Joint Resolution of March 3, 1865. With an Appendix. Senate Report 156. 39th Congress. 2nd Session. 1867. Washington: GPO, 1867.

U.S. Department of the Interior, Bureau of Indian Affairs, *Report of the Commissioner of Indian Affairs, 1865.* Washington: GPO, 1865.

U.S. War Department. The War of the Rebellion: A Compilation of the Official Records of the Union and Confederate Armies. Washington: GPO, 1880-1901.

Dissertations

Roberts, Gary Roberts. "Sand Creek: Tragedy and Symbol," A Dissertation Submitted to the Graduate Faculty in Partial Fulfillment of the Requirements for the Degree of Doctor of Philosophy, Norman, OK: 1984.

Books, Journals, and Miscellaneous Sources

American Psychiatric Association. *Diagnostic and Statistical Manual for Mental Disorders DSM III-R* Washington, D.C.: American Psychiatric Press, 1987.

Appleby, Joyce, Lynn Hunt, and Margaret Jacob. *Telling the Truth About History.* New York: W. W. Norton & Company, 1994.

Athearn, Robert G. *William Tecumseh Sherman and the Settlement of the West.* Norman, OK University of Oklahoma Press, 1995.

"The Backfire Effect" *You Are Not So Smart A Celebration of Self Delusion,* June 10, 2011. http://youarenotsosmart.com/2011/06/10/the-backfire-effect/.

Bain, David H. Bain. *Empire Express Building the First Transcontinental Railroad.* New York: Viking, 1999.

Barry, Louise. "The Ranch at Great Bend," *Kansas Historical Quarterly*, 39, no. 1 (Spring 1973).

———. "The Ranch at Walnut Creek Crossing." *Kansas Historical Quarterly* 37, no. 2 (Summer 1971).

Bennett, Deborah J. *Randomness.* Cambridge, MS: Harvard University Press, 1998.

Berthrong, Donald J. *The Southern Cheyennes.* Norman, OK: University of Oklahoma Press, 1963.

Bloch, Marc. *The Historian's Craft.* New York: Vintage Books, 1953.

Breakenridge, William M. *Helldorado: Bringing the Law to the Mesquite.* Lincoln, NE: University of Nebraska Press, 1992.

Breisach, Ernst. *Historiography Ancient, Medieval, and Modern.* Chicago, IL: University of Chicago Press, 1983.

Broome, Jeff. "Indian Massacres in Elbert County, Colorado: New Information on the 1864 Hungate and 1868 Dietemann Murders." *The Denver Westerners Roundup* Vol. LX, no. 1 (January–February 2004).

Brown, Dee. *Bury My Heart at Wounded Knee*. New York: Holt, Rinehart & Winston, 1970.

Butler, Christopher. *Postmodernism: A Very Short Introduction*. New York: Oxford University Press, 2002.

Carey, Raymond G. "Colonel Chivington, Brigadier General Connor, and Sand Creek," in *Westerners Brand Book 1960*. Guy M. Herstrom, ed. Boulder, CO: Johnson Publishing Co., 1961.

Carr, Nicholas. *The Shallows What the Internet is Doing to Our Brains*. New York: W. W. Norton & Company, 2011.

Carroll, John M., ed. *The Sand Creek Massacre: A Documentary History*. New York: Sol Lewis, 1973.

Chabris, Christopher, and Daniel Simons. *The Invisible Gorilla How Our Intuitions Deceive Us*. New York: Broadway Books, 2009.

Coel, Margaret. *Chief Left Hand: Southern Arapaho*. Norman, OK: University of Oklahoma Press, 1981.

Coffin, Morse H. *The Battle of Sand Creek*. Waco, TX: W.M. Morrison, 1965.

"Cognitive Dissonance and Self-Perception Theory." *eLearnPortal*. www.elearnportal.com/courses/psychology/social-and-community-psychology/soci al-and-community-psychology-cognitive-dissonance-and-self-perception-th.

Collins, Loren. *Bullspotting Finding Facts in the Age of Information*. Amherst, NY: Prometheus Books, 2012.

Condorcet, Marquis de. "The Future Progress of the Human Mind." in Isaac Kramnick, ed. *The Portable Enlightenment Reader*. New York: Penguin Books, 1995.

Cooper, Joel. *Cognitive Dissonance Fifty Years of a Classic Theory*. London: Sage Publications Ltd., 2007.

Coward, John M. *The Newspaper Indian Native American Identity in the Press, 1820–1890*. Urbana, IL: University of Illinois Press, 1999.

Craig, Reginald S. *The Fighting Parson: The Biography of Colonel John M. Chivington* (Tucson, AZ: Westernlore Press, 1959.

Dippie, Brian. *The Vanishing American White Attitudes & U. S. Indian Policy*. Lawrence, KS: University Press of Kansas, 1982.

Dunn, J. P. Jr. *Massacres of the Mountains: A History of the Indian Wars of the Far West 1815-1875*. New York: Harper and Brothers, 1886.

Dunn, Lt. Col. William R. *I Stand by Sand Creek: A Defense of Colonel John M. Chivington and the Third Colorado Cavalry*. Fort Collins, CO: The Old Army Press, 1985.

Elson, Ruth Miller. *Guardians of Tradition American Schoolbooks of the Nineteenth Century*. Lincoln, NE: University of Nebraska Press, 1964.

Engel, George L. *Psychological Development in Health and Disease*. Philadelphia, PA: W. B. Saunders Company, 1962.

Engelhardt, Laura. "The Problem with Eyewitness Testimony Commentary on a talk by George Fisher and Barbara Tversky." *Stanford Journal of Legal Studies* Vol. 1:1, April 5, 1999. http://agora.stanford.edu/sjls/Issue%20One/fisher&tversky.htm.

Evans, Richard J. "Postmodernism and History." *Butterflies & Wheels*, October 22, 2002. www.butterfliesandwheels.org/2002/postmodernism-and-history/.

Festinger, Leon, Henry W. Riecken, and Stanley Schacter. *When Prophesy Fails*. Foreword by Elliot Aronson. London: Pinter & Martin, 2005.

Fischer, David Hackett. *Historians' Fallacies: Toward a Logic of Historical Thought*. New York: Harper & Row, 1970.

Foote, Kenneth E. *Shadowed Ground America's Landscapes of Violence and Tragedy*. Austin, TX: University of Texas Press, 1997.

Foxhall, Kathryn. "Suddenly, a Big Impact on Criminal Justice." *American Psychological Association*, Vol. 31, no. 1, January 2000. Www.apa.org/monitor/jan00/pi4.aspx.

Frederick, J. V. *Ben Holladay: The Stagecoach King*. Glendale, CA: Arthur H. Clark Co., 1940. Reprint, Lincoln, NE: University of Nebraska Press, 1989.

Frost, S. E. Jr. *Basic Teachings of the Great Philosophers* (New York: Anchor Books, 1989

Fukuyama, Francis. *The End of History and the Last Man*. New York: Avon Books, 1992.

Fussell, Paul. *Wartime Understanding and Behavior in the Second World War*. New York: Oxford University Press, 1989.

Gabriel, Richard A. *No More Heroes Madness and Psychiatry in War*. New York: Hill and Wang, 1987.

———. *The Painful Field The Psychiatric Dimension of Modern War*. Westport, CT: Greenwood Press, 1988.

Gardner, Daniel. *The Science of Fear How the Culture of Fear Manipulates Your Brain*. New York: Plume, 2009.

"The ghosts of Sand Creek." www.examiner.com/article/the-ghosts-of-sand-creek

Ginsburg, Herbert R. and Silvia Opper. *Piaget's Theory of Intellectual Development*. Englewood Cliffs, NJ: Prentice Hall, 1988.

Gorman, James. "Scientists Trace Memories of Things That Never Happened." *New York Times*, July 25, 2013. www.nytimes.com/2013/07/26/science/false-memory-planted-in-a-mouse-brain-study-shows.html?_r=0

Greene, Jerome, ed. *Lakota and Cheyenne Indian Views of the Great Sioux War, 1876–1877*. Norman, OK: University of Oklahoma Press, 1994.

Greene, Jerome A., and Douglas D. Scott. *Finding Sand Creek History, Archaeology, and the 1864 Massacre Site*. Norman, OK: University of Oklahoma Press, 2004.

Grinnell, George Bird. *The Cheyenne Indians Their History and Ways of Life Vol. I.* Lincoln, NE: University of Nebraska Press, 1972.

Grossman, Dave, Lt. Col. *On Killing The Psychological Cost of Learning to Kill in War and Society*. Boston MS: Little, Brown & Company, 1995.

Hallinan, Joseph T. *Why We Make Mistakes*. New York: Broadway Books, 2009.

Hardorff, Richard G., ed. *Lakota Recollections of the Custer Fight New Sources of Indian-Military History*. Spokane, WA: Arthur H. Clark Company, 1991.

"A Historian Looks at Hegel Philosophically: Critical Examination of Hegelian Dialectic, Determinism, and Contingency." www.historicalinsights.com/dave/hegel.html

Hoig, Stan. *The Sand Creek Massacre*. Norman, OK: University of Oklahoma Press, 1961.

———. *The Western Odyssey of John Simpson Smith Frontiersman, Trapper, Trader, and Interpreter*. Glendale, CA: The Arthur H. Clark Company, 1974.

Hood, Bruce M. *Supersense Why we Believe in the Unbelievable*. New York: HarperOne, 2009.

Howbert, Irving. *The Indians of the Pike's Peak Region*. New York: Knickerbocker Press, 1914. Reprint, Glorieta, NM: The Rio Grande Press, Inc., 1970.

Huston, Matt. "Now It's Personal Arguments are Harder to Resolve when Values are on the Line." *Psychology Today* 47, no. 3 (May/June 2014).

Hyde, George E. *Life of George Bent Written From His Letters*. Savoie Lottinville, ed. Norman, OK: University of Oklahoma Press, 1968.

Kahana, Eva, et al., "Coping with Extreme Trauma." In *Human Adaptation to Extreme Stress from the Holocaust to Vietnam*. John P. Wilson, Zev Harel, and Boaz Kahana, eds. New York: Plenum Press, 1988.

Kammen, Michael. *Mystic Chords of Memory The Transformation of Tradition in American Culture*. New York: Vintage Books, 1993.

Keegan, John. *The Face of Battle*. Middlesex, UK: Penguin Books, 1976.

Kelman, Ari. *A Misplaced Massacre Struggling over the Memory of Sand Creek*. Cambridge, MS: Harvard University Press, 2013.

Kelsey, Harry E, Jr. *Frontier Capitalist: The Life of John Evans*. Denver: State Historical Society of Colorado, 1969.

Keohane, Joe. "How Facts backfire." *The Boston Globe*, July 11, 2010.

Lavender, David. *Bent's Fort*. Lincoln, NE: University of Nebraska Press, 1972.

Liberty, Margot, and John Stands in Timber. *Cheyenne Memories*. Lincoln, NE: University of Nebraska Press, 1972.

Lieberman, Matthew D., et al. "Do Amnesics Exhibit Cognitive Dissonance Reduction? The Role of Explicit Memory and Attention in Attitude Change." *Psychological Science*, 12, no. 2, March 2001: 135-140. http://pss.sagepub.com/content/12/2/135.full.pdf

Limerick, Patricia Nelson. *The Legacy of Conquest: The Unbroken Past of the American West*. New York: W. W. Norton & Co., 1987.

Linenthal, Edward T., and Tom Engelhardt, eds. *History Wars The Enola Gay and Other Battles for the American Past*. New York: Metropolitan Books, 1996.

Linenthal, Edward Tabor. *Sacred Ground Americans and Their Battlefields*. Urbana, IL: University of Illinois Press, 1991.

Loftus, Elizabeth F., Julie Feldman, and Richard Dashiell. "The Reality of Illusory Memories." In *Memory Distortion How Minds, Brains, and Societies Reconstruct the Past.* Daniel L. Schacter, ed., 47–68. Cambridge, MS: Harvard University Press, 1995.

Loftus, E. F. & J. C. Palmer. "Reconstruction of auto-mobile destruction: An example of the interaction between language and memory." *Journal of Verbal Learning and Verbal Behavior,* 13, 1974.

Lukacs, John. *Historical Consciousness or the Remembered Past.* New York: Schocken Books, 1985.

McCrone, John. *The Ape that Spoke Language and the Evolution of the Human Mind.* New York: William Morrow and Co., Inc., 1991.

McLeod, Saul. "Eyewitness Testimony." *Simply Psychology,* 2009. www.simplypsychology.org/eyewitness-testimony.html

Marshall, S. L. A. *Men Against Fire: The Problem of Battle Command in Future War.* Gloucester, MA: Peter Smith, 1978.

Michno, Gregory F. *Battle at Sand Creek The Military Perspective.* El Segundo, CA: Upton and Sons, 2004.

———. *The Deadliest Indian War in the West The Snake Conflict, 1864–1868.* Caldwell, ID: Caxton Press, 2007.

———. *Encyclopedia of Indian Wars Western Battles and Skirmishes, 1850–1890.* Missoula, MT: Mountain Press, 2003.

———. *The Mystery of E Troop Custer's Gray Horse Company at the Little Bighorn.* Missoula, MT: Mountain Press, 1994.

———. "Ghostbusters Busted at Sand Creek," *Skeptic,* Vol. 19, no. 1, 2014: 52–56.

Michno, Gregory F. and Susan J. Michno. *Forgotten Fights: Little-Known Raids and Skirmishes on the Frontier, 1823–1890.* Missoula, MT: Mountain Press, 2008.

Milavec, Pam. "Jesse S. Haire: Unwilling Indian Fighter." *Prologue* 43, no. 2 (Summer 2011).

Miller, Greg. "How Our Brains Make Memories Surprising new research about the act of remembering may help people with post-traumatic stress disorder." *Smithsonian Magazine,* May 2010. www.smithsonianmag.com/science-nature/how-our-brains-make-memories-14466850/

Mlodinow, Leonard. *The Drunkard's Walk How Randomness Rules Our Lives.* New York: Vintage Books, 2009.

Monahan, Doris. *Destination: Denver City. The South Platte Trail.* Athens, OH: Ohio University Press, 1985.

Mooney, Chris and Sheril Kirschenbaum. Unscientific America How Scientific Illiteracy Threatens our Future. New York: Basic Books, 2009.

"My Mind Is Made Up. Don't confuse Me With the Facts." *Quote Investigator.* http://quoteinvestigator.com/2013/02/13/confuse-me/

"Mystery History the Paranormal and More." http://mysteryandhistory. blogspot.com/2011/05/ghosts of-sand-creek.html.

Nichols, David A. *Lincoln and the Indians Civil War Policy and Politics*. Urbana, IL: University of Illinois Press, 2000.

Nyhan, Brendan. "Does Fact-Checking Work? False Statements are Wrong Metric." *Columbia Journalism Review*. http://www.cjr.org/united_states_project/ does_ factchecking_work_false.php

Payne, Jessica D. et al. "Stress administered prior to encoding impairs neutral but enhances emotional long-term episodic memories." *Learning & Memory*, 14 (12), December, 2007: 861-868. http://www.ncbi.nlm.nih.gov/pmc/articles/ PMC2151024/

Perrigo, Lynn I. "Major Hal Sayr's Diary of the Sand Creek Campaign." *Colorado Magazine* 15, no. 2 (March 1938).

Popkin, Richard H. and Avrum Stroll. *Philosophy Made Simple*. New York: Broadway Books, 1993.

Powell, Father Peter John. *People of the Sacred Mountain*, Vol. 1. San Francisco, CA: Harper & Row, 1981.

Pratkanis, Anthony R. and Elliot Aronson. *Age of Propaganda The Everyday Use and Abuse of Persuasion*. New York: W. H. Freeman and Company, 1992.

Qin, Shaozheng, et al. "Understanding Low Reliability of Memories for Neural Information Encoded Under Stress: Alterations in Memory-Related Activation in the Hippocampus and Midbrain." *Journal of Neuroscience*, 32 (12), March 21, 2012: 4,032-4,041. www.jneurosci.org/content/32/12/4032.full.

Raine, Adriane. *The Anatomy of Violence The Biological Roots of Crime*. New York: Vintage Books, 2014.

Roberts, Gary L. and David Fridtjof Halaas. "Written in Blood The Soule-Cramer Sand Creek Massacre Letters. *Colorado Heritage* (Winter 2001).

Robertson, James Oliver. *American Myth American Reality*. New York: Hill & Wang, 1980.

Ropeik, David. "Why Changing Somebody's Mind, or Yours, is Hard to Do." *Psychology Today*, July 13, 2010. Http://www.psychologytoday.com/blog/how-risky-is-it-really/201007/why-changing-somebody-s-mind-or-yours-is-hard-do.

Rosenberg, Bruce A. *Custer and the Epic of Defeat*. University Park, PA: Penn State University Press, 1974.

Russell, Bertrand. *A History of Western Philosophy*. New York: Simon and Schuster, 1945.

Sand Creek Massacre Project. Vol I: Site Location Study. Denver, CO: National Park Service, 2000.

Sanford, Mollie D. *Mollie: The Journal of Mollie Dorsey Sanford in Nebraska and Colorado Territories 1857–1866*. Lincoln, NE: University of Nebraska Press, 1976.

Schacter, Daniel L. *Searching for Memory: The Brain, the Mind, and the Past*. New York: Basic Books, 1996.

Schacter, Daniel L. "Memory Distortion: History and Current Status." In *Memory Distortion How Minds, Brains, and Societies Reconstruct the Past*. Daniel L. Schacter, ed. 1–43. Cambridge, MS: Harvard University Press, 1995.

Shaw, Luella. *True History of Some of the Pioneers of Colorado*. Hotchkiss, CO: W.S. Coburn, John Patterson, and A.K. Shaw, 1909.

Schlesinger, Jr., Arthur. "What Should We Teach Our Children About History?" *American Heritage*. (February-March 1992).

Shermer, Michael. *The Believing Brain*. New York: St. Martin's Griffin, 2011.

Shopes, Linda. "Making Sense of Oral History." *Oral History in a Digital Age*. http://ohda.matrix.msu.edu/2012/08/making-sense-of-oral-history/

Singer, Peter. *Hegel: A Very Short Introduction*. New York: Oxford University Press, 1983.

Smith, Gary. "How to Lie with Statistics," *Skeptic*, Vol. 19, no. 4 (2014): 44–48.

Smith, Thomas T. *The Old Army in Texas A Research Guide to the U.S. Army in Nineteenth-Century Texas*. Austin, TX: Texas State Historical Association, 2000.

Stout, Martha, Ph.D. *The Sociopath Next Door The Ruthless Versus the Rest of Us*. New York: Three Rivers Press, 2005.

Tanner, Michael. *Nietzsche A Very Short Introduction*. New York: Oxford University Press, 1994.

Tavris, Carol, and Elliot Aronson. *Mistakes Were Made (But Not By Me): Why we Justify Foolish Beliefs, Bad Decisions, and Hurtful Acts*. Orlando, FL: Harcourt, Inc., 2007.

"10 Research Findings About Deception That Will Blow Your Mind," http://liespotting.com/2010/06/10-research-findings-about-deception-that-will-blow-your-mind/

Thean, Tara. "Remember That? No You Don't. Study Shows False Memories Afflict Us All," *Time*, November 19, 2013. http://science.time.com/2013/11/19/remember-that-no-you-dont-study-shows-false-memories-afflict-us-all/

Varley, *James F. Brigham and the Brigadier: General Patrick Connor and his California Volunteers in Utah and Along the Overland Trail*. Tucson, AZ: Westernlore Press, 1989.

Vasicek, Donald. "Donald L. Vasicek: The Zen of Writing." http://donvasicek.com/uncategorized/1516/

Vyse, Stuart A. *Believing in Magic: The Psychology of Superstition*. New York: Oxford University Press, 1997.

Watts, Duncan J. *Everything is Obvious* Once You Know the Answer*. New York: Crown Business, 2011.

"The West: Episode Four (1856–1868) Death Runs Riot." www.pbs.org/weta/thewest/program/episodes/four/whois.htm

Wetherington, Richard K. and Frances Levine, eds. *Battles and Massacres on the Southwestern Frontier. Historical and Archaeological Perspectives.* Norman, OK: University of Oklahoma Press, 2014.

White, Lonnie J. *Hostiles and Horse Soldiers: Indian Battles and Campaigns in the West.* Boulder, CO: Pruett Publishing Company, 1972.

Williams, Scott C., ed. *Colorado History Through the News (A Context of the Times.) The Indian Wars of 1864: Through the Sand Creek Massacre.* Aurora, CO: Pick of Ware Publishing, 1997.

Wilson, Elinor. *Jim Beckwourth: Black Mountain Man and War Chief of the Crows.* Norman, OK: University of Oklahoma Press, 1972.

Wiseman, Richard. *Paranormality Why We See What Isn't There.* Lexington, KY: Spin Solutions Ltd., 2010.

Wynkoop, Edward W. *The Tall Chief: The Autobiography of Edward W. Wynkoop.* Edited and with an Introductory Biography by Christopher B. Gerboth. Denver, CO: Colorado Historical Society, 1994.

Index

Award-winning author Gregory F. Michno is a Michigan native and the author of three dozen articles and many books dealing with World War II and the American West, including *USS Pampanito: Killer-Angel*, *Lakota Noon*, *Battle at Sand Creek*, *The Encyclopedia of Indian Wars*, *The Deadliest Indian War in the West*, *Circle the Wagons*, and *Dakota Dawn: The Decisive First Week of the Sioux Uprising, August 17-24, 1862*. Greg helped edit and appeared in the DVD history "The Great Indian Wars: 1540-1890." He lives in Colorado with his wife Susan.